"*Teaching STEAM Through Hands-On Crafts* is a must-have for any STEAM teacher! The authors are long-time experts in all of the traditional crafts as well as being expert STEAM educators. The lessons in the book, backed by extensive research, deftly connect practical and historical knowledge to formal STEAM knowledge in a way that will help students understand and appreciate the details of everyday materials and objects."

   Erin Peters-Burton Ph.D., Donna R. and David E. Sterling Endowed Professor in Science Education, *George Mason University, USA.*

"The multitude of activities my teacher used from *Teaching STEAM Through Hands-On Crafts* engaged your brain and way of thinking, as well as brought to light a new hobby or pastime that otherwise would've been hidden. I especially enjoyed weaving and bread making. It utilizes both the left and right sides of your brain. You learn the history, technology, and chemistry of it all. It was a class that I truly enjoyed and looked forward to every day. I now have an otherwise unknown interest in these many activities. The activities were wonderful, and I am glad I had the opportunity to experience them."

   Blaise Bruni, 7th Grade Student, *Discovery Middle School, Madison, Alabama, USA.*

Teaching STEAM Through Hands-On Crafts

Help your students connect historic technologies with today's STEAM concepts through the lens of crafting! This book, written by a science education professor and a middle school STEM teacher, provides guidance for turning classic crafts into transdisciplinary STEAM lessons for grades 3–8. Ready-to-use lessons outline the history, science, mathematics, and engineering embedded within ten hands-on crafts from around the world. Each chapter outlines the history of a craft, its social impact, and the mathematics, engineering, and scientific concepts and skills embedded in the craft. Content standards from art, history, English language arts, technology, mathematics, and science are embedded within each unit. Lessons are supplemented with ready-to-photocopy handouts, guiding questions, and logistical support such as shopping lists and safety procedures. Activities have all been classroom-tested to ensure appropriate leveling and applicability across STEAM disciplines. Ideal for any STEM or STEAM classroom across upper elementary and middle schools, this book helps make STEM concepts meaningful and tangible for your students. Rather than just reading about science, technology, mathematics, or engineering, students will become makers and engage in STEAM directly, just as original crafters have done for centuries.

Additional instructional materials are available at: https://steamcrafts.weebly.com/

Christine G. Schnittka is the Emily R. and Gerald S. Leischuck Professor of Critical Needs in Education in Auburn University's College of Education, USA.

Amanda Haynes is the STEM teacher at Discovery Middle School in Madison, Alabama, USA.

Other Eye On Education Books Available from Routledge

(www.routledge.com/eyeoneducation)

Everyday STEAM for the Early Childhood Classroom: Integrating the Arts into STEM Teaching
Margaret Loring Merrill

STEAM Teaching and Learning Through the Arts and Design
Debrah Sickler-Voigt

A Sensory Approach to STEAM Teaching and Learning
Kerry P. Holmes, Jerilou J. Moore and Stacy V. Holmes

The A in STEAM: Lesson Plans and Activities for Integrating Art, Ages 0–8
Jerilou J. Moore and Kerry P. Holmes

Getting Started with STEAM: Practical Strategies for the K–8 Classroom
Billy Krakower and Meredith Martin

Hands-On STEAM Explorations for Young Learners: Problem-Based Investigations for Preschool to Second Grade
Allison Bemiss

Inspiring Innovation and Creativity in Young Learners: Transforming STEAM Education for Pre-K-Grade 3
Allison Bemiss

STEM by Design: Strategies and Activities for Grades 4–8
Anne Jolly

Teaching STEAM Through Hands-On Crafts

Real-World Maker Lessons for Grades 3–8

Christine G. Schnittka and Amanda Haynes

NEW YORK AND LONDON

Designed cover image: Christine G. Schnittka

First published 2025
by Routledge
605 Third Avenue, New York, NY 10158

and by Routledge
4 Park Square, Milton Park, Abingdon, Oxon, OX14 4RN

Routledge is an imprint of the Taylor & Francis Group, an informa business

© 2025 Christine G. Schnittka and Amanda Haynes

The right of Christine G. Schnittka and Amanda Haynes to be identified as authors of this work has been asserted in accordance with sections 77 and 78 of the Copyright, Designs and Patents Act 1988.

All rights reserved. No part of this book may be reprinted or reproduced or utilised in any form or by any electronic, mechanical, or other means, now known or hereafter invented, including photocopying and recording, or in any information storage or retrieval system, without permission in writing from the publishers.

Trademark notice: Product or corporate names may be trademarks or registered trademarks, and are used only for identification and explanation without intent to infringe.

ISBN: 978-1-032-54964-4 (hbk)
ISBN: 978-1-032-54965-1 (pbk)
ISBN: 978-1-003-42831-2 (ebk)

DOI: 10.4324/9781003428312

Typeset in Palatino
by codeMantra

Access the Support Material using this link: https://steamcrafts.weebly.com/ or scanning the QR code below:

Dedication

We dedicate this book to our crafty ancestors for making our world, to our children Jess, Andrea, Daniel, Ryan, and Maddy for being the best things we have ever made, to Dan and Eric for patiently holding down our respective forts, feeding the cats and the chickens while we made messes in our kitchens, to all the teachers everywhere who let their students make stuff, and finally to all the kids at Discovery Middle School in Madison, Alabama, who dove right in and made ALL the things in this entire book and taught us a thing or two!

Contents

Preface   x
Acknowledgments   xii
Meet the Authors   xiii
Online Support Material   xv

1 **Introduction to STEAM Crafts**   1

2 **Twisty Twine**   7

3 **Warp and Weft**   31

4 **Clean Chemistry**   57

5 **Practical Paper**   82

6 **Brilliant Beeswax**   110

7 **Plant Pigments**   136

8 **Milk Metamorphosis**   164

9 **Fungal Food**   190

10 **Clay Creations**   216

11 **Conclusion**   244

Preface

Long ago, a family was getting ready to eat dinner and relax for the day. Grandmother stood over the fire and stirred the warm milk, making a soft cheese to accompany the crusty bread she made that morning. Mother was spinning the last bit of fiber that she had collected the day before so she could start weaving the summer clothes before it got too hot. Daughter was making paper—so she could write about and preserve memories of her family. Son was busy sloshing fresh butter in the churn that Father had made—he was almost done! Father was dyeing the cloth that Mother had just woven, to sew a satchel to carry his collection of musical flutes that Grandfather made. Soap was ready and waiting to clean up all this fun after the day was done. Within this family, our human family, lies the collective knowledge and effort made by them all: the pieces made with clay to make music and hold water, the light blanket woven to keep cozy on a cool night, the rug in front of the fireplace to protect the wooden plank floor from sparks, and the plants drying upside down that the Father had collected for the dye vat, simply because they added color and cheer to their lives.

This scene of the human family at work is changing. All around us, technology is being innovated and invented, which is ideally a good thing, but in today's modern world, apps, devices, and software are where the money is being spent and where the schools are focusing their efforts. All the while, the material intelligence that our ancestors passed down, this generational knowledge, is largely lost on today's youth.

In recent years, an emphasis has been placed on interactive computer technologies in the classroom and one-to-one tablet or device initiatives. STEM is the golden phrase for grant funding and buy-in from stakeholders. In the effort to prepare today's youth for tomorrow's jobs, in the effort to be "college or career ready," we have unintentionally moved away from who we really are: talking primates with opposable thumbs and a fancy neocortex who make things to improve our lives. We have factories making computers, smartphones, and the devices which sit on our kitchen counters to tell us the day's weather and news. These devices take a trip across the ocean or land, enter our homes and schools and workplaces, and occupy our hands and our minds. **Meanwhile, our minds and our hands are starving for the work they were designed to do.** So, they play with fidget spinners, type on keyboards, and touch screens most of the day. What if we are starving a part of ourselves in the process of growing an advanced society?

Get ready … you may just be on the precipice of a shift in the way you think about STEAM education. If you read this book and try the lessons within, you just might see your students come alive and thrive in a way you have never seen before. Your school administrators may start poking their heads in your classrooms saying, "Your kids made <u>what</u>?" and parents may start sending you nice notes about how delightful it is at home now that their children have new hobbies. Teachers down the hall may be asking to borrow all your looms and soap molds to give it a go. These are not NEW ideas. But they are a new approach to getting kids to think critically, solve problems, develop resilience, design solutions, and use their imagination to create things that they can appreciate, hone, use in their daily lives, and improve upon.

Acknowledgments

Chris would like to lovingly acknowledge all the makers in her family who have been inspirational in so many ways: Ursula, Dan, Daniel, Andrea, Jessica, Nana and Grandaddy, Matt, Jeff, Amanda S., Grandma Gwen, Stacey, Kate, Marlene, and her adopted son, Cheikhouna Ka, who contributed to the final chapter. Chris is indebted to her late cousin, Vicki Cobb, for inspiring her to write. She would also like to deeply thank her Schnittkid, Amanda Haynes, who has been the perfect partner on this journey into the intersection of crafts, science, history, engineering, and teaching.

Amanda would like to thank Chris Schnittka for teaching her everything she knows, believing in her, and entrusting her with helping to carry this gem across the finish line—this has been your dream for a long time, and as always, I'm just happy to help. So many lessons learned throughout this process!

We both would like to acknowledge Auburn University's College of Education and the Department of Curriculum and Teaching, without which we would never have met or had the opportunity to collaborate on this project.

Meet the Authors

Christine G. Schnittka is the Emily R. and Gerald S. Leischuck Professor of Critical Needs in Education at Auburn University and has spent the last 20 years preparing future science teachers to teach with creative enthusiasm. She co-directs AUTeach, a teacher preparation program for science majors. She develops and researches design-based curriculum units for elementary and middle school youth, targeting key science concepts through a maker lens. Her research has focused on engineering education in K-12, energy literacy, informal STEM education, and most recently, the affective benefits of hand-making or hand-crafting. Her curricula have been used by teachers in more than 33 states and 13 countries. Prior to her career in higher education, Dr. Schnittka was a middle school teacher in Charlottesville, Virginia where she earned both a master's degree in mechanical engineering and a PhD in science education at the University of Virginia. As a middle school teacher fresh out of engineering school, Chris taught integrated STEM before it was even an acronym.

When Chris is not working with her students, engaged in research, attending meetings at work, or playing with her five grandchildren, she is busy making or designing something. Whether knitting socks, dyeing with indigo, reclaiming clay from scraps, making mugs and bowls on the potter's wheel, designing and 3D printing pottery tools, or fermenting sourdough starter for the next loaf of crusty bread, when she is not busy making something, she is planning the next thing she will make!

Chris decided to write *Teaching STEAM Through Hands-On Crafts: Real-World Maker Lessons for Grades 3-8* as a way to document and share the science, history, and technology of the crafting activities she loves. Over the years, she has conducted these activities with graduate students, afterschool youth, adult learners, family and friends, and local Girl Scouts. Amanda Haynes, her dear friend and former graduate student, has adapted these activities for elementary and middle school classroom settings.

Chris and her husband, Dan, have three grown children, three grown children-in-law, five adorable grandchildren, and two annoying cats. They live in the small, southern college town of Auburn, Alabama where Chris was raised with her sisters, where students still roll the oaks on Toomer's Corner every fall, where the sultry scent of gardenias still perfumes the humid air every spring, and where the high-pitched cries of tree frogs and cicadas echo off the loblolly pines on summer evenings.

Amanda Haynes is an enthusiastic STEM educator currently shaping young minds at Discovery Middle School in Madison, Alabama. Equipped with an MEd degree in Secondary Science Education from Auburn University, Amanda is deeply committed to fostering a love for science and technology in her students. Her dedication to excellence in education is exemplified by her achievement of the Dimensions of Success STEM Certification from the PEAR Institute. Daily, she strives to create new STEM experiences and challenges for her students to bolster their critical thinking, collaboration, and communication skills.

As a former science teacher, and with collaborations with her co-author and mentor, Amanda brings experience and innovative teaching strategies to her classroom. Beyond her professional endeavors, she finds joy in hobby farming, exploring new vacation destinations, and expressing her creativity through singing. Family and friends are also an integral part of her daily life and responsibilities as she is married with two children and a large extended family.

In co-authoring *Teaching STEAM Through Hands-On Crafts: Real-World Maker Lessons for Grades 3-8*, Amanda Haynes utilized her classroom and her students' experiences to inform the creation of the work, and to create companion documents that effectively turn the book from a concept into a ready-to-teach curriculum! Through her work, Amanda continues her attempt to impact the next generation of scientists, engineers, and innovators.

Online Support Material

Additional resources for this book can be accessed online by visiting this page: https://steamcrafts.weebly.com/ or scanning the QR code below.

1

Introduction to STEAM Crafts

The oldest musical instrument that has ever been discovered is a small flute with five finger holes made from the thin radius bone of a vulture's wing (Figure 1.1). It has been dated to be 35,000 years old. Discovered in a cave in Germany, what does this discovery tell us about the knowledge held by early humans (Bonvillain, 2013)?

Figure 1.1 Vulture's wing flute from 35,000 years ago. Image drawn by author Christine Schnittka from a photograph at the University of Tübingen. Used with permission. (Conard et al., 2009).

These early craftspeople may not have understood the science and mathematics of sound, harmonics, vibrating air inside a hollow column, frequency, pitch, waves … but this ancient craft is an example of human technology. Only stone tools were in existence at the time, and the craftsperson had to use sharp stones to wear away at the bone and create the holes and v-shaped mouthpiece so that air could be blown across the opening to make musical notes. Our ancestors possessed keen material intelligence (Adamson, 2018), creativity, and engineering skills. Material intelligence is "a deep understanding of the material world around us, an ability to read that material environment, and the know-how required to give it new form" (Adamson, 2018).

DOI: 10.4324/9781003428312-1

The oldest sandals ever discovered were found in 1938 in Fort Rock Cave in Oregon covered in a layer of ash. Carbon dated to be 9,000 years old, the ash they were buried under was deposited by the volcano, Mount Mazama, which erupted over 7,000 years ago. These shoes were meticulously crafted from twisted and woven fibers from the bark of the sagebrush plant (Connolly, 2018). While humans have been twisting fibers to make string for 40,000 years, there is evidence that our Neanderthal cousins twisted fibers as well. These early shoemakers undoubtedly did not understand the microscopic features of the cellulose material they were using, nor did they know the physics we use today to explain the strength of twisted twine. The Native Americans who made those sandals had deep material intelligence, creativity, and engineering skills.

When we touch clay, wood, and rocks, we cannot see the microscopic features that give the materials their properties, but they are there. These microscopic features are studied by materials scientists, chemists, and engineers. The molecular arrangement of cellulose makes it good for paper or rope, and the hydrogen atoms lining the cellulose molecule make it perfect for bonding to other cellulose molecules. All ancient crafts are an art form infused with science, technology, engineering, and mathematics lessons that have the potential to be engaging, motivating, and related to everyday life.

Material intelligence was once universal in humans (Adamson, 2018). Before the industrial age, people had to possess the ability to use the materials around them to solve their problems. People had to knit warm garments from raw sheep's wool to stay warm, dig clay from the Earth and fire it into watertight vessels to hold water, hollow out trees to make canoes, and evaporate sea water to make salt to preserve meat. Today, we go to a store to purchase clothing, food storage containers, inflatable rafts, and iodized salt. Most people have no idea where these common items come from or how they are made, and do not think about the sustainability of the materials that go into making the objects … and most importantly … the general populace have no idea how to make these items for themselves (Figure 1.2).

In Finland, a craft education course called "slöjd" (pronounced *sloyd*) is mandatory for school children. Finnish youth have been taking this class since 1866. Slöjd is also taught in Sweden, Iceland, Denmark, Norway, and other Nordic countries. Slöjd is not typically integrated into other school subjects, but it could be. If Slöjd students were making baskets from wire, they could ask questions like,

> Why does wire flatten when hammered, but twine does not? What properties do different kinds of wire have (thermal, electrical, oxidation)? Why does gold wire not rust? When you build a basket from

wire, why does the wire break if it's bent back and forth too much? What is the ideal distance between wires when weaving? Why does wire get stiffer when it's bent a few times? Can wire be used as thread?

Think about the traditional crafts that our ancestors practiced for their very survival: making butter, cheese, and bread, pickling vegetables and fish, making fishing nets and sails for boats, making soap and candles, weaving rugs and cloth, spinning fibers into string, tanning leather, metalworking, woodworking, basket weaving, making and firing pottery, tying knots, sewing, whittling, and more. Modern industrialization has taken the production of these materials out of our everyday lives. Most of them are lost arts (Freidenrich, 2019; McGovern, 2008). This ancestral knowledge is most especially lost on the youth of today. Youth in modern societies might associate craft making with creating slime or making things out of Play-Doh, yet the essence of our humanity, one of the key elements that make us different from other life forms, is our ability to use higher order thinking to create tools that allow us to perform incredible tasks. It is in our "bones" to use these skills to solve problems (Kojonkoski-Rannali, 1998; McGaw, 2014; Spencer-Wood & Burke, 2019).

Figure 1.2 Material intelligence in the human family. Image created by author Christine Schnittka.

Our ancestors survived because they knew this knowledge and skill. Perhaps reviving these skills for youth can help them develop skills, positive attitudes, and content knowledge.

Craft education in the Nordic countries was designed to develop self-esteem through skill building, as well as decision making, problem solving, technical literacy, and independence (Autio et al., 2016). Is there a relationship between craft skills and success in school? Making things certainly helps people feel in control, it helps them express themselves creatively and artistically, and it gives them a sense of purpose (Pöllänen, 2009). Making things gives people a chance to think, process emotions, and feel better (Bathje, 2012). It lowers heart and breathing rates, helps with anxiety and depression, and helps people think positive thoughts (Pöllänen, 2009). Perhaps teaching school subjects through traditional crafts would be good for students' minds **and** spirits.

Glenn Adamson, in his book, *Fewer, Better Things, Better, Fewer Things,* said of craft making that "We're not doing what our brains and bodies were developed to do." Andy Hargreaves of Boston College, in his book, *Teaching in a Knowledge Society* said, "A modern society requires creative, inventive and self-confident citizens to meet the eternal changing conditions for modern life in an uncertain world (Hargreaves, 2003)." Motivating youth through crafts to see how school subjects relate to their lives, how they are practical and not just abstractions, and are useful in solving everyday problems, is very important, as crafting is rooted in our history as a species.

Crafting in schools may be what kindergarten children do with glue sticks and construction paper, but it is so much more than that. Langlands (2017) describes the fact that the Anglo Saxon word, "Craeft," from the middle ages, meant having wisdom about the natural world, understanding materials, and understanding the properties of objects made from natural materials. People engaged in Craeft possessed power, strength, and skill, which is quite different from what people think of today when they purchase a craft kit to make a predefined object. Matter becomes material when someone sees its potential and acts on it to transform it. If crafting is intrinsically human, why are youth in the United States spending more time touching screens than transforming their surroundings (Sparks, 2022)?

In this book, teachers will be guided through the process of making ten different traditional crafts. They will learn the science, technology, and history embedded in each of them, as well as learn about contemporary crafting practices. The lessons in this book can be used with youth of all ages but will be aligned with the needs and talents of upper elementary and middle school youth.

Why STEAM? Why include the arts in science, technology, engineering, and mathematics education? One rationale is to infuse the STEM disciplines with creativity, a most valued and important human talent (Trilling & Fadel, 2009). Another rationale is for motivation. When students see value and usefulness in the school subjects they learn, and when they feel success in learning them, they are more motivated to learn (Jones, 2009). Integrating the arts into STEM lessons is one way to enact STEAM education. STEAM can be seen as transdisciplinary, transcending any one component of the acronym (Liao, 2016). This transdisciplinary approach elevates the value of creativity in contemporary problem solving, and places it on an equal footing with the science, technology, math, and engineering disciplines.

The philosophy of the curricula in this book is based on the social constructivist theory of learning (Vygotsky, 1978). The lessons in this book are designed around the BSCS 5E instructional model designed by the Biological Sciences Curriculum Study (Bybee, 2009). Based on Dewey's model of reflective thinking (Dewey, 1938), Piagetian theory (Piaget, 1955), and other learning cycle models that followed, the five phases of this model are: Engage, Explore, Explain, Elaborate, and Evaluate. This approach allows students to work collaboratively in groups or with their parent or teacher to solve problems and construct solutions, and they also learn certain skills through the modeling of their teacher. When students are involved in open-ended activities, learning as apprentices once did, they are not being told what to do—they are creating and innovating, and making decisions based on their underlying knowledge. Furthermore, allowing students to take ownership of their learning, and their inevitable product, fosters a sense of empowerment and increased intrinsic motivation. The role of the teacher is to guide students through their decision-making processes and model new skills to be learned.

This book is not a kit with step-by-step instructions. It is a guide that gives the teacher or parent enough of a diving board to jump into the deep end. It spells out the history of the craft, the science embedded in the craft, basic instructions for giving the craft a try, and an example project that can be adapted to fit the needs of the classroom setting. Accompanying documents, presentations, and examples are provided on our website steamcrafts.weebly.com and can help to make the content in this book more accessible and easier to adapt. However, this book also provides suggestions for scientific inquiries, mathematical endeavors, engineering challenges, and more. It also connects you and your students with people who are practicing each craft as an art form. It is our hope that this book helps you, the teacher or parent, use crafts as educational contexts to empower, motivate, enrich, and educate today's youth.

References

Adamson, G. (2018). *Fewer, better things*. Bloomsbury Publishing.

Autio, O., Thorsteinsson, G., & Olafsson, B. (2016). Examining technological knowledge and reasoning in Icelandic and Finnish comprehensive schools. *Design and Technology Education: An International Journal, 21*(2), 59–68.

Bathje, M. (2012). Art in occupational therapy: An introduction to occupation and the artist. *The Open Journal of Occupational Therapy, 1*(1), 8.

Bonvillain, N. (2013). *Cultural anthropology*. Pearson.

Bybee, R. W. (2009). *The BSCS 5E instructional model and 21st century skills*. National Academies Board on Science Education.

Conard, N. J., Malina, M., & Münzel, S. C. (2009). New flutes document the earliest musical tradition in southwestern Germany. *Nature, 460*(7256), 737–740.

Connolly, T. J. (2018). Fort Rock sandals. https://oregonencyclopedia.org/articles/fort_rock_sandals/#.XUm21ZPYrOQ

Dewey, J. (1938). *Experience and education*. Macmillan.

Freidenrich, E. (2019). *Almost lost arts: Traditional crafts and the artisans keeping them alive*. Chronicle Books.

Hargreaves, A. (2003). *Teaching in a knowledge society*. Teachers College Press.

Jones, B. D. (2009). Motivating students to engage in learning: The MUSIC model of academic motivation. *International Journal of Teaching and Learning in Higher Education, 21*(2), 272–285.

Kojonkoski-Rannali, S. (1998). *The idea in our hands: An analysis of the meaning of the concept of handicraft, Research Number 185*. Publications of the University Turku.

Langlands, A. (2017). *Craeft: An inquiry into the origins and true meaning of traditional crafts*. W.W. Norton and Co.

Liao, C. (2016). From interdisciplinary to transdisciplinary: An arts-integrated approach to STEAM education. *Art Education, 69*(6), 44–49.

McGaw, J. (2014). Mapping 'place' in Southeast Australia: Crafting a possum skin cloak. *Craft Research, 5*(1), 11–33.

McGovern, U. (2008). *Lost crafts: Rediscovering traditional skills*. Chambers.

Piaget, J. (1955). The construction of reality in the child. *Journal of Consulting Psychology, 19*(1), 77.

Pöllänen, S. (2009). Contextualising craft: Pedagogical models for craft education. *International Journal of Art & Design Education, 28*(3), 249–260.

Sparks, S. D. (2022). Students are behaving badly in class. Excessive screen time might be to blame. *Education Week*. https://www.edweek.org/leadership/students-are-behaving-badly-in-class-excessive-screen-time-might-be-to-blame/2022/04

Spencer-Wood, S. M., & Burke, C. (2019). Epilogue: The future of craft research. In Burke, C., & Spencer-Wood, S. (Eds) *Crafting in the world* (pp. 255–287). Springer Nature.

Trilling, B., & Fadel, C. (2009). *21st century skills: Learning for life in our times*. Jossey-Bass.

Vygotsky, L. S. (1978). *Mind in society: Development of higher psychological processes*. Harvard University Press.

2
Twisty Twine

Introduction

When was the first time you thought about string, yarn, rope, or thread? I remember going to the fabric store as a young mother to purchase thread and fabric to make baby clothes, looking at the vast array of threads on display, and feeling overwhelmed not knowing which to choose. Quilting thread? Polyester? Cotton? All Purpose? Heavy duty? In picking out rope for the swing my husband and I hung from a bent tree in our front yard, the same decision was faced. Jute? Sisal? Nylon? Polyester? Cotton braided? Plaited? Twisted? Double braided? After learning to crochet and knit, similar decisions had to be made when choosing yarn. Should I purchase cotton or wool? Worsted, DK, or fingering weight? Handspun or machine made?

These long stringy things: thread, rope, and yarn, are important components of our lives (Figure 2.1). Chances are, you are touching hundreds of these items right now! There is plenty of science, mathematics, history, and engineering embedded in the ancient craft of stringy things.

Fiber History

People have been using fibers to make rope and string for a very long time. Some fibers are already long and stringy, like blades of tall grass. Some fibers are naturally short, like the tiny fibers in a fluffy ball of cotton. Whether

DOI: 10.4324/9781003428312-2

8 ◆ Twisty Twine

Figure 2.1 The rope swing. Image created by author Christine Schnittka.

initially long or short, twisting fibers together makes them longer and stronger. When you think about the earliest tools that humans made, string is a significant tool that gave humans a real advantage. They could make knots, tie things together, create fishing nets, and secure large items for lifting or dragging. If you were stranded on a deserted island, one of the first things you would need to do is make some rope.

Because rope and string that are made from plant materials rot and disintegrate over time, it is rare to find very old samples of them. However, we have evidence of rope imprinted into clay as well as evidence in terms of tools used to make and use rope. There are sewing needles made from bone, dated to be 61,000 years old (Backwell et al., 2008). However, people may have been sewing with strands of leather, or single blades of grass, so the needle is not definitive evidence of string that old. Japanese pottery from 10,000 BCE called Jomon Pottery contains imprints of twisted cords. In Finland, remnants of a fishing net made from willow rope are estimated to have been made in 8540 BCE. An impression of twisted rope was found on a clay pot found in Scotland, believed to be 5,300 years old. In Egypt, people were twisting strands of papyrus into rope in 2000 BCE and flax into rope in 1500 BCE, and this evidence is found in paintings on ancient pottery and in ancient tombs.

More recent evidence from 1350 BCE in Tell-el-Amarna, in Israel, is found in actual ropes and knots made from grasses.

Tools for Making String

The history of string and rope is intimately tied up with the history of the devices used to twist fibers into string and rope. What tool would you create to help you twist fibers into rope and string?

Hands alone work just fine to make rope and string, especially when people work together. But if you try to twist plant fibers together into a long rope by yourself, you will find the need for some kind of tool to help you. The first rope-making tool may have simply been a stick to wind the completed rope around. Put a notch at the top of your stick to secure the end of the rope, and wind the rest of the rope around it for safekeeping. This stick could also be useful in helping you do the twisting. Tie a knot at the end of your new rope and secure in the notch, then roll the stick against your thigh to give it a good twist, and wrap your new rope segment around the stick as you go. You can try this right now with a pencil and some string. Cut a slit in the pink pencil eraser, slide your string into it, and roll the pencil along your thigh to twist the string.

Another innovation for making rope may have been a stick or bone with several holes in it. After one string has been spun, several strings are then twisted together to make a strong rope. A piece of mammoth ivory with four notched holes found in southwestern Germany may have been used for such rope twisting. This tool is believed to be 40,000 years old (Conard & Malina, 2016; Figure 2.2).

Figure 2.2 Mammoth bone tool for making rope. Image drawn by author Christine Schnittka from a photograph at the University of Tübingen (Conard & Malina, 2016). Used with permission.

Twisting fibers into string is a time-consuming task. What can speed up the process? Science! Gravity and inertia were not concepts discussed thousands of years ago, but people knew from experience that a stick with a weight on it would spin longer than a stick alone. Around 5,000 years ago, people started adding weights to their spindles. Roll the spindle along your thigh with your dominant hand, just as before, while holding the new string in your non-dominant hand, but then let the spindle drop and continue to spin. These drop spindles, made from a stick and a "whorl," were quite the innovation (Figure 2.3).

Figure 2.3 Peruvian woman with drop spindle. Image created by author Christine Schnittka from the photograph, "Old female with drop spindle on Taquile island Peru" by Peter van der Sluijs is licensed under CC BY-SA 3.0.

While these ancient spindle shafts would break and rot and return to the soil, the whorls often remained. Made from clay or rocks, ivory or bone, or even metal, these whorls have been found all over the world. In the Ashalim Cave in southern Israel in the Negev Desert, a spindle made from a branch of the small Tamarisk tree was discovered with fibers of flax nearby. Still attached to this spindle was a whorl made from lead. Using Carbon-14 dating, this spindle/whorl combination is estimated to be from 4325 BCE. Notice how the spindle even has a notch at the top for the string (Langgut et al., 2016; Figure 2.4).

In the Indus Valley, in what is today Pakistan, people of the ancient Harappan civilization used spindles and whorls to spin cotton. Dated to be from around 3300 BCE, people there used ceramic to make their whorls (Kenoyer, 2010). The Near East is not the only place that ancient spindles and whorls have been found. Seventeen ceramic spindle whorls were found at Chichen Itza in Mexico, probably from around 500 BCE (Ardren et al., 2010).

Even with a drop spindle, spinning animal fur or plant fibers into string still took a lot of time. Eventually, the spinning wheel was invented. This tool

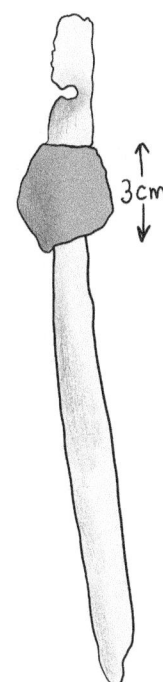

Figure 2.4 Ancient drop spindle. Image created by author Christine Schnittka from photograph in Figure 6, Langgut et al. (2016). Used with permission.

may have been first invented in India between 500 and 1000 CE, or it may have been invented in China at about the same time. The spinning wheel worked with the simple machine, the pulley. One person would crank a handle to spin a large wheel. A belt connected the large wheel with a small one, which made the small wheel spin much much faster. If the diameter of the large wheel was 10 times the diameter of the small wheel, the small wheel spun ten times faster than the large one. For every one spin of the large wheel, the small one would spin ten times (Figure 2.5).

While one person spun the larger wheel, a second person would use the smaller, faster wheel to spin fibers into string. A well-coordinated person might spin the large wheel with one hand while manipulating the fibers and string with the other. In his later years, the great Indian leader Mohandas Gandhi would sit and spin cotton for an hour each day in this fashion, both as a spiritual practice and also as a protest against British rule and their control of the textile trade.

This hand-operated spinning wheel was used all across China, India, and the Middle East for a very long time. In the 14th century, a water powered spinning wheel was invented in China, and in the 16th century, a foot-pedal-operated spinning wheel was invented in Germany. Pressing a pedal with the foot operated a lever attached to the axle of the large wheel.

12 ◆ Twisty Twine

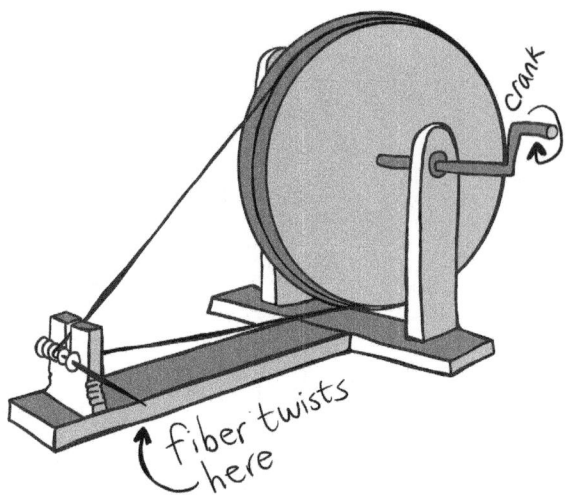

Figure 2.5 Spinning wheel. Image created by author Christine Schnittka of an image in the public domain from The Wesleyan Juvenile Offering, September 1852.

This simple machine, combined with the inertia of the spinning wheel, kept the wheel going as long as the pedal was pushed repetitively. These innovations, the treadle and the use of water power, made it easier for one person to operate the machine, and in the case of the foot-powered machine, a bobbin was incorporated to store the newly spun string.

During the Middle Ages in Europe, easier-to-operate spinning wheels meant more yarn was produced. More yarn meant more fabric. More fabric created more rags, and more rags meant more paper! Textiles directly increased the amount of "text" that could be printed with the 15th century invention of the printing press!

In 1720, the Englishman James Hargreaves invented a machine which could spin eight spools of yarn at a time. He wanted to keep his invention a secret so that only he could benefit from it. Because he could make so much more yarn than his competitors, the price of yarn fell, and the other spinners in England got angry. They broke into his house to see what his secret spinning machine looked like, and eventually started copying the design. Hargreaves patented his "Spinning Jenny" in 1770, and tried to sue all the spinners who had copied his machine.

In 1793, the American Eli Whitney invented a machine which would remove the seeds from cotton. This cotton "Gin" used brushes and hooks to pull the cotton through a mesh screen while leaving the seeds on the other side of the screen. The words, "Jenny" and the "Gin" come from the word, "Engine." These two inventions made spinning quicker and easier.

One would think only good things would come from these inventions, but that is not the case. If you could process cotton faster and spin it faster, you would want more cotton in your warehouses. In the late 1700s, a lot of cotton was grown in the southern United States. I'll leave it to you to imagine what happened next.

Back in England in the early 1800s, these new machines meant that fewer people were needed to pick seeds from cotton and spin all sorts of fibers into yarn. People were losing their jobs and they were not happy. One group of angry textile workers who called themselves Luddites started protesting the use of all these machines and would sneak into the textile mills at night and break them. The textile mill owners started shooting at the Luddites, and many Luddites were arrested. Eventually the British army got involved. What a mess! Today we call a person who opposes technological advancements, a "Luddite." The Luddites of today are worried about the impact that robots, computers, and Artificial Intelligence will have on human workers (Figure 2.6). Will our world soon no longer need people who make things by hand?

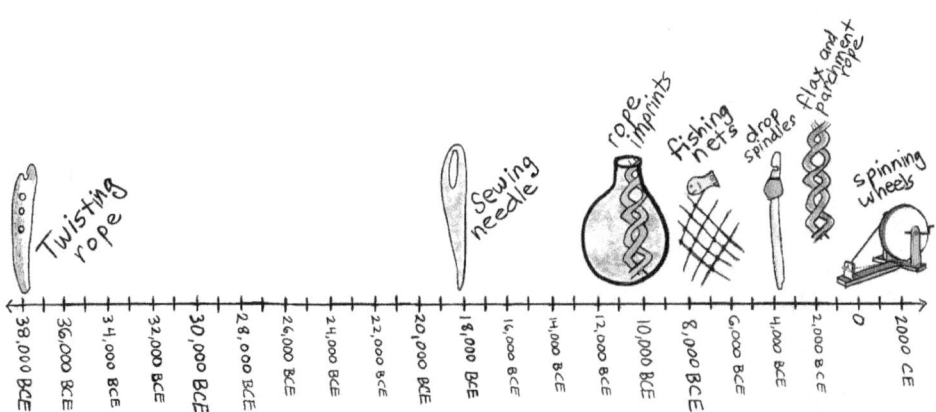

Figure 2.6 Timeline of fiber history. Image created by author Christine Schnittka.

Meeting the Standards

Teaching this chapter as written focuses on STEAM principles that include: historical elements that influenced technological advancements, engineering principles including iterative design, criteria and constraints, and scientific measurement principles as well as data collection and analysis. For more detailed information regarding which specific standards are covered in this unit, please refer to our website: https://steamcrafts.weebly.com/.

14 ◆ Twisty Twine

Materials

- A variety of strings, ropes, and yarns
- Handheld magnifying lenses
- Digital microscope plugged into a computer
- Small rulers
- Cotton balls
- Cotton fabric swatch
- Dryer lint
- Wool or flax or linen roving
- Cotton balls
- Pipe cleaners
- Yarn
- Small looms
- Scissors
- Large rocks
- Epoxy or E6000 glue
- Paints to decorate rocks
- Wool roving or flax roving for each group of students
- A drop spindle for each group of students
- String
- Paper clips

Safety

- Be sure no students have wool allergies before using wool.

The Lesson

The BSCS 5E Instructional Model for String Making

The lessons in this book are designed around the BSCS 5E instructional model designed by the Biological Sciences Curriculum Study (Bybee, 2009). Based on Dewey's model of reflective thinking (Dewey, 1938), Piagetian theory (Piaget, 1955), and other learning cycle models that followed, the five phases of this model are: Engage, Explore, Explain, Elaborate, and Evaluate. The purpose and summary for each phase are explained in the sections that follow.

- To find accompanying presentations, student handouts, and more be sure to visit our website: https://steamcrafts.weebly.com/.

Engage: String Play

Purpose
The purpose of this phase of the lesson is to build excitement about what strings are made from, and to initiate curiosity about them and how they are made. It's also a chance for the teacher to find out what prior knowledge students have.

Overview
Students explore various kinds of string, dissecting them and determining what each string is made from.

Bring a collection of various strings, ropes, and yarns to class. Distribute samples of these items to each student along with rulers. Challenge students to dissect these stringy things, to untwist the plied yarn to separate the singles. Are the singles twisted the same way? Then, challenge them to untwist the singles. Notice how easily they separate when pulled apart? Ask students to try and find the length of the "staple" on each different kind of string or yarn. The staple is the fiber that the yarn is made from. A cotton staple may be 25 mm long whereas a wool staple might be 100 mm long (Figure 2.7).

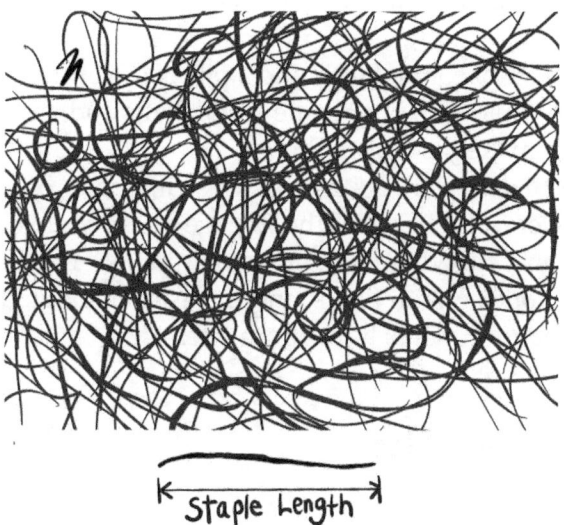

Figure 2.7 A pile of fibers and staple length. Image created by author Christine Schnittka.

Probing Questions to Ask

What makes each staple stick to the others and form a string that you can pull on and not break?

- Students will think that the staples are sticky, or they will just say that the twisting makes them stick together.

Pass out magnifying lenses or have digital microscopes at a station for students to examine the fibers closer.
How are the fibers different from each other?

- Some fibers may be curly, others straight. Some may be smooth, and others bumpy.

How do you think the different properties of the fibers affect the strength and behavior of the string when it's made?

- Students may think that what is apparent at the micro level will be apparent at the macro level, so a bumpy fiber will make a bumpy yarn.

Look around the room. What do you see that might be made from these fibers?

- Carpeting, clothing, curtains … students will miss some items. Do a pre-check yourself.

Now, hold up a piece of cotton fabric and a pile of cotton balls. Ask, how do we go from "this" to "this"? Pass out some cotton balls and challenge students to figure out how to make yarn from them.
Tell students that they are going to make string, rope, or yarn from scratch, from raw fiber. Here, at the end of the Engage phase of this lesson, by asking these questions and allowing students to manipulate fibers, students should be interested in working with fibers, and the teacher should have determined any prior knowledge students have about fibers.

Explore: Manipulating String

Purpose
The purpose of this phase of the lesson is to allow students to all have experiences with the phenomenon prior to learning any new content. Some students have different levels of experience with fibers. This phase attempts to level

that field of knowledge in order to have a more concrete foundation to build further understanding.

Overview

After demonstrating how to twist fibers into string with one's fingers, and demonstrating how to use a drop spindle, students will try their hands at spinning fibers with drop spindles.

Begin the lesson with a demonstration of taking dryer lint and twisting it into a "string" and then taking a common cotton ball purchased from the drug store, and twisting it also into a string.

Next, demonstrate the drop spindle. If the teacher is not sufficiently skilled, a video found online can be helpful. The easiest material to work with is wool roving separated into finger-width sections about 15 cm (6″) long. The wool roving can be pulled gently from one end, and a thin amount will cling together enough to be spun into yarn (Figure 2.8).

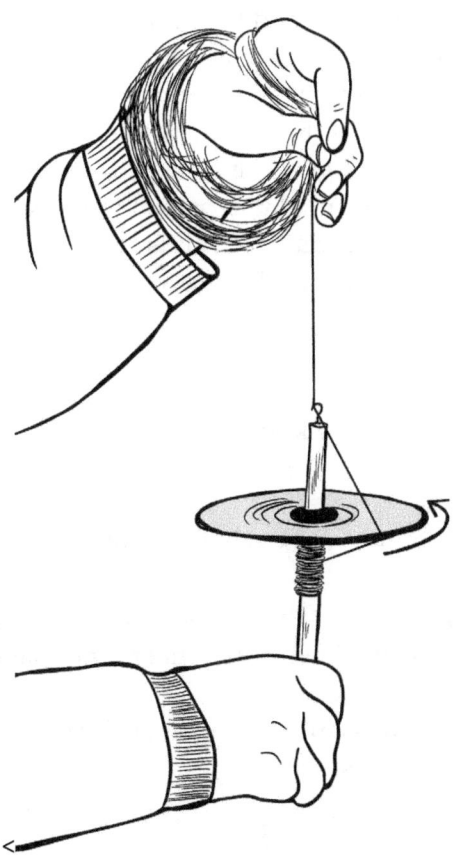

Figure 2.8 Drop spindle. Image created by author Christine Schnittka.

After demonstrating, provide students with drop spindles and wool roving. If any one student has a wool allergy, substitute linen or flax roving. Drop spindles can be purchased or made from simple materials. A wooden dowel with a wooden toy wheel near the top and a cup hook at the very top works just fine. In a pinch, a pencil with a cup hook screwed into the eraser can even work. The steps for using a drop spindle are as follows:

1. Create a slip knot in a piece of yarn about 20 cm (8") long and attach it to the cup hook on the drop spindle. This is the "lead" used to initially attach the fibers.
2. Pull out some of the fibers from the roving and twist them into the yarn lead by twisting the drop spindle in your hand.
3. Pull out more roving and twist the drop spindle so that a twisted strand is formed. The drop spindle can just be twisted by hand, or it can be rolled along the thigh when seated. Expert spinsters will get the spindle going and then just let it spin in the air while hanging there.
4. Once about 2 feet of twisted strand has been created, wind it around the dowel of the spindle and then hook the twisted strand around the cup hook a couple of times.
5. Repeat steps 3 and 4 until all the roving has been spun.
6. Two people are needed to ply one twisted string into a two-stranded string. Have one person unwind the yarn from the spindle, being careful not to untwist it, with a person holding each end. Then, fold the strand in half (meeting both ends together) so that the two halves twist around each other and make a plied piece of string that will not unravel.

As students are exploring this process with the spindles, you can ask some questions to find out what they know.

Probing Questions to Ask

Why do you think twisting works to hold the fibers together?

- Twisting applies a force which presses the fibers closer to each other. This increases the friction between fibers and makes the string stronger.

Newly spun yarn tends to just unravel again. How do you think you can keep your new string from untwisting?

- String must be plied. That means that two twisted strings must be twisted together.

Why do you think you have to ply the string to keep it from unraveling?

- When you twist the fibers, you are putting energy into them. Twisted fibers can untwist easily after you let go of the new string. The new string acts like a spring when it's all twisted up, and will easily unravel. Plying two twisted strings that are twisted in <u>opposite</u> directions means that each will try to untwist in different directions. Since they are doing this at the same time, the plied yarn does not untwist at all.

Do you think you could ply 2-strand string into 4-strand string?

- If you have two 2-ply strings, they will just sit next to each other unless each is twisted in opposite directions.

How strong is your string? What could you use it for?

- You can measure the strength of your string by pulling on it. Try tying one end of it to a hook on the wall or in the ceiling, and the other end to a bucket handle. Fill the bucket until the string breaks. Then you will know how strong your string is!

Where do you think dryer lint comes from?

- Dryer lint comes from clothes which are tumbled in a dryer. Tiny fibers get dislodged from the strings that are made into clothing, and these tiny fibers collect in a screen as "lint." Some lint is from cotton plants or linen plants, and some is from animal fur, and some is from materials such as polyester and nylon. You can try twisting dryer lint into string!

- A student handout with the instructions and visuals of this process is available on our website https://steamcrafts.weebly.com/.

Explain: The STEAM Concepts

Purpose
The purpose of this phase of the lesson is to allow students to gain new scientific knowledge and understanding of how fibers, string, and fabrics work in order to make informed design decisions in a later phase.

Overview
A presentation of this content can be found on our website https://steamcrafts.weebly.com/. In this phase of the lesson, you should ask your students to explain their new reasonings and understandings. It's very important in this phase of the lesson to find out what students are thinking before teaching them the STEAM concepts of fibers, strings, and fabrics. What follows is a discussion of the basics and the details of fiber science.

Fiber Science: The Basics
Why does a twist make a fiber stronger? Friction!

Parallel fibers have some friction between them because they are touching, but friction increases between things as the force pushing them together increases (Figure 2.9). Think about how there is more friction between your hands the harder you push them together. Well, spinning fibers packs them tight against each other. Pulling only makes the twisted fibers pack tighter, increasing the friction more. The bumpier the surface of the fiber, the more friction it can have.

Figure 2.9 The s and z twists. Image created by author Christine Schnittka.

Demonstrate this with three long pipe cleaners. Show how a twist makes them able to form a long piece of rope. Take a stack of pipe cleaners and place them next to each other and draw them out so that you have a meter-long string of them. Even though the pipe cleaners are bumpy and tend to stick to each other, you cannot pull on this new string at all. There isn't enough friction to counteract the pulling force. But, if you twist the pipe cleaners together, you will create friction everywhere that two of the pipe cleaners are forced together tightly. Add all these little friction forces together, and you have the strength of your new rope!

Galileo knew about the strength of the twist. In 1638 he said,

> But in the case of the rope the very act of twisting causes the threads to bind one another in such a way that when the rope is stretched with a great force the fibers break rather than separate from one another.

Here is a list of interesting facts about fibers:

1. Cotton fibers are 88%–97% cellulose. The remainder is waxes, proteins, and pectins.
2. Cotton fibers grow out of a cotton seed, with 16,000 fibers per seed.
3. A cotton fiber is one cell. The cell walls strengthen, then get layers of cellulose.
4. A cotton fiber is only 25 micrometers wide, and can be 3.5 cm (1 1/3") long.
5. A cotton fiber grows for 50 days, then the cell dries out.
6. Other plant fibers such as flax, jute, ramie, and kenaf are derived from the stalks of the plants. They are about 75% cellulose.
7. Cotton fibers are hollow. They can hold water 24–27 times their own weight.
8. Fibers stick to each other when wet, and then stay stuck after the water evaporates due to hydrogen bonds.
9. The United States produces primarily short staple cotton.
10. Wool fibers have scales that trap dirt and keep an animal's skin clean.
11. The friction when you smooth your fingers down a wool fiber is less than when you smooth your fingers up a wool fiber, and this is called the directional friction effect.
12. When wool gets wet, the diameter increases by 16% and the length increases by 1%.
13. Wool can absorb 35% of its weight in water, and is made of the protein keratin.

14. Wool is hygroscopic—water actually bonds to the fiber.
15. Silk, the fiber that silkworms make to form their cocoons, is made the protein fibroin.

Fiber Science: The Details
Plant-based Fibers

Cotton and hemp and bamboo are made from cellulose, the same thing paper is made from. Cellulose is made by combining glucose (sugar) molecules into a chain, which is called a polymer (meaning many units). Cotton is 90% cellulose (Figures 2.10 and 2.11).

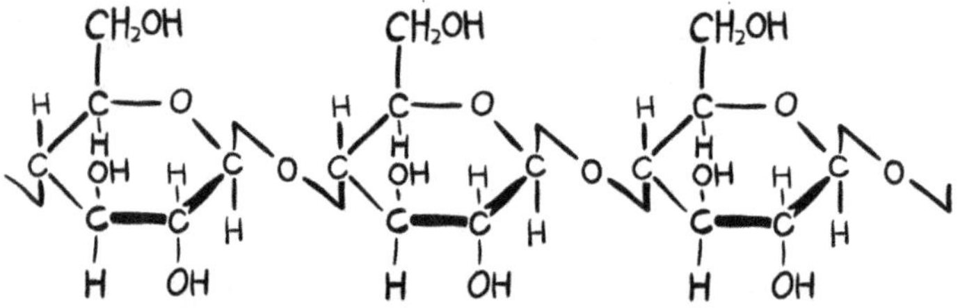

Figure 2.10 The structure of cellulose. Image created by author Christine Schnittka.

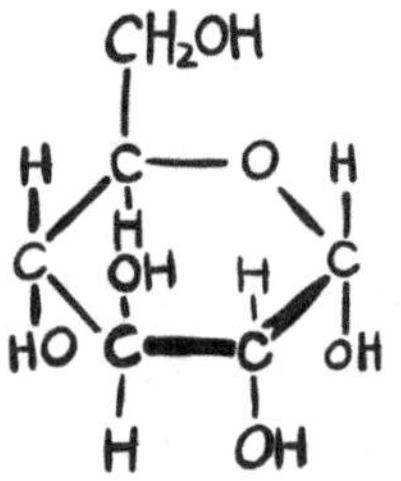

Figure 2.11 The structure of glucose. Image created by author Christine Schnittka.

What elements are used to make the cellulose in cotton, bamboo, and hemp?

- (C, H, O).

Where do these elements come from?

- CO_2 is in the air and H_2O is in water.

What process combines the CO_2 and H_2O and makes glucose and cellulose?

- Photosynthesis.

Animal-based Fibers

Silk comprises fibroin protein (see Figure 2.12), while wool (see Figure 2.13) is composed of keratin, the same material in hair and fingernails. Keratin is a protein made up of multiple amino acids. If you have ever smelled wool burning, the scent is from the sulfur in the wool producing sulfur dioxide.

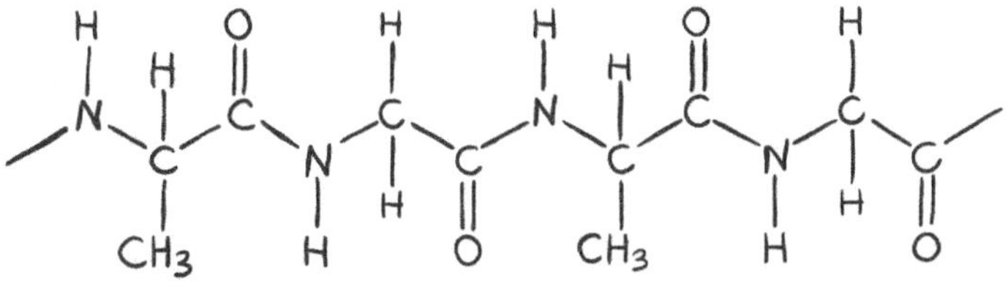

Figure 2.12 The chemical structure of silk. Image created by author Christine Schnittka.

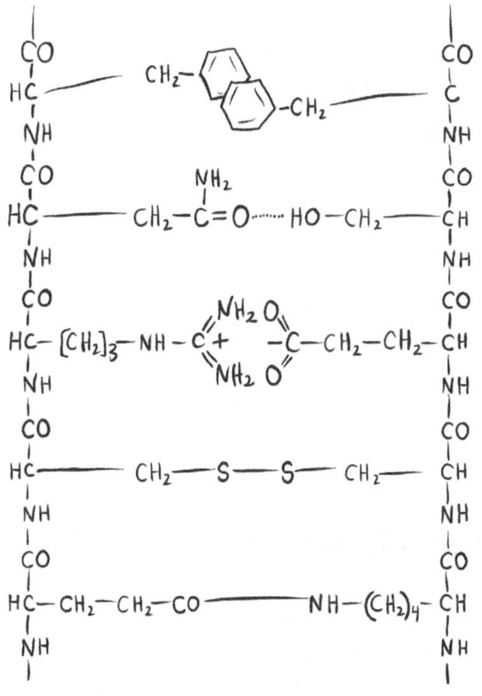

Figure 2.13 The chemical structure of wool protein. Image created by author Christine Schnittka.

Synthetic-based Fibers

Acrylic and nylon and polyester are polymers made from petroleum oil. As seen in Figure 2.14, they contain the elements C, H, and O. Petroleum oil is made from decaying plant and animal matter, and so it contains the same elements as plants and animals, which includes nitrogen. Polyester, derived from petroleum, looks very different than natural fibers do (Figure 2.15).

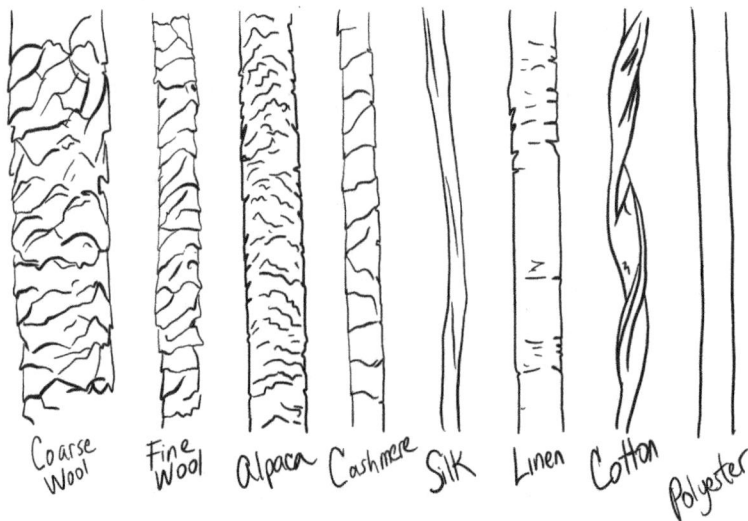

Figure 2.14 The chemical structure of acrylic. Image created by author Christine Schnittka.

Coarse Wool | Fine Wool | Alpaca | Cashmere | Silk | Linen | Cotton | Polyester

Figure 2.15 Comparing fibers microscopically. Image created by author Christine Schnittka.

Elaborate: Fiber Art, Craft, Technology, and Engineering

Purpose
The purpose of the Elaborate phase of this lesson is to apply the science of fibers to craft, art, technology, and engineering. Now that your students have experimented with fibers and learned about the science of fibers, it's time to engineer some string and fabric! After making a string or fabric by following some specific instructions, students can engineer their own to meet certain specifications.

Overview
Students listen to the story of Rockpunzel (Rapunzel but with a character change). The story about Rapunzel was written by The Brothers Grimm in

1812, but instead of Rapunzel letting down her hair to allow others to climb up into her locked tower, Rockpunzel cuts off her hair and spins it into a rope so she can escape! Students are given a sample of her hair to make their own rope for Rockpunzel.

The Challenge

There is an ancient story that many people have heard, about a young woman with long hair who is trapped in a tower. The tower has a window, and the young woman stays in the tower, wistfully gazing out of the window, letting down her hair for the sorceress to climb up and bring her food, until a prince climbs up her hair to rescue her.

In this challenge, the young woman is named Rockpunzel. She is made of rocks! And instead of waiting for a prince to rescue her, she cuts off her hair and spins it into a rope. She then uses the rope to rescue herself!

Probing Questions to Ask

What materials do you think Rockpunzel has up in that tower?

- She has her hair!

What would make a good rope for her to use to rescue herself?

- It would need to be strong, and ideally it would have knots to help her climb down.

The teacher should make Rockpunzel from a large, heavy rock. I like to use two rocks glued together with strong adhesive, and then glue some "hair" on top. See Figure 2.16. Be sure to have a string with a hook (a bent paper clip) attached to Rockpunzel so she can "climb" down the rope. Place Rockpunzel up on the top of a bookshelf or other high place, representing her tower. The tower must have something to tie a rope to, like a nail or screw or hook.

Give each student group the same amount of fiber. Wool or flax work the best for this challenge to represent Rockpunzel's hair. Challenge students to work together to make a rope that is long enough for Rockpunzel to get down from her tower without falling. The rope has to be strong enough not to break, and it has to have several knots along the length.

When a group has created a rope, secure it to the top of the "tower" and using the hook attached to Rockpunzel, have her climb down the rope. If she can successfully cling to each knot, and if the rope reaches the floor, the student group has successfully completed the challenge (Figure 2.17).

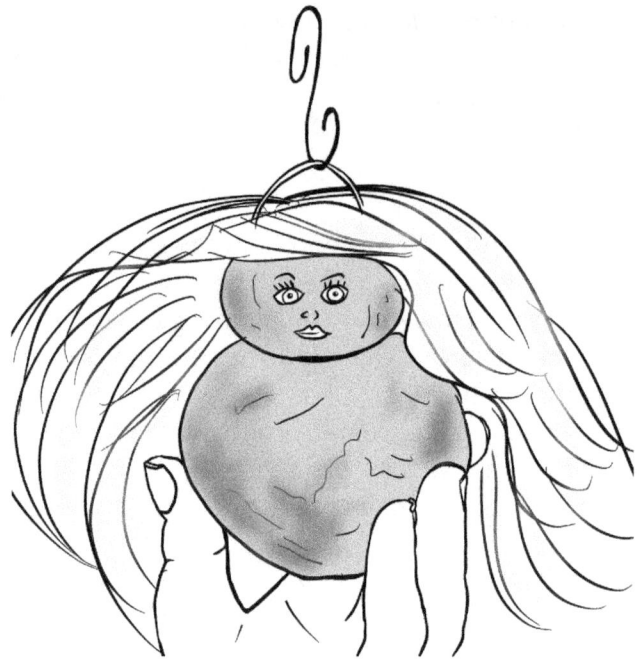

Figure 2.16 Rockpunzel. Image created by author Christine Schnittka.

Figure 2.17 Rockpunzel descending from her tower. Image created by author Christine Schnittka.

Probing Questions to Ask

How are ropes used in real life to rescue people?

- ♦ Ropes are used to rescue people trapped in a situation they can't escape from. A helicopter can fly overhead and lower a rope for them to climb up.
- ♦ People who climb mountains tie a rope to their waists and secure it to the mountain so if they fall, they will only fall as far as the rope.
- ♦ People who live in buildings that are too high to jump from will often have a rope ladder they can throw out the window in case of a fire.

- A student handout with the story of Rockpunzel and a description of this challenge is available on our website https://steamcrafts.weebly.com/.

Evaluate: What Did They Learn?

After making strings, rope, and yarn, ask your students to write the answers to the following questions to see what they learned. A form to collect the answers to these questions from your students is provided on our website https://steamcrafts.weebly.com/.

1. Why is it rare to find samples of rope or yarn that are thousands of years old?

    - ♦ Ropes and strings that are made from plant materials rot and disintegrate over time, so it is rare to find very old samples of them.

2. What artifacts have people found that indicate rope, string, or yarn was around?

    - ♦ There are sewing needles made from bone, dated to be 19,000 years old. Japanese pottery from 10,000 BCE contains imprints of twisted cords. An impression of twisted rope was found on a clay pot found in Scotland, believed to be 5,300 years old. In Egypt, evidence is found in paintings on ancient pottery and in ancient tombs.

3. What was the first rope-making tool?

   ◆ The first rope-making tool may have simply been a stick to wind the completed rope around. Put a notch at the top of your stick and it can be useful in helping you do the twisting. Tie a knot at the end of your new rope and secure in the notch, then roll the stick against your thigh to give it a good twist, and wrap your new rope segment around the stick as you go.

4. How does a drop spindle work?

   ◆ A drop spindle is a stick with a whorl and a hook or notch on it. Hook your fibers to the top of the stick and spin it to make yarn. Inertia will keep the spindle going while you feed more fibers into the newly made yarn.

5. How does a spinning wheel work?

   ◆ A spinning wheel uses a belt that surrounds a large wheel and a small one. When the large wheel turns, the small one turns much much faster. A spindle on the small wheel is used for spinning fibers.

6. What is a staple length?

   ◆ A staple is a small piece of fiber which is spun into a string. A staple length is the average length of this small piece.

7. What makes each staple stick to the others and form a string that you can pull on and not break?

   ◆ As the staples are pressed to each other by twisting them, friction keeps them together.

8. Why do you have to ply newly made string to keep it from unraveling?

   ◆ When you twist the fibers, you are putting energy into them. Twisted fibers can untwist easily after you let go of the new string. The new string acts like a spring when it's all twisted up, and will easily unravel. Plying two twisted strings that are twisted in <u>opposite</u> directions means that each will try to untwist in different directions. Since they are doing this at the same time, the plied yarn does not untwist at all.

9. What are plant fibers like cotton, bamboo, and hemp made from?

    ◆ Cellulose

10. What are wool and silk made from?

    ◆ Wool is made from keratin and silk is made from fibroin. These chemicals are both proteins.

Summary

The history of using fibers to make stringy things is long, and yet unfinished as new, innovative, high-tech fibers for rope making are invented. Ropes, string, threads, and yarn play vital roles in our lives today as they have for thousands of years. There is science spun into string!

Contemporary Fiber Artists

Today, artists use rope in all sorts of ways. Check out our website for links to some amazing modern fiber artists. It's possible to make rope or string from many types of materials such as old candy wrappers, newsprint, used grocery bags, and many types of plant material. So, use some science, math, and engineering design techniques to make some rope, string, yarn, or twine today!

References

Ardren, T., Manahan, T. K., Wesp, J. K., & Alonso, A. (2010). Cloth production and economic intensification in the area surrounding Chichen Itza. *Latin American Antiquity, 21*(3), 274–289.

Backwell, L., d'Errico, F., & Wadley, L. (2008). Middle stone age bone tools from the Howiesons Poort layers, Sibudu Cave, South Africa. *Journal of Archaeological Science, 35*(6), 1566–1580.

Bybee, R. W. (2009). *The BSCS 5E instructional model and 21st century skills*. National Academies Board on Science Education.

Conard, N.J., & Malina, M. (2016). Außergewöhnliche neue Funde aus den aurignacienzeitlichen Schichten vom Hohle Fels bei Schelklingen, *Archäologische Ausgrabungen in Baden-Württemberg*, 2015, 60–66.

Dewey, J. (1938). *Experience and education.* Macmillan.

Galilei, G. (1638). *Dialogues concerning two new sciences.* Leyden [Translated by A. DeSalvio and A. Fabaro (1914)].

Kenoyer, J. M. (2010). Measuring the Harappan world: Insights into the Indus order and cosmology. In: Morley, I., & Renfrew, C. (Eds) *The archaeology of measurement: Comprehending heaven, earth and time in ancient societies* (pp. 106–121). Cambridge University Press.

Langgut, D., Yahalom-Mack, N., Lev-Yadun, S., Kremer, E., Ullman, M., & Davidovich, U. (2016). The earliest Near Eastern wooden spinning implements. *Antiquity, 90*(352), 973–990.

Piaget, J. (1955). The construction of reality in the child. *Journal of Consulting Psychology, 19*(1), 77.

3

Warp and Weft

Introduction

My first experience working with weaving was in a hot, summertime field across the street from my house in Georgia when I was about eight or nine years old. I remember pulling up the tall grasses, laying them flat on the ground, and weaving them into a mat for my "fort" in the woods. I could roll it up and carry it from the field to the woods. The distinct memory I have was the feeling of accomplishment, joy, and pride. Nobody taught me how to make a rug from tall grasses, but I figured it out. My fort was much more pleasant to play in with a woven covering over the pebbles, leaf litter, and red clay (Figure 3.1).

If you look around for things that are woven, you see them everywhere. You see fabric on people, windows, floors, furniture, beds, and in bathrooms. You might also see chair seats woven from grasses or twisted paper, as well as woven baskets. Some of your clothes have been woven and some have been knitted. (Your t-shirt is most likely knitted, whereas your blue jeans are most likely woven.) If you've followed the thread of a conversation, read a text, spun a yarn, gotten tangled up in a web of lies, unraveled the mystery of life, had your mind warped, went batty, woven an idea into a line of thought, or wound it all up into a neat ball, you've experienced the idea of weaving. Weaving is the act of interlacing one-dimensional objects like string or straw so that they form a two-dimensional sheet that is held together by friction. In this chapter, students explore the idea of weaving, investigate woven fabrics,

DOI: 10.4324/9781003428312-3

Figure 3.1 Weaving in a field of tall grasses. Image created by author Christine Schnittka.

learn about the ancient history of fabrics, learn about the science of fabrics, and create their own woven item just as I did all those years ago in a hot, summertime field in Georgia.

 Weaving History

Weaving fibers is a technology that has been around for tens of thousands of years. Weaving was invented independently in all the cultures of the world. People may have gotten the idea to weave from birds, as there are many species of weaver birds who weave twigs, grass, and other fibers into intricately shaped nests (Figure 3.2).

People first wove shelters and baskets from natural materials like branches and grasses like weaver birds do, and I did as a child. Then, after people figured out how to twist thinner natural fibers like flax, wool, and cotton into string, more types of weaving were invented. There is evidence that thin plant fibers were first twisted on purpose 34,000 years ago. Small samples of twisted wild flax, grown in what is today the country of Georgia, were found in soil samples taken from the floor of the Dzudzuana Cave in the foothills of

Figure 3.2 Weaver bird. Image created by author Christine Schnittka.

the Caucasus Mountains (Kvavadze et al., 2009). Some of these fiber remnants even appear to be dyed! The twisted fibers may have been used to make rope, or woven, we can't be sure.

While fragments of weaving have disintegrated, imprints of woven fabric in clay have been found in an archeological dig in what is now the Czech Republic (Soffer, 2004). The hunter-gatherers who left these textile imprints lived 27,000 years ago. Even though fabrics made from plant or animal fibers disintegrate, samples of weaving have been found all over the world which are thousands of years old.

The oldest *evidence* of woven fibers in China is a piece of woven silk fabric, found in the tomb of a child buried over 5,600 years ago (Vainker, 2004). A v-neck linen dress over 5,100 years old was discovered in an Egyptian tomb, and it is now on display in a London museum (Stevenson & Michel, 2016). While remnants of weaving from that time have deteriorated in India, evidence of weaving over 4,000 years ago is on statues and in the text, *Arthashastra,* written in Sanskrit between 3000 BCE and 2000 BCE (Wilson, 1979). In the English translation of *Arthashastra*, it says, "The Superintendent of Weaving shall employ qualified persons to manufacture threads (sútra), coats (varma), cloths (vastra), and ropes." The book mentions weaving with silk, linen, and wool. Wearing woven fabrics was more comfortable than wearing furs in warm climates. Plus, all those Egyptian mummies had to be wrapped in woven linen! One mummy needed approximately 372 m² (4,000 square feet) of woven linen. Weaving in Africa from linen and cotton, and in China and India from silk, are ancient traditions. While the cotton plant seems to have originated in Africa, it somehow migrated to South America where it was used for weaving there as well.

Weaving in South America is as ancient as the people who migrated there from Asia. Cloth samples woven by people living in the Andes mountain region, which runs the length of the western portion of the continent, have been preserved for 6,000 years (Stone, 2012). Woven from cotton, alpaca, or llama wool, textiles were used in this region for much more than clothing and blankets. Woven items were traded and used to show status, and in a culture that did not use the written word to communicate or leave behind thoughts and ideas, woven textiles filled that function. The backstrap loom was commonly used. As seen in Figure 3.3, the loom was attached to a structure such as a tree at one end, and a strap wrapped around the weaver's back kept the loom taught.

Figure 3.3 Inca weaver with backstrap loom. Image adapted from a photo in the public domain by author Christine Schnittka.

Tools for Weaving

The history of the loom is as rich as the history of weaving itself. A loom is simply a technology which facilitates weaving. A loom stretches out the long yarns, called the warp, so that the weft can be woven between them. Simple looms can be built with four sticks in the ground, and a stick crossways at each end to hold the textile in place. Horizontal looms with treadles were used in Egypt in 4400 BCE. Treadles were pushed with the feet in order to lift some of the warp threads and make it easier to pass the weft threads over and under (Bruno, 1997).

Another early loom design was used vertically instead of horizontally. The warp was kept taught with clay weights tied to the end of each warp string. These looms have long since disintegrated, but the weights have been unearthed in archaeological digs all over Europe that date to 7,000 years ago. In today's northern Croatia, in the town of Zadubravlje near the border with Bosnia and Herzegovina, the oldest loom weights have been unearthed (Minichreiter, 2001). Figure 3.4 depicts a Greek woman weaving on a loom with weights in 540 BCE.

Figure 3.4 Vertical loom with weights. Image adapted from photo in the public domain by author Christine Schnittka.

Looms entered the computer age in the 19th century when punched cards were used to control the pattern made by the loom. These looms, named after their inventor, Joseph Marie Jacquard, demonstrate an early type of computer programming. The warp threads passed through holes in small, cardboard cards, which acted as the hardware. When the cards were twisted to raise and lower different threads, patterns were created when the weft was woven. The pattern of holes on the cards acted as the software because they could be easily manipulated and changed. This type of loom was the inspiration for the first computer, the Analytical Engine, invented by Charles Babbage in 1837.

Throughout history, woven materials have been used for applications such as medical bandages, food storage, ship sails, and fishing nets in addition to clothing, bedding, and mummy wrapping. Weaving was a slow process, often done by women at home. Weaving the sail on a ship might take more time than building the ship! The industrialization of weaving, with mechanized looms, mechanized processing of raw fibers, and mechanized spinning of fibers into yarn, created the modern world (Figure 3.5).

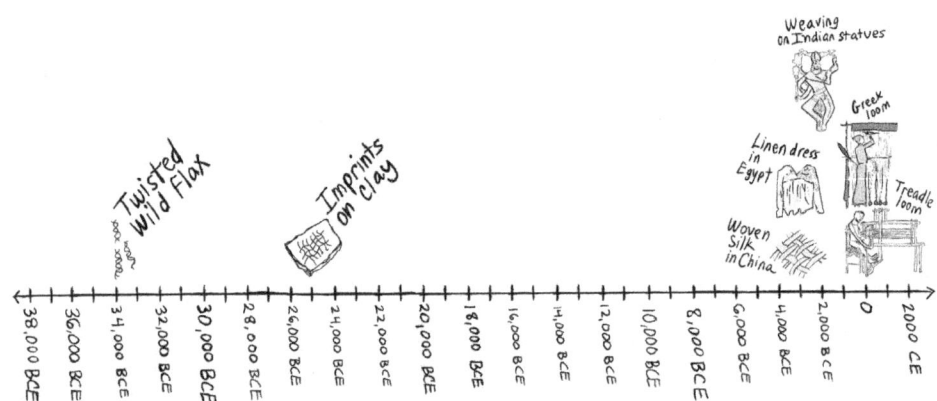

Figure 3.5 Timeline of weaving history. Image by author Christine Schnittka.

Meeting the Standards

Teaching this chapter as written focuses on STEAM principles that include: historical elements that influenced technological advancements, engineering principles including iterative design, criteria and constraints, and scientific measurement principles as well as data collection and analysis. For more detailed information regarding which specific standards are covered in this unit, please refer to our website: https://steamcrafts.weebly.com/.

Materials

- Assortment of woven materials (fabric samples)
- Assortment of ribbon, yarn, string, rope, twine, thread, etc.
- Digital projector display for teacher presentation(s)
- Magnifying lenses
- Paper (copy paper is fine)
- Scissors (for student use)
- Glue (tacky glue or other liquid craft glue)
- Tape (masking or cellophane are fine)
- Optional materials: 3D printer, one or many digital microscopes
- 3D printed shuttles, looms, and heddles.
- Printed copies of handouts found on our website: https://steamcrafts.weebly.com/

Safety

- Be careful when using scissors to cut materials.
- Use caution when 3D printing and keep hands away from the build plate and heated nozzle while printing.

The Lesson

> **The BSCS 5E Instructional Model for Weaving**
>
> The lessons in this book are designed around the BSCS 5E instructional model designed by the Biological Sciences Curriculum Study (Bybee, 2009). Based on Dewey's model of reflective thinking (Dewey, 1938), Piagetian theory (Piaget, 1955), and other learning cycle models that followed, the five phases of this model are: Engage, Explore, Explain, Elaborate, and Evaluate. The purpose and summary for each phase are explained in the sections that follow.

- To find accompanying presentations, student handouts, and more be sure to visit our website: https://steamcrafts.weebly.com/.

Engage: Weaving Ways

Purpose

The purpose of this phase of the lesson is to build excitement about weaving, to initiate curiosity about weaving and the process of creating something. It's also a chance for the teacher to find out any prior knowledge students have about weaving. Students should observe woven materials at a macro scale (with their eyes) as well as on the micro scale (with a zoomed in image or with a microscope).

Overview

Students should examine different woven textiles and make observations about the material used as well as the pattern used to create the woven product. If available, digital microscopes can be used to examine different woven products in the room—students' shirts, pants, etc. Being able to see these items at 200x magnification is very interesting. Once students see the items that they experience on a daily basis close-up, they will be shocked at how different they look on a microscopic scale versus a macroscopic scale. Encourage students to attempt to draw the patterns that they find (Figure 3.6).

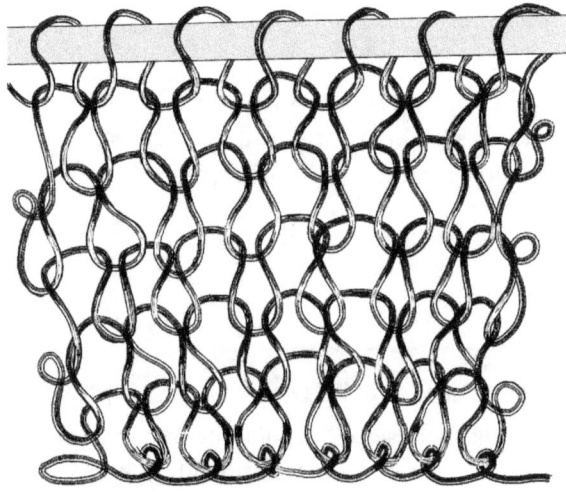

Figure 3.6 Knitted textile. Image created by author Christine Schnittka.

If digital microscopes are not available or affordable, students can still use handheld lenses and think about how the different products they have encountered have different weaving patterns and resulting properties. Using the printable resources found on our website https://steamcrafts.weebly.com/ students can begin to make connections between the small scale arrangement of materials and how that plays a role in the eventual resulting product.

Probing Questions to Ask
What do you think makes these textiles behave differently from each other?

- ◆ Woven fabrics will be stiff in the x and y directions while knitted or crocheted fabrics will be stretchy.

Most students have never considered why their t-shirts are stretchy and a woven pillowcase is not.

Why would you want some textiles to behave like knitted fabrics and some like woven ones?

- ◆ The stretchiness of knitted material is important in tight-fitting garments, whereas the stiffness of woven materials is important for clothing that needs to drape a certain way and hide what is underneath it.

How would you make each of these fabrics, the stretchy ones and the non-stretchy ones?

- ◆ See if students know about woven and knitted materials and can articulate the methods of knitting, crocheting, or weaving.

Explore: Weaving With Purpose

Purpose
The purpose of this phase of the lesson is to allow students to try their hand at creating different weaving patterns and physically experience how the warp and weft work together to make a design.

Overview
Students can use the handouts found on our website https://steamcrafts.weebly.com/ to try various mini challenges. They can use pieces of paper of varying widths, or they can use different gauges of string or yarn. In addition to this, students will also examine the properties of different materials such as drape, strength, and transparency by looking at examples of woven textiles.

Pass out a collection of different types of woven fabric to students. Include woven medical bandaging, thin fabric that you can see through, as well as thick fabric used for upholstery. Be sure to source a variety of materials such as cotton, wool, and polyester. Add a sample of knitted cotton fabric to the collection as well. Be sure that each sample is the same size, such as a square 10cm x 10cm (4" x 4"). Also distribute a data table for collecting data on each type of fabric.

Drape
Ask students to place each sample on their fingertip and describe the way it behaves. Some fabrics will fall straight down on all sides of the finger, but others will almost stay flat. Have students create a record of the fiber type, the yarn thickness, and the amount of drape they observe.

Textile engineers measure drapability by measuring the area of the shadow created by a light source. The bigger the shadow, the stiffer the textile. The smaller the shadow, the more the textile drapes (Figure 3.7).

Ask students:

What do you think causes some fabrics to be good at draping while others are not?

Figure 3.7 The shadow caused by fabric drape. Image created by author Christine Schnittka.

- The drape of a textile depends on the thickness of the fiber or string it is made from. The thinner the fiber, the more flexible the material and the more it drapes. If you make a tablecloth from thick fibers, it will not drape over the edges of the table very well. Drapability is also dependent on the amount of twist in the yarns used, plus the type of fiber used. Yarns become stiffer when they are more tightly twisted.

Have students rate the drapability of each sample.

Strength

Ask students to take each sample of fabric and try to rip it. Some samples may rip easily while others will not rip without scissors.

Have them add a column to their data chart to document the "rippability" or strength of the fabric.

Ask students:

What do you think makes some fabrics stronger than others?

- Tearing strength is the strength a material has when subject to opposing forces that might cause it to tear. Twill fabrics like blue jeans have a higher tearing strength than plain woven ones because the weft yarns that run side to side jump over and under two warp yarns which run top to bottom. Since more weft is exposed, and there are fewer tight intersections between the yarns, they can slide against each other easier. Tight intersections of weft and warp make tearing easier.

Why would you want some fabrics to resist tearing?

- A fabric used for something like a tablecloth is not subjected to forces over and over again, but fabric used to make pants needs to resist tearing since it is stretched and bent over and over. A textile that is bent and pulled on a lot needs to resist tearing or else it will fail. Other examples of fabrics that need to resist tearing are book covers, seat cushions, and even backpacks.

What makes a fabric strong?

- Friction holds the fibers in the yarn together, and friction holds the yarns together as they cross each other. Friction is a force that can oppose motion, and the more tight, overlapping fibers there are, the stronger the woven material.

Transparency

For the final exploration, have students try to look through their fabric samples and describe how see-through or transparent each sample is. Have them collect this data and add it to their table.

Ask students:
What do you think makes some fabrics see-through and others not?

- ◆ Woven materials are porous. In-between each vertical and horizontal thread is a small gap. The size of the gaps in woven fabric impacts things like breathability, resistance to abrasion, and strength. When weaving, the weft materials can be pushed tightly together or not. The warp threads can be close together or wider apart. This factor impacts how much materials drape, shrink when washed, and allow air and liquids to pass through.

Why would you want some fabrics to be transparent and others not?

- ◆ When transporting coffee beans, a woven sack keeps the beans together, but allows any moisture in the beans to evaporate.
  When brewing a cup of tea, the tea bag keeps the leaves from floating into your drink but allows water to get the leaves wet and remove the flavor. Conversely, umbrellas need to keep out water and sun!

- Two versions of this lesson are available on our website https://steamcrafts.weebly.com/. One utilizes digital microscopes, one uses concepts within this chapter to help students make connections between the properties of woven materials and their applications.

Explain: The STEAM Concepts

Purpose

The purpose of this phase of the lesson is to allow students to gain new scientific knowledge and understanding of how fibers, string, and fabrics work in order to make informed design decisions in a later phase. Students should understand that different types of materials, and different weaving patterns, will impart different properties on the final product. Lastly, they should understand how looms can make weaving easier, but require the production of a corresponding heddle.

Overview

A presentation found on our website https://steamcrafts.weebly.com/ discusses different examples of weaving science that can be used to show students the science embedded in woven technology. In this phase of the lesson, you should first ask your students to explain their new reasonings and understandings. It's very important in this phase of the lesson to find out what students are thinking before teaching them the STEAM concepts of fibers, strings, and fabrics. What follows is a discussion of the basics and the details of fiber science.

Make Weaving Science: The Basics

The fibers in woven materials are oriented *orthogonally*. That means that the fibers are oriented 90 degrees from each other. The warp is placed first (strung from top to bottom) and then the weft is woven in from right to left, then from left to right, over and over again.

There are many different ways to weave fibers. The plain weave is what you are used to: over, under, over. under. Twill is different: over two, under two. When the start and stop of the weft are offset, this creates diagonal lines on the fabric surface. Denim jeans are usually woven in twill.

Look at the two drawings of fabric in Figure 3.8. Which is twill and which is plain?

Ship sails might be tightly woven so as to catch the wind, whereas medical bandages might be loosely woven to allow air to circulate. Fishing nets are SO loosely woven that water easily passes through but fish do not.

Figure 3.8 Plain weave and twill weave. Image created by author Christine Schnittka.

Woven materials are generally not elastic in either the horizontal or the vertical directions, unless elastic yarns are used in the warp or weft. However, woven materials do have elasticity in the diagonal direction as the yarns pivot where they overlap. Today's blue jeans are usually made of cotton and a stretchy fiber like Lycra, so that they stretch a bit. Before Lycra was used in blue jeans, they did not stretch much at all and jeans had to be "broken in" before they were comfortable.

Weaving Science: The Details

Today, the airbags in your cars that keep you safe in an accident are made from woven materials. Seatbelts are made from woven materials. The suits that astronauts wear are made from woven materials. Even surprising items such as umbrellas are often woven. Sometimes, woven materials are embedded inside plastic or rubber. You can see this in car tires and in the grocery store belt that moves your items along after you place them on it. Did you know that duct tape also has woven materials embedded in there?

Ask students:

Why do you think woven materials are used in these technologies?

- ◆ Strength and flexibility are properties that can be obtained by weaving.

Let's explore some specific fibers and how they are used to create woven fabrics with helpful properties.

Nomex

Nomex is a flame and heat resistant synthetic fiber similar to nylon. However, unlike nylon, Nomex fibers do not melt or burn. Nomex can be used to make solid objects, but it can also be used to make thin fibers. These fibers do not conduct electricity, and they are chemical resistant. Nomex fabrics are used in clothing for firefighters, military pilots, and racecar drivers. The properties of Nomex fibers make them good for automotive, aerospace, military, law enforcement, fire fighter, and other first responder industries. Nomex can be woven to create personal protective equipment (PPE) clothing for any workers that are subject to flame, heat, and arc flash risks.

Teflon

Teflon Polytetrafluorethylene (PTFE) is a hydrophobic (water repelling) polymer that is most commonly associated with non-stick cookware. However, Teflon PTFE also exists in a fiber form! PTFE was originally discovered by Roy. J Plunkett in 1938 while he was researching refrigerants during his time at DuPont. The non-stick and non-slip properties of Teflon polymer are retained in the Teflon fiber. It is important to note that Teflon is a brand name of

PTFE fibers. Other companies also use PTFE fibers. Fabrics woven from these fibers are chemical, flame, and abrasion resistant. In fact, NASA chose Teflon fibers for their Apollo Flight Suit. Teflon fabrics can be combined or bonded to other materials for multifunctional applications. Teflon fabrics are used in self-lubricating/maintenance-free bearings in aerospace and automotive industries as well as in office equipment and off-road equipment.

Kevlar

Stephanie Kwolek invented the polymer Kevlar ($C_{14}H_{14}N_2O_4$) while she was working for DuPont as a chemist in the 1960s. She had been asked to invent a super strong fiber to make tires out of, and she came up with something even better. The fiber she invented has been woven into fabrics so strong, they can stop a speeding bullet. The tensile strength of Kevlar is five times that of steel! Her invention and the woven materials made from it have saved thousands of lives. The woven fabric is also used inside tires, as protective gloves, for fireproof clothing, and more. Kevlar is an expensive fabric. However, don't plan on cutting it or sewing with it. If it stops a speeding bullet, imagine how it responds to a pair of scissors and a needle. Not well!

Carbon Nanotubes

Scientists at Rice University in Houston, Texas, and in Tokyo, Japan, have figured out that when special nanosized carbon tubes are woven into fabrics, the fabric can convert heat into electricity. Thermocouples are devices made from two different types of metal wire. When the junction where the two metal wires are soldered together gets hot, an electrical voltage is produced. The hotter the temperature, the higher the voltage. As for the nanosized carbon tubes in fabric, a similar method is used. Carbon nanotubes are connected to steel threads. When the fabric heats up, it produces a voltage where the carbon nanotube is joined to a steel thread. While weaving is not necessary for this technology, it may bring a lot of innovative applications to woven fabrics in the future.

Ask students after this lesson:
What makes something woven?

- ◆ The orthogonal interlacing of long, flexible materials such as string makes something woven.

Define warp and weft.

- ◆ Warp is the component of a woven item which remains stationary as the weft is placed under and over it. Weft is the component of a woven item which goes under and over the stationary weft.

What are some properties of woven materials?

- Woven materials are flexible but strong. They are often somewhat porous and can be made from animal, mineral, or plant materials.

Describe some high-tech woven materials.

- Kevlar is so strong, it cannot be cut with regular scissors. Teflon fabrics are very tough. Nomex materials are flame and heat resistant. Carbon nanotubes can be woven into fabrics and produce electricity.

Elaborate: Weaving Art, Craft, Technology, and Engineering

Purpose
The purpose of the Elaborate phase of this lesson is to apply the science of fibers to craft, art, technology, and engineering. Now that your students have experimented with fibers and learned about the science of fibers, it's time to engineer some fabric!

Overview
After making a fabric by following some specific instructions, students can engineer their own to solve specific problems they have. Perhaps they want to create coasters for drinks so the table stays dry. Perhaps they want to gather a small piece of fabric around each leg of their desk chair to make it slippery. Perhaps they wish to create a small, soft washcloth or a tough pot holder.

Weaving Ways
Before delving into the fabric-making project, ask:

If you had to write a computer program to describe different weaving patterns, what would it be?

For example, twill might be woven with this computer program:
START
2 OVER 2 UNDER REPEAT 2X
REPEAT ABOVE LINE
2 UNDER 2 OVER REPEAT 2X
REPEAT ABOVE LINE
REPEAT ABOVE 4 LINES 2X
END

Plain woven fabric might be woven with this computer program:
START

OVER UNDER REPEAT 10X
REPEAT ABOVE LINE 10X
END
Ask students:
What would be the computer programs for these materials in Figure 3.9?

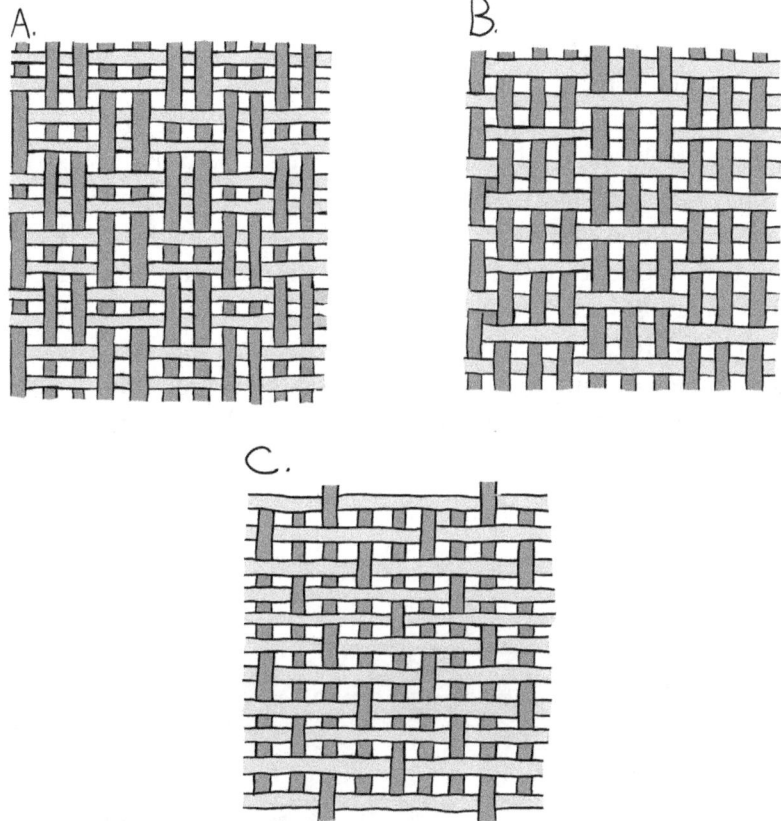

Figure 3.9 Different weaves. Image created by author Christine Schnittka.

Looms

Weaving uses "software" like the above text describes and can be accomplished with no tools at all—just fingers and hands. Have you ever made a friendship bracelet like the one below? You most likely did not use a loom, and you may have thought you were braiding, not weaving. Braiding is weaving! My middle school students used to make these simply by taping the warp to their desks and passing it back and forth AS THE weft. That's what braiding is … taking the warp and using it as weft (Figure 3.10).

Figure 3.10 Friendship bracelet. Image created by author Christine Schnittka.

Give students a piece of tape and six long strings. Have them tie a knot in the six strings at one end and tape the knot to the table in front of them. Instruct them to take the string on the right and weave it over and under the other strings, going right to left. They can repeat this over and over again, taking the string on the right, one of the warp strings, and weaving it as if it were weft. They will end up with a bracelet similar to the one in Figure 3.10!

A loom is a technological innovation that makes weaving easier and faster. A traditional way to weave is similar to the braiding technique used for making bracelets, but one end of the warp is attached to a stick held against the body, and the other end of the warp is tied around one's foot. This might be considered the most basic kind of loom. (Figures 3.11 and 3.12).

Some looms are large and complex with heddles that raise and lower the warp so that the weft can be passed under easily. The loom in Figure 3.13 has spools for wrapping the warp and the finished textile. As you let out the warp from the rear spool, you wind up the finished textile on the front spool.

Figure 3.11 Peruvian girl weaving. Image adapted by author Christine Schnittka inspired by photograph by Rob Young which is licensed under CC BY 2.0.

Warp and Weft ◆ 49

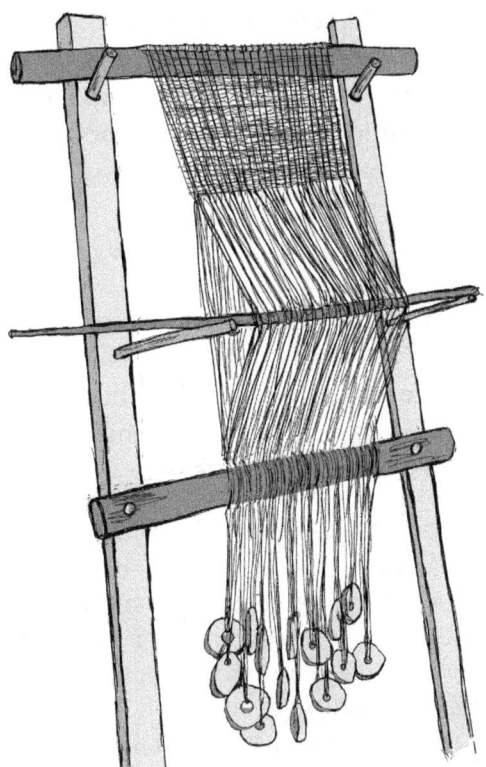

Figure 3.12 Weighted loom. Image adapted by author Christine Schnittka inspired by a photograph in the public domain.

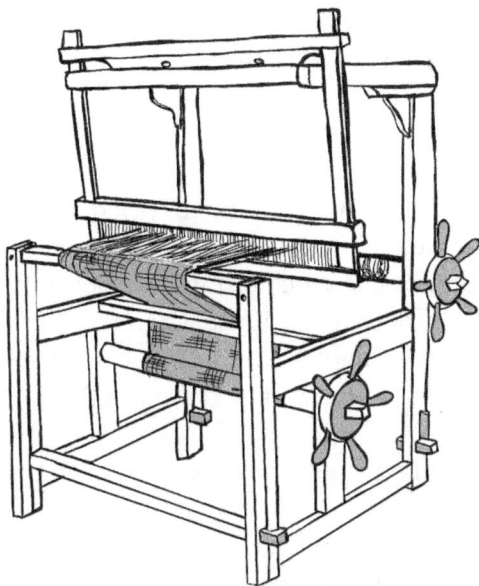

Figure 3.13 Loom with heddle. Image adapted by author Christine Schnittka by image entitled "Looms" by bonaircat which is licensed under CC BY 2.0.

- A student handout is provided on our website https://steamcrafts.weebly.com/ in order to help students conceptualize the relationship between weaving patterns and computer coding. The pattern of a weave can impart different qualities on a woven product, and therefore the pattern should be carefully considered when making a woven product that is made for a given purpose.

The Challenge

The challenge for this phase of the lesson is to have students create a unique woven product. They can create an advertisement, a price point, a material to use, a pattern, and even create a custom heddle to help produce their product. See https://steamcrafts.weebly.com/ for additional student handouts that help to establish the deliverables of this challenge.

> Many years ago when I was a very busy and distracted middle school teacher, the mother of one of my students set up her loom near my classroom for students to try out. I found time during my break one day to weave a long strip of fabric, about 9" long and 3" wide. After removing it from the loom, I folded it up and stitched it into a pocket with a long cord attached to it. I would wear this pocket around my neck during the school day, and I kept a small audio recorder in it to capture my thoughts, to-do items, and things to remember throughout the day.

Many problems can be solved with a small piece of woven fabric. When one takes the small square and sews a running stitch around the perimeter, it can be cinched into a small baggie (Figures 3.14 and 3.15).

Other Ideas

- Design a piece of fabric to hold scented, dried flowers so that the flowers are contained.
- Design a piece of fabric to cinch around the bottom of a classroom chair leg to reduce friction and noise when the chair is moved.
- Design a soft and absorbent cloth that can be used to wash one's face.
- Design a piece of fabric that can be placed in the back of a shoe to prevent blisters.
- Design a piece of fabric that can be used for a tea bag to brew a cup of herbal tea.
- Design a coaster for a drink which does not allow fluid to reach the table.
- Design a small potholder one can use with a hot beverage.
- Design a small pocket that can be sewn to a backpack for storing an ID card.

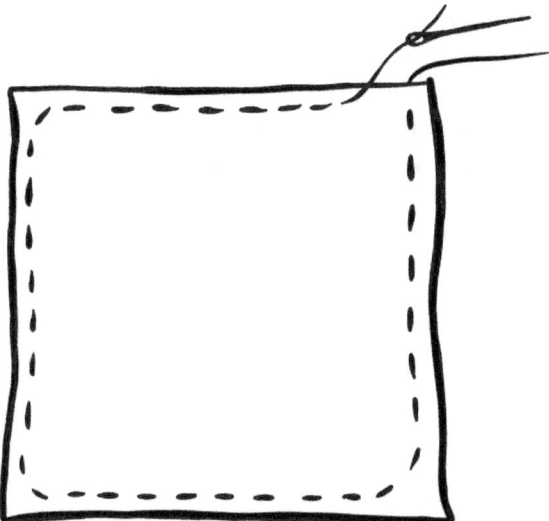

Figure 3.14 Running stitch around a small square of fabric. Image created by author Christine Schnittka.

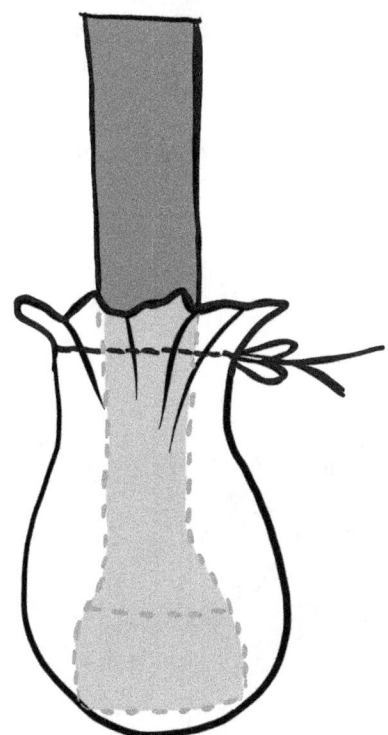

Figure 3.15 Chair leg protector. Image created by author Christine Schnittka.

To weave this small piece of fabric, students can use commercially purchased looms, or they can invent their own looms, or the teacher can 3D print looms for them.

To invent one's own loom, students can use old picture frames or they can recreate some of the looms they learned about in this chapter (Figures 3.16 and 3.17).

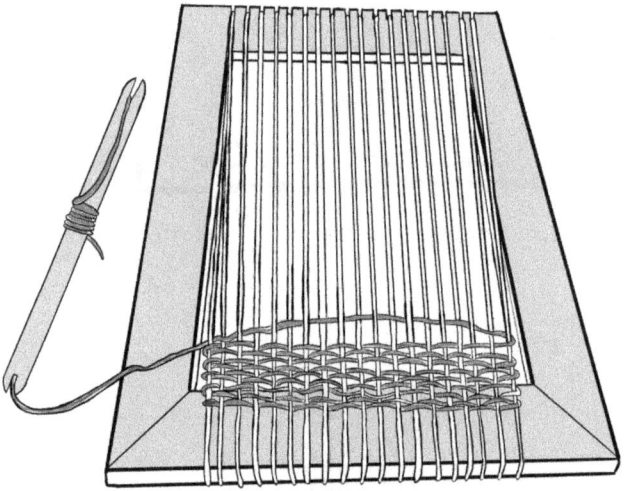

Figure 3.16 Loom made from picture frame. Image created by author Christine Schnittka.

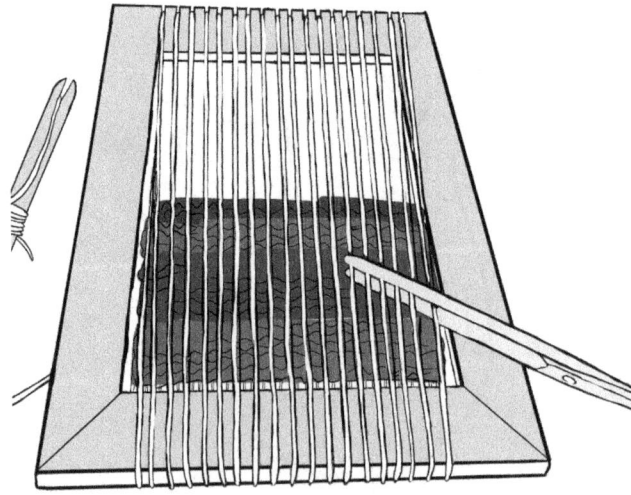

Figure 3.17 The back of the loom made from a picture frame. Image created by author Christine Schnittka.

Directions for a Frame Loom

1. Warp your loom by wrapping yarn around the frame, aligning the yarn with notches created with a file or other sharp object.
2. Weave your weft back and forth across and under the warp. If you wish, you can use a popsicle stick as a shuttle.
3. For additional help, use a heddle to raise and lower odd and even warp. A heddle has notches that raise the even strings of warp when it is in one orientation. Turn the heddle to the other side and you raise the odd strings.
4. When you are done weaving, cut the strings on the back of the loom.
5. Take 2–3 of the loose warp strings and tie a knot close to the woven fabric. Repeat this across the top and bottom of your piece.
6. Take a needle and weave in any loose weft strings so that they are hidden.
7. Trim all loose strings!

A very simple loom can be made from cardboard as shown in Figure 3.18.

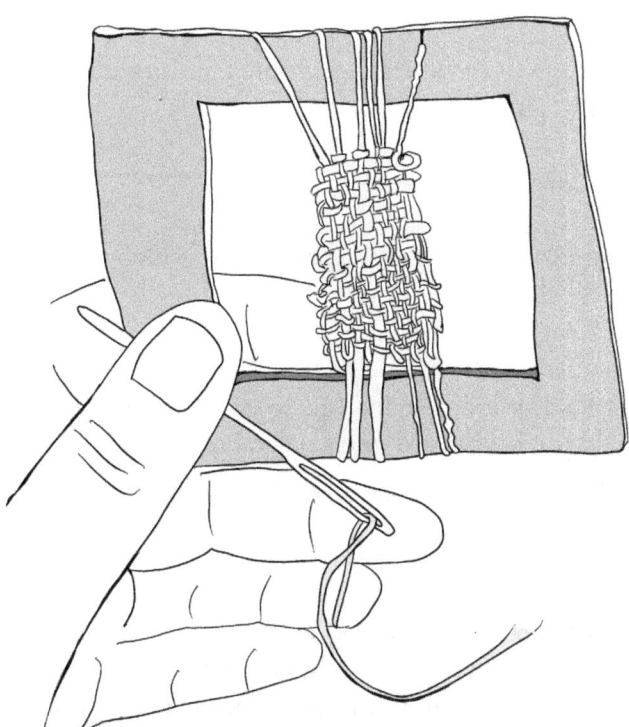

Figure 3.18 Simple loom made from cardboard. Image created by author Christine Schnittka.

3D Printed Looms

We have designed looms, shuttles, and heddles that can be 3D printed. Different heddles can be used to create patterns with the weft.

After students have completed their projects, give them the opportunity to share their design and their product with the class. This can be done poster-style with drawings, text, and images, or it can be done digitally as a presentation.

- The 3D design files as well as handouts to organize student effort can be found on our website: https://steamcrafts.weebly.com/.

Evaluate: What Did They Learn?

After making their fabric and turning it into a problem-solving device, ask your students to write the answers to the following questions to see what they learned. A form to collect the answers to these questions from your students is provided on our website https://steamcrafts.weebly.com/.

1. The first clothing was probably made from fur or animal skin. Why do you think people started weaving clothing?

    - Wearing woven fabrics was more comfortable than wearing furs in warm climates.

2. What is a loom?

    - A loom is an invention, a technology, which makes weaving easier.

3. What is a backstrap loom?

    - A backstrap loom is tied to a tree or a door or even one's foot, and then tied behind one's back. It's a portable loom one can use anywhere.

4. Why might looms use weights?

    - Weights can be tied to the different warp threads to keep them vertical and taught while a person weaves. It may be easier to weave standing up than sitting on the ground or bending over a low, horizontal loom.

5. What makes woven fabric strong?

    ◆ The friction between crossing warp and weft creates strength in a fabric.

6. What makes fabric stiff and not drape well?

    ◆ The thicker the yarn and the tighter the twist of the yarn contributes to the stiffness of the fabric.

7. What is "orthogonal"?

    ◆ The fibers in woven materials are oriented *orthogonally*. That means that the fibers are oriented 90 degrees from each other.

8. What is a shuttle and what is a heddle?

    ◆ A shuttle is a device that the weft yarn is wrapped around. It is passed under and over the warp yarn. A heddle is a device that lifts some warp yarns so you can easily pass the shuttle under them.

Summary

The history of weaving is long, and yet unfinished as new, innovative, high-tech textiles are invented. Textiles and other woven materials play vital roles in our lives today as they have for thousands of years. There is science buried in those orthogonally oriented yarns … science that helps textiles resist fire, speeding bullets, and a cold winter chill. Woven materials' strength, flexibility, durability, and versatility are something worth noticing and appreciating.

Contemporary Weaving Artists

Weaving is still a relevant art and craft today. Artists and craftspeople around the world weave and do fascinating things with what they make.

For links to examine modern weaving artists, please see our website https://steamcrafts.weebly.com/.

References

Bruno, L. C. (1997). Science and technology firsts. *Gale Publishing*. https://lccn.loc.gov/96043595

Bybee, R. W. (2009). *The BSCS 5E instructional model and 21st century skills*. National Academies Board on Science Education.

Dewey, J. (1938). *Experience and education*. Macmillan.

Kvavadze, E., Bar-Yosef, O., Belfer-Cohen, A., Boaretto, E., Jakeli, N., Matskevich, Z., & Meshveliani, T. (2009). 30,000-year-old wild flax fibers. *Science*, *325*(5946), 1359–1359.

Minichreiter, K. (2001). The architecture of early and middle neolithic settlements of the Starčevo culture in Northern Croatia. *Documenta Praehistorica*, *28*, 199–214.

Piaget, J. (1955). The construction of reality in the child. *Journal of Consulting Psychology*, *19*(1), 77.

Soffer, O. (2004). Recovering perishable technologies through use wear on tools: Preliminary evidence for Upper Paleolithic weaving and net making. *Current Anthropology*, *45*(3), 407–413.

Stevenson, A., & Michel, W. D. (2016). Confirmation of the world's oldest woven garment: The Tarkhan Dress. *Antiquity Project Gallery*, *90*, 349.

Stone, R. (2012). *Art of the Andes: From Chavin to Inca*. Thames & Hudson.

Vainker, S. (2004). *Chinese silk: A cultural history*. Rutgers University Press.

Wilson, K. (1979). *A history of textiles*. Westview Press.

4

Clean Chemistry

Introduction

Some of my earliest childhood memories involve bathtubs and bubbles. I would soap up a washcloth and then blow through it from the other side, producing mounds and mounds of bubbles to add to my bathwater. When I demonstrate this for my grandchildren today, they shriek with joy! We humans just love our bubbles (Figure 4.1).

Soap is probably the first human-made chemical that ever touched your skin. Think about it. You were born, you snuggled with your mother, and then you probably went off to the nursery for a bath. Where would we be without soap? We would be dirtier and germier for sure, our clothing would be permanently soiled, and our bedsheets, towels, and dishcloths would stink. Bet you never stopped to thank soap for all the good it does. One would think that we humans have been using soap for a very long time, but it's a somewhat recent invention in the grand scheme of things, particularly for personal hygiene. As recently as 1846, doctors were delivering babies without even washing their own hands, much less the babies and their mothers. Surprisingly, scientists had yet to deduce the germ nature of disease. That year, the Hungarian doctor Ignaz Semmelweis tried to figure out why so many women died from blood infections after giving birth. He tried switching the birth position, and even tried keeping the noise down, but still, women who gave birth in hospitals were dying in great numbers. It was the accidental prick of a pathologist's finger with a blood sample from the cadaver of a deceased mother (and the pathologist's subsequent death) that sparked the idea that "cadaver

Figure 4.1 Blowing bubbles. Image created by author Christine Schnittka.

particles" were the root cause of maternal death. After Dr. Semmelweis instructed his staff to wash their hands with soap, water, and chlorine to remove these cadaver particles, the maternal death rate plummeted. However, people have a habit of not agreeing with scientific discoveries in the beginning because the new ideas disrupt their mental models about how the world works. The other doctors at the hospital did not like being blamed for the spread of germs and eventually stopped hand washing. Dr. Semmelweis lost his job. Poor Dr. Semmelweis did not fare well after this rejection of his discovery and died at age 47 in a mental institution from … you guessed it … a blood infection (Davis, 2015; Kadar et al., 2018).

So, wash your hands and get ready to learn how to teach your students all about life saving, good smelling, bubbly soap.

 Soap History

Cleansing agents were invented independently around the world by people from several different cultures using simple materials they had access to. And funny enough, these cleansing agents were made from two waste products commonly found around a campfire.

Five thousand years ago, the Babylonians left behind a clay tablet with a recipe for us. If you can read Sumerian, have a go at it! You can take a look at this tablet on the University of Pennsylvania's Penn Museum website linked on our website, www.steamcrafts.weebly.com/.

In case you can't read Sumerian, I think it says to take ashes from a false carob tree, mix them with dried figs and salt, and boil them in water, and with this water, wash the diseased place. The clay tablet even mentions beer and bat dung for cleansing (Civil, 1960).

After the Babylonians were cleaning their diseased places with ash water, there was a recipe written in the Book of Numbers in the Hebrew Bible (perhaps dated to 520 BCE) for making the same thing, what we now call lye. The ashes of a red heifer were mixed with water, and then a person dipped a hyssop branch into this liquid and sprinkled it on things to purify them. Konkol and Rasmussen (2015) point out that the word hyssop and soap sound similar.

> A person who is clean shall take hyssop, dip it in the water, and sprinkle on the tent and on all the vessels and people who were there, or on him who touched the bones or the person who was killed or died naturally or the grave.
>
> (Numbers 19: 18)

Dousing your skin or your hair or your clothing with what is essentially drain cleaner to kill germs works. It's not that different from what Dr. Ignaz Semmelweis wanted doctors to do with bleach. However, if you have ever accidentally encountered a strong basic solution, like bleach or drain cleaner, you will know that it can be painful. Combining lye with fat or oil is what truly makes soap, "soap," the gentle cleanser.

There was a medical document found on papyrus in Egypt from 3,500 years ago, describing how to cure all sorts of ills, from blindness to cancer. We call this "The Ebers Papyrus" because Georg Ebers bought the 20-meter-long scroll back in the 1800s. In this scroll there are recipes for treating just about every possible human ailment, from bleary eyes to constipation. Ingredients used for these medicines were things such as "an old book cooked in oil," castor oil, myrrh, and wax. The recipe for a face wash found in section 718 includes whipped ostrich egg, salt, oil, and natron. Natron is a hydrated sodium carbonate, very similar to baking soda (sodium bicarbonate). Our chemical symbol for sodium, Na, is derived from the word natron. When natron is dissolved in water, the solution is alkaline. When this recipe for face wash was followed, something that approximated soap was created when the oil mixed with the alkaline natron solution. Whip up some chicken egg, salt, olive oil, and baking soda just to see if it cleans your face! (Figure 4.2)

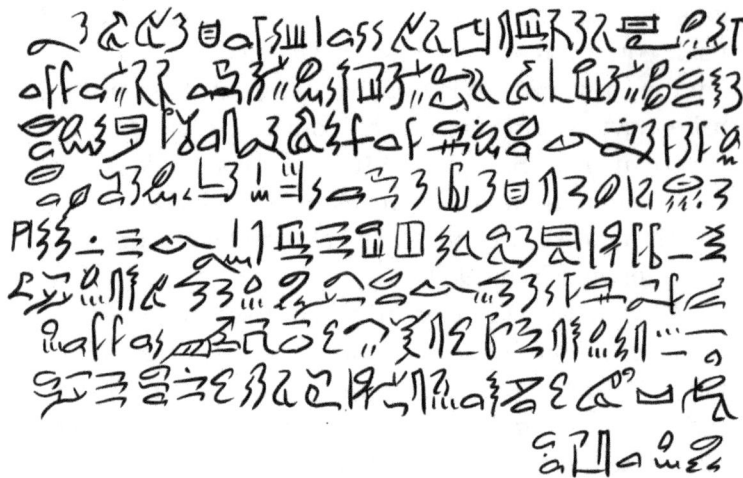

Figure 4.2 Section of the Ebers Papyrus from 1550 BCE. Image adapted by author Christine Schnittka from image in the public domain.

The Roman author, Pliny the Elder, who wrote *Naturalis Historia* in 77 CE wrote that soap was invented by the Gauls for washing hair, and that they used goat fat (called tallow) and beechwood tree ashes. These Gauls lived in modern-day France, where some of the best soaps are still made.

During the Middle Ages, folks in the Middle East were soaping up, but it seems that using soap in European countries fell out of fashion among "common folk" for some time, potentially contributing to the epidemic of Bubonic Plague that ravaged China, India, the Middle East, and particularly Europe during the late Middle Ages. Most of us were taught in school that the Bubonic Plague, caused by the bacteria *Yersinia pestis*, was spread by fleas on rats in Europe, but Dean et al. (2018) used mathematical models to analyze the historical data, and theorized that human lice and human fleas were the vector. What could have helped rid people of all those parasites? Soap!

Soap manufacturing returned to Europe in the 1400s with an industrialized model and factories that produced it by the ton. The knowledge of soap soon spread to China, where clothing, hair, and skin had been cleansed by a mixture of pig pancreas and dried bean powder called Zaodou (澡豆) or by a mixture of plant ash and burned shell ashes (Jiahui, 2023).

Soap didn't make its way to India until the late 1800s, where it was made from coconut oil and lye. Prior to this, people on the subcontinent cleansed their bodies with the ashes of the soapwort plant. People there usually belonged to one of three religions: Hinduism, Buddhism, or Jainism, and they were primarily vegetarians. So, inventing soap from lard or tallow just was not a likely event. However, coconut oil worked great! Likewise, people indigenous to the Americas often used the roots of the yucca plant to cleanse themselves, which produced a foamy lather (Wilson, 2023). They did not invent soap because they lacked an excess supply of animal fats. What fat they did have from small mammals or deer was consumed as a source of dietary calories.

The final story of soap comes from West Africa, where people today still make and sell their signature "black soap" made from the ashes of plantain peels, palm oil, and possibly cocoa powder, honey, and shea butter. It is not certain when the Yoruba people invented this soap because theirs was an oral, not a written, culture, but in the 1300s they were leading a sophisticated, urban life, and I'd like to think that soap played a role in their ability to live closely together in such a modern way. We made this soap outside on a gas grill, from water leached through wood ashes, a variety of oils, and shea butter, and it indeed worked great. You can find a video of our process on our website: https://steamcrafts.weebly.com/.

When you think about it, soap had to play an important role in human civilization once it was invented, as it significantly mitigated disease. Soap is one of the first medical interventions, invented by people who had an excess of fats and ashes, and happened to combine the two and discover all the potential they had working together synergistically (Figure 4.3).

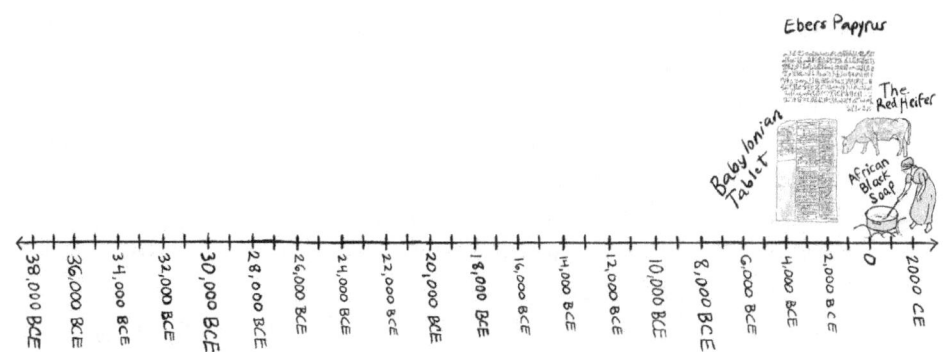

Figure 4.3 Timeline of soap. Image created by author Christine Schnittka.

When teaching about the history of soap, we suggest that this information is shared during the Explain portion of the unit. For a presentation outlining this information, be sure to visit our website: https://steamcrafts.weebly.com/.

Meeting the Standards

Teaching this chapter as written focuses on STEAM principles that include: historical elements that influenced technological advancements, engineering principles including iterative design, criteria and constraints, and scientific measurement principles as well as data collection and analysis. For more detailed information regarding which specific standards are covered in this unit, please refer to our website: https://steamcrafts.weebly.com/.

Materials

- Food grade NaOH pellets can be purchased online from several sources
- Fluorescent product such as Glo Germ, GLO Effex Glow in the Dark Paint
- UV Flashlights (ideally one per student group)
- Two digital scales: one for massing the NaOH pellets and one for massing the fat/oil
- Graduated cylinder for measuring the volume of water
- Variety of fats and oils (e.g. shortening, olive oil, coconut oil, canola oil)
- Glass bowl for mixing oils and NaOH solution
- Glass beaker for water
- Gloves, chemical goggles, lab apron
- Assortment of different soaps (e.g. bar soap, hand soap, dish soap, orange pumice, Dr. Bronner's, Tecnu)
- Glass beaker for measuring the mass of NaOH
- Immersion blender or handheld battery operated whisk (optional but highly recommended)
- Wooden spoon or wooden sticks used ONLY for soapmaking
- Styrofoam cups for making individual round bars of soap
- Melt-and-pour soap base—enough for each student to have one 50 gram bar of soap.
- Wooden craft sticks for mixing soap
- Optional: fragrances or essential oils, natural mica pigment powders for coloring the soap, and exfoliants such as oatmeal, poppy seeds, cornmeal, cinnamon, cocoa, or coffee grounds

Safety

- Soap is made to be used on the face, in the hair, and on the skin. So, soap in and of itself is not dangerous. However, soapmaking often involves chemicals that are caustic.
- Always use precautions when demonstrating soapmaking with caustic chemicals. These precautions include eye protection and skin protection as well as an apron to protect clothing.
- Keep children at a safe distance when demonstrating soapmaking with caustic chemicals. After soap has been made, it takes a few weeks for the pH value to fall into a safe range. Do not allow students to use soap that has not cured for the appropriate amount of time. Making soap in the "melt and pour" method is safe and appropriate for youth.
- Protect youth from heat sources and melted soap that is too hot for skin contact.
- Making soap from scratch requires the use of a strong base such as NaOH, sodium hydroxide, often called lye or drain cleaner. Using the right precautions, you can use NaOH safely. However, it may not be appropriate for students to use NaOH, and the teacher may have to complete the steps involving NaOH instead. Here are safety instructions for using NaOH. You MUST read this section if you are to purchase and/or use NaOH.

  - Purchase food grade NaOH pellets and store the container in a locked cabinet so that students do not access it.
  - Keep NaOH pellets in their original container. Keep the top screwed on at all times unless pouring out the pellets. You want to keep humidity out.
  - Wear medical-grade gloves, splash-proof goggles, and a lab coat when handling NaOH pellets or solutions of NaOH.
  - NEVER pour water onto NaOH pellets, <u>ONLY pour them into the appropriate amount of water.</u> If you pour water onto them, you will start off with a VERY concentrated solution of NaOH, which is not wise.
  - NaOH solutions in water look clear and harmless, but they are most definitely not. So, never leave a NaOH solution unattended. After making your NaOH solution, immediately use it by pouring it into the collection of fats and oils, as seen in Figure 4.10.
  - When working with NaOH, be near a source of water. If your classroom does not have a sink or an eye-wash station, do not use

NaOH. It is ideal to have absorbent powder available in case there is a spill. This powder can be purchased from any hardware store.

- CAUTION: If a NaOH pellet falls onto the counter or floor, do not pick it up with bare hands. If skin contacts a NaOH pellet, immediately shake it off then rinse the skin with water. A pellet will not burn unless the skin is sweating. However, if it remains on the skin, the skin will sweat, a chemical reaction will commence, heat will be generated, and the skin will be severely burned.
- CAUTION: If a NaOH solution gets in someone's eyes, remove contacts, peel back the lids, and flush with running water for 30 minutes. Seek medical attention as the eyes are being flushed.
- CAUTION: If a NaOH solution gets on someone's skin, remove any clothing that got wet, and immediately rinse the affected skin under running water for 30 minutes.
- CAUTION: If a NaOH solution spills, move people away from the spill immediately. Make sure you are wearing gloves, splash-proof goggles, and a lab coat. Bring a trash can (with a trash bag inside it) close to the spill. If you have absorbent powder (e.g. Spill Sorbent) pour it onto the spill and then move the powder into the trash can. If you do not have absorbent powder, drop paper towels or newsprint onto the spill to absorb the liquid. Do NOT pour water onto the spill. Using a gloved hand, place the wet paper into a trash can and seal the bag. Bag the trash a second time before disposal.
- CAUTION: Never let anyone have the opportunity to drink a NaOH solution. However, if someone accidentally ingests a NaOH solution, immediately give them water to drink, and then call Poison Control 1-800-222-1222. Do not induce vomiting.

The Lesson

> ### The BSCS 5E Instructional Model for Soap Making
> The lessons in this book are designed around the BSCS 5E instructional model designed by the Biological Sciences Curriculum Study (Bybee, 2009). Based on Dewey's model of reflective thinking (Dewey, 1938), Piagetian theory (Piaget, 1955), and other learning cycle models that followed, the five phases of this model are: Engage, Explore, Explain, Elaborate, and Evaluate. The purpose and summary for each phase are explained in the sections that follow.

- To find accompanying presentations, student handouts, and more be sure to visit our website: https://steamcrafts.weebly.com/.

Engage: Experience Soap

Purpose
The purpose of this phase of the lesson is to build excitement about soap and allow students to begin thinking about the variety of soaps there are, and wondering how it is made. It's also a chance for the teacher to find out what students know about soap and how it's made.

Overview
Students will apply a substance to their hands which glows when exposed to UV light. Then, they will wash their hands with various substances to see which soaps work best.

To begin, ask students when they last washed their hands? Their hair? Their car? Their dishes? Did they use soap? Have they ever tried washing something without soap? How effective was it? What do they think soap actually does to help clean things? This kind of questioning can get students thinking about experiences they have had involving soap. Once students have been reflective about their experiences, it is time to introduce the activity.

Introduce a fluorescent glow gel/paint/spray. This should be a substance that goes on essentially clear when applied to the hands (while being non-toxic of course), and then when exposed to UV light, shows up as a fluorescent stain on the hands. Some drying may be required to let the material set, but it should not be overly obvious that the product is on the hands unless it is shown under the UV light.

Explain that you are going to conduct an experiment on the effectiveness of soap versus the effectiveness of using just water on your hands to remove dirt and germs.

Provide the fluorescent staining agent, and have the students apply it to a small area of their hand—just make sure that it is applied in a uniform manner. Perhaps students could press a rubber stamp onto a sponge soaked in the fluorescent staining agent, and then stamp the back of their hand. Once they have applied the stain, students can blow on or wave their hands to let it dry. Next, have the students shine UV flashlights on their hands and reveal the fluorescent stain. They will be amazed at how the stain lights up so differently under UV light than under ordinary lights. If available, students can also take a picture of the staining agent on their hands before any is removed in the activity that follows. After they are finished confirming that the stain is working, then they should split into two groups. Half the students should wash their hands with just water, while the other half should use soap and water. Students should not use abrasive paper towels to dry off their hands, in order to keep the frictional removal of the stain out of the experiment.

Once the students have attempted their washing assignment (water or water and soap), have them shine the UV light on their hands a second time. Who still has the stain on their hands? Did any of the stain remain with the soap and water group? Did any of the stain get removed from the water only group? If so, did that student do anything different from the others? There should be a clear dichotomy between the two groups of students. The stain should still remain on the group who only washed with water, while the group that used soap and water may have some, most, or all of the stain removed.

Once all the materials are cleaned up and students are intrigued by seeing the difference that soap makes on cleanliness, the teacher can return to questioning students about their understanding of what occurred.

We asked three students some questions about soap, and their answers are shown in Figure 4.4.

Question Asked:	Lily (Kindergarten)	Zoey (3rd Grade)	Emma (6th Grade)
What is soap?	Something you make to wash your hands.	Soap is something you use to wash your hands and body, and you can use it to make bubbles.	Something to clean your hands and body.
What do you think it's made of?	Wet bath bombs	A liquid	Water and sodium
Where do we use soap?	At the sink or bath	On your body, your hair, and for bubbles	In bathrooms
Do you think that soap was discovered or invented?	Invented	Discovered	Invented
What are the good things that soap does?	That you yourself better.	Cleans you and have fun with bubbles.	Cleans and is good for making slime sometimes.
What are some bad things that soap does?	It can spill and get messy.	If you get it in your eye it stings, and it tastes bad in your mouth.	If you don't wash it off, it can make your skin red.
What would our lives be like if we didn't have any soap at all?	We wouldn't really be clean.	We would be smelly and dirty.	We would use hand sanitizer or we would be dirty

Figure 4.4 Table of student responses about soap. Image created by author Christine Schnittka.

Probing Questions to Ask

What is soap?

- ◆ Students will likely not know that it is a substance with polar molecules which are alkali salts of fatty acids. They will likely simply know it's a substance that cleans things.

What do you think it is made of?

- ◆ Students will likely not know that soap is made from an oil or fat blended with a strong alkaline solution like lye. They will likely not know that they can make soap from ashes collected from the fireplace and grease or fat that gets thrown away after cooking meat.

Where do we use soap?

- ◆ Students will be able to identify kitchen, bathroom, and outdoor uses as well as personal hygiene uses. They will likely not know that soap is also used as a lubricant, and a thin layer works well on eyeglasses to keep them from fogging up. Some people rub soap on furniture that their dogs like to chew on, and gardeners use a dilute soap solution on their plants to keep aphids off! If you have ever cooked over a campfire, you may know that if you rub soap on the bottom of your kettle, it will not collect soot.

Do you think that soap was discovered or invented?

- ◆ Many students will think that soap was discovered, as if it has always existed in some form, but soap is definitely a human invention.

What are the good things that soap does?

- ◆ Soap cleans, lubricates, protects, and makes for good clean fun!

What are some bad things that soap does?

- ◆ Soap can dry out one's skin. When soap gets into our waterways, it can cause problems with aquatic life. However, soap is biodegradable and causes fewer problems than detergent does. Liquid soaps come in plastic containers that must be manufactured, and are then discarded, so soaps in plastic containers have environmental impacts. The lowest environmental impact is from a bar of handmade soap!

What would our lives be like if we didn't have any soap at all?

- ◆ Without soap, we would have difficulty keeping our skin, hair, dishes, and clothes clean. This lack of sanitation would lead to increased spread of disease!

- A student handout is provided on our website https://steamcrafts. weebly.com/ to help guide students through this introductory activity and get them thinking about the properties and effectiveness of soap.

Explore: Soap Stations

Purpose
The purpose of this phase of the lesson is to give students the opportunity to compare and contrast different soaps. By seeing all the ways that soaps are different, they can be ready to understand the unifying concepts in the next lesson.

Overview
Students will move through different stations to experience different types of soap. They will make observations about different properties of soap and begin to compare and contrast the soaps and what, specifically, makes them different.

Using the lab sheet on our website: https://steamcrafts.weebly.com/students can move through the stations and collect information about what they experience.

Each station should be numbered or labeled and contain a soap, a basin of water, and towels for drying (Figure 4.5).

Tell the students that they are going to be soap testers or soap connoisseurs.

Have students go to the wash stations set up around the room and wash their hands to experience the different soaps. Make sure they dry their hands between washings, and that they record their observations on their lab sheet.

The soap stations that you set up can vary depending on what you are able to collect, but some examples for different stations include: soft hand soap that is foamy, soft hand soap that is a gel form, bar soap, Dr. Bronner's, Tecnu, orange pumice, dish soap, or hand-crafted soap. You can even have them try to wash their hands with some of the products that go into making soap such as olive oil, shortening, oatmeal, shea butter, or coconut oil. Try to have at least five different "soaps" available for students to try.

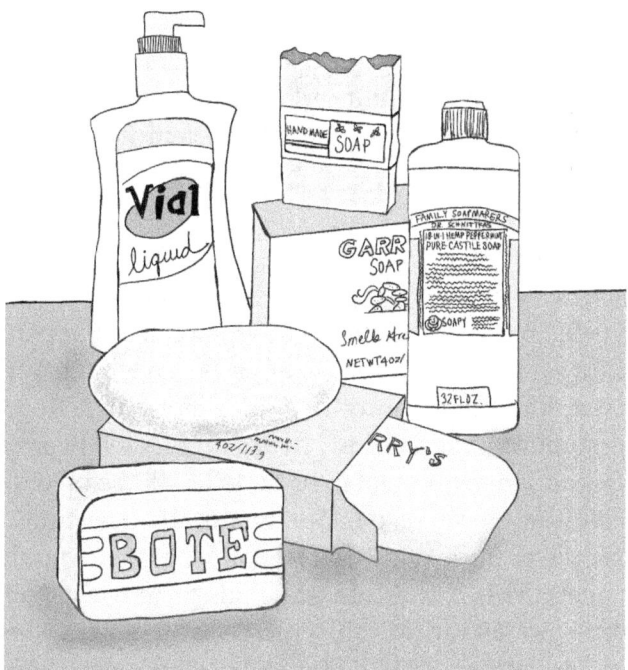

Figure 4.5 An assortment of soaps. Image created by author Christine Schnittka.

Probing Questions to Ask

After students are done exploring soap, ask these questions:

Which soap made the most bubbles?
Which soap felt the best on your hands?
Which soap did you like the best?
What do you think makes each of these soaps different from each other?

- A student handout is provided on our website https://steamcrafts.weebly.com/ in which students can evaluate the effectiveness of different soaps and compare their results to their classmates' results.

Explain: The STEAM Concepts

Purpose

The purpose of this phase of the unit is to allow students to gain new scientific knowledge and understanding of how soap works in order to make informed design decisions in a later phase.

Overview

A presentation found on our website https://steamcrafts.weebly.com/ discusses the science of soapmaking. Saponification, the process of breaking an oil or fat up into soap and glycerin, is explained. Ancient ways of soapmaking are described.

Soap Science: The Basics
Saponification

Saponification is the name of the chemical reaction that happens when soap is made. Saponification happens when an oil or fat (called a triglyceride) breaks apart into a glycerol molecule and three soap molecules. In soapmaking, an alkaline metal solution, like sodium hydroxide (NaOH) or potassium carbonate (K_2CO_3) is added to oil or fat in order to break the oil or fat molecule up into parts. Saponification can also happen naturally over time, as old oils can get rancid when one or more of the fatty acids separates from the glycerol and floats around freely. This makes old, stale oils taste really bad …. like soap! The oils in grains can get rancid too, which is why old crackers, old oatmeal, and old cookies can taste rancid. In Figure 4.6, you can see how a triglyceride like oil or fat is broken up into soap molecules and a glycerol molecule when an alkaline metal solution is added.

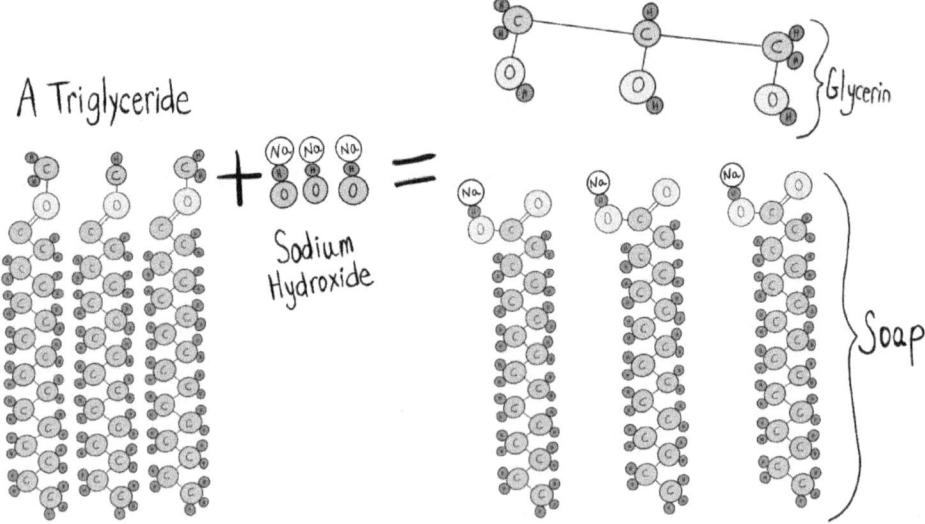

Figure 4.6 How a triglyceride becomes soap. Image created by author Christine Schnittka.

Soap Science: The Details

Where did the inventors of soap get an alkaline metal solution from? One way to make a potassium carbonate solution is to pour hot water over ashes from a wood fire, and let the water drain through them. When wood is burning, the cellulose is chemically converted into carbon dioxide gas. After burning, what's left is what did not combine with oxygen and then turn into a gas. Wood ashes contain between 5% and 7% potassium, and ~2% phosphorus. Hardwood ashes contain more potassium than softwood ashes. Wood ashes contain small amounts of iron, silicon, aluminum, zinc, manganese, arsenic, cadmium, copper, lead, nickel, and chromium. A quarter of wood ash is calcium carbonate, $CaCO_3$. Where does a plant get these metals like silicon, aluminum, and zinc from? From the soil!

When hot water is poured through ashes, the metals and minerals are carried away by the water, namely the potassium and sodium salts, but the silica and calcium carbonate are not. The resulting solution, a sort of wood ash "tea," has all sorts of minerals dissolved in it. When you boil this solution, you end up with a concentrated potassium carbonate solution with other elements floating around. If you evaporate all the water off the solution, you are left with a white powder called potash, from the Dutch words "pot ash." A potash solution is very basic or alkaline and contains the metals calcium, sodium, potassium, and phosphorus, iron, aluminum, zinc, copper, etc. Yes, calcium is a metal! Mixing four parts of oil or fat with three parts of concentrated potash solution and cooking it over heat will saponify the fats and result in soap. The cooking speeds up the chemical reaction of saponification.

Potash can also be mined! The largest potash mine in the world is in Canada, and there are large mines in Russia and Belarus as well. These deposits of potash formed millions of years ago when inland seas dried up, leaving behind lots of potassium salts. In northern Ethiopia along the shores of the Red Sea, there is a very large deposit of potash in a region called the Danakil Basin. This other-worldly place looks like a cross between the Moon and Mars, with volcanoes, lava lakes, sulfur-rich hot springs, and colorful yellow and green salt deposits. Potash from this area has historically been used to make a lovely, creamy, black soap.

How Soap Cleans

You might be wondering how a saponified fat works to clean dirt, grime, and germs off surfaces. A saponified fat has two parts: glycerol and a fatty acid. The glycerol is colorless, odorless, and sweet-tasting, and does not contribute to the cleansing action of soap. It's the fatty acids that do all the soapy work.

> You may have seen glycerol used as a sweetener in food. It is usually removed in the industrial manufacture of soap, but moisturizing soaps and clear glycerin soaps do contain it. Historically, glycerol was collected as a byproduct of saponification and used as antifreeze, which is why antifreeze is sweet, and thus dangerous for people and animals to drink. Glycerol is used to produce nitroglycerin, which is both an explosive and a heart medicine.

A fatty acid is a little molecule shaped like a pin, with a head and a tail. The head contains hydrogen and oxygen atoms, and it is polar, meaning it has an electric charge, and the tail, made of carbon and hydrogen, is non-polar. Those little polar heads are attracted to other polar molecules, namely water. The little non-polar tails are attracted to non-polar molecules like dirt, grime, sweat, and oils as well as bacteria and viruses. So, the little fatty acids grab hold of dirt particles or germs, and when you rinse the soap off your face or garment, those dirt particles and germs get rinsed off too. The tails of the soap molecules even poke holes in the lipid membranes of bacteria and some viruses (Jabr, 2020). There are eight different kinds of fatty acids, and you will see them named on the ingredient list of soaps you purchase: myristic, lauric, stearic, palmitic, oleic, linoleic, linolenic, and ricinoleic. Vegetable oils will contain different fatty acids than fats from animal sources. One bar of soap may contain several different types of fatty acids (Figure 4.7).

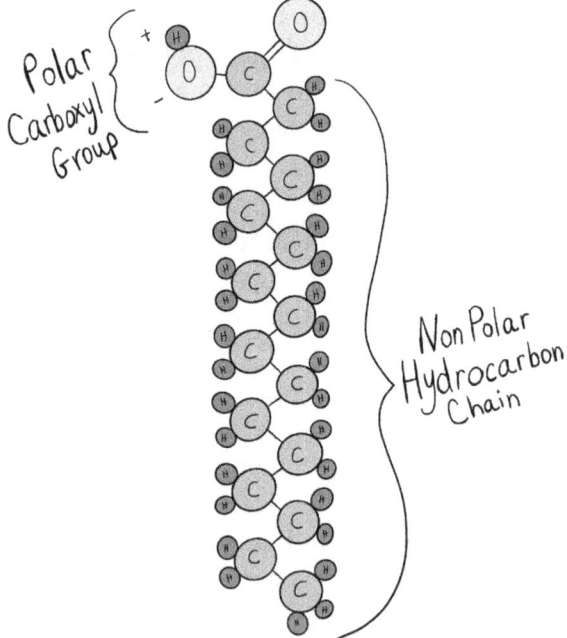

Figure 4.7 A soap molecule. Image created by author Christine Schnittka.

The little soap molecules tend to group up together in an arrangement called a micelle. The polar heads are attracted to each other and form a sphere, while the dirt is attracted to the tails, and gets trapped inside of the micelle. When you wash your hands, hair, or clothes, these little micelles get washed away carrying the dirt and germs with them (Figure 4.8).

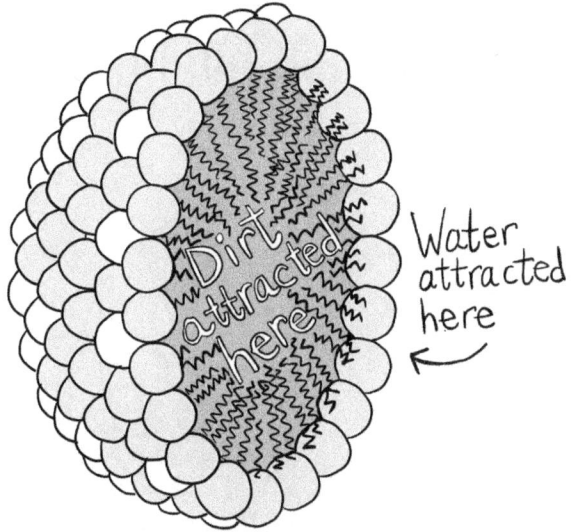

Figure 4.8 A micelle. Image created by author Christine Schnittka.

Why Does Soap Bubble?
Bubbles form when soap molecules form a sandwich instead of a small micelle. The sandwich is possible because of a layer of water trapped in between each soapy film. Without the layer of water, the soapy film would not exist … the soap molecules would form micelles. See Figure 4.9 to understand how a soap bubble is structured.

Elaborate: Making Soap

Purpose
The purpose of the Elaborate phase of this lesson is to apply the science, art, technology, and engineering of soap. Now that your students have experimented with soap and learned about the science of soap, it's time to engineer some soap!

Overview
After making soap by following some specific instructions, students can engineer their own to meet certain specifications. Younger students will use a

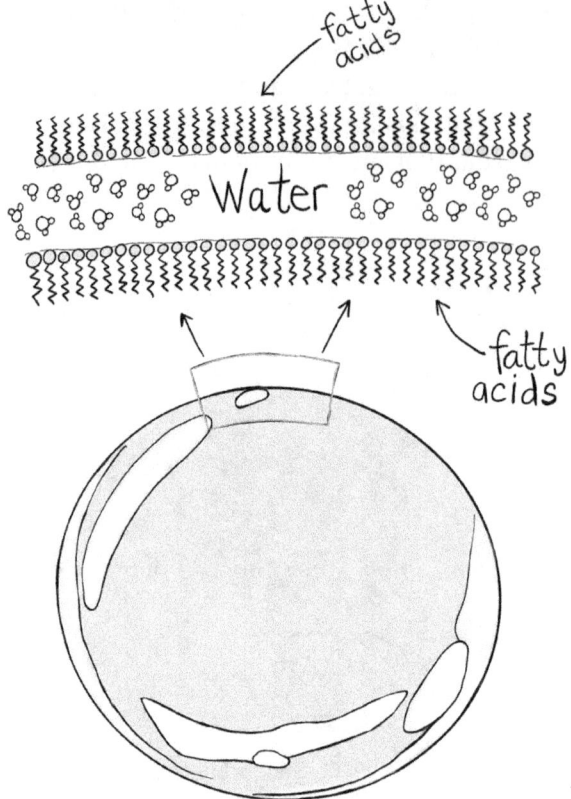

Figure 4.9 A spherical sandwich of soap molecules and water. Image created by author Christine Schnittka.

melt-and-pour base and add ingredients to it, and older students can make their own soap with enough supervision.

Clean Chemistry

For Younger Students

When working with younger students, only the teacher should access sodium hydroxide and freshly made soap, as it will have a high pH for several weeks (Figure 4.10). The teacher, wearing personal protective equipment (PPE) including lab apron, splash-proof goggles, and long gloves, can demonstrate for the class how to combine the ingredients, and allow students to see the mixture begin to thicken and solidify into soap. The teacher can pour the soap into a mold, and the students can take turns stirring scents, colors, or exfoliants into the soap with direct supervision of the teacher. Young students, however, CAN work with a "melt and pour" soap base since its pH has had

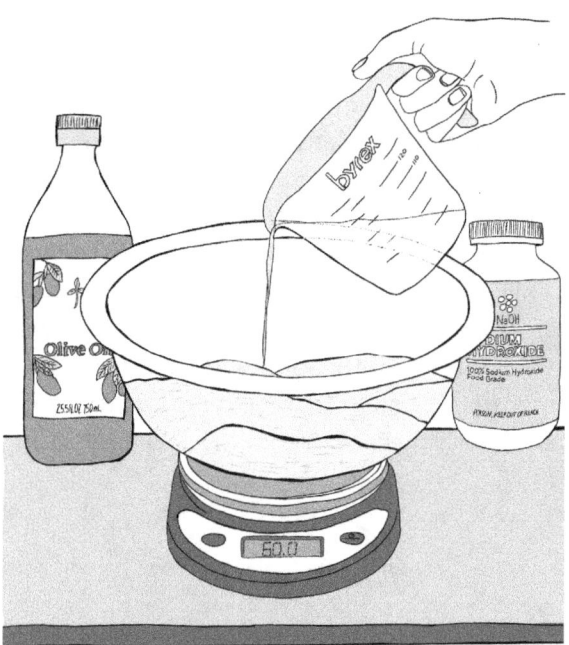

Figure 4.10 Making soap. Image created by author Christine Schnittka.

time to neutralize. If the teacher demonstrates making soap, make sure to have a source of running water in the room, as well as a trashcan and paper towels in case there are accidents or spills.

Teachers with younger students who wish to demonstrate soapmaking, should read the section that follows, but only <u>demonstrate</u> soapmaking, and have their students customize their own bar of soap, using a "melt and pour" soap base. The soap base is melted over low heat, poured into molds, and then additives are stirred in with a wooden stick. We use Styrofoam cups as molds, and pour in about an inch of soap base. The teacher can pour the melted soap base into Styrofoam cups, and students can safely hold the cup, and add special ingredients to the base while stirring with a craft stick. These ingredients could be things like poppy seeds, coffee grounds, oatmeal, clay, colored mica powders, essential oils, shea butter, or vitamin E.

For Older Students

Older students may be mature enough to handle a NaOH solution under direct supervision if there is only one group accessing the NaOH at a time, and a teacher is with the students at all times while they are using the NaOH pellets or solution. It is a good idea to have extra help in the classroom in order to be sure that all safety precautions are followed.

Set up stations around the room and have students move in small groups of 3–4, one group at a time. This is not an appropriate lab for all the students to be engaged with at the same time due to safety issues. The teacher can assign reading or some other quiet desk work as groups move through the stations under teacher supervision, particularly at STATION 3. The amounts used at each station need to be precisely measured, and the amounts can be calculated for different types of soap. Recipes follow the station descriptions.

STATION 1: This station needs to be at a counter or table with access to electricity. Measure the oil/fat in grams on a digital scale and then heat it up a bit in a beaker (to 55°C, 131°F) if the fat is solid, so that it is liquid. I like to use a coffee cup warmer for this step. Using oven mitts or tongs, take this beaker to STATION 3 and leave it there. Next, go to STATION 2 (Figure 4.11).

Figure 4.11 Coffee cup warmer melting oils in a beaker. Image created by author Christine Schnittka.

STATION 2: Measure your water in a graduated cylinder. Remember, 1 ml = 1 gram of water. Pour your water into a beaker and take the beaker with you to STATION 3.

STATION 3: Wearing a lab safety coat, safety gloves, and safety splash-proof goggles, measure the mass of your NaOH pellets in a DRY beaker or little cup. Make sure goggles are on the face! Pour the NaOH pellets slowly into the water beaker and stir with a wooden stick until all the pellets are dissolved. Never pour water onto the pellets. Combining NaOH with water will produce a hot, exothermic reaction! Once dissolved, slowly pour the NaOH solution into the beaker of warmed oil from STATION 1. Start stirring the mixture, and then carefully take the mixture to STATION 4 and continue stirring with the beaker on a table. It may take 20 minutes of stirring for the soap to begin solidifying. This stage is called "trace" because at this stage, one can trace a shape in the soap and it will be visible.

STATION 4: After you have reached "trace," add any colorings or essential oils, mix, and pour into a Styrofoam cup. Label your Styrofoam cup with your name.

Multiple groups of students can be at STATION 4 if all students are seated and wearing their PPE.

After all students have completed their soap, the cups should be placed in a cabinet or other secure place for a few weeks until the oils are fully saponified and the pH is 8. This can be tested by wetting a pH strip with water and touching it to the soap.

Soapmaking Recipes and Math

Soap recipes can be calculated using an online calculator. There are several, so see our website https://steamcrafts.weebly.com/ for links to our favorites.

Soap recipes can also be calculated easily by hand. Since each fat or oil has a different saponification (SAP) value, the amount of NaOH needed will be different for each recipe. The basic formula is:

_____ g of oil × SAP value _____ = _____ g of NaOH

Some common oil SAP values are:

Oil	SAP value
Avocado	.133
Coconut	.190
Corn	.136
Olive	.134
Canola	.124
Soy	.135
Crisco	.136
Beeswax	.069

The next step is to add the mass of the oil and the mass of the NaOH = _____.

So, if you used 100 grams of olive oil, you would need 13.4 grams of NaOH since 100 × .134 = <u>13.4 grams of NaOH.</u>

With 100 grams of oil and 13.4 grams of NaOH, the total mass is now 113.4 grams, and you calculate 30% of this mass to determine the amount of water to use.

113.4 grams × .30 = mass of the water to use = <u>34.02 grams of water</u>

At STATION 1, measure 100 grams of olive oil on a digital scale.

At STATION 2, measure 34.02 ml of water (since the density of water is 1 g/ml).

At STATION 3, measure 13.4 grams of NaOH and add it to the water.

At STATION 4, stir until trace is achieved, and then add scents, colors, or exfoliants such as oatmeal, poppy seeds, or clay.

The total mass of soap will be 147 grams, the exact size of some commercial bars of soap. When poured into Styrofoam cups, this will make 3 small bars of soap.

If you have multiple oils, determine the total mass of all of them, and the percentage of each. If you have 50 g Crisco, 35 g olive, and 15 g coconut, this adds up to 100 g. Here is how to calculate the amount of NaOH:

[Percent of the whole × (entire mass × SAP)] + [percent of the whole × (entire mass × SAP)] = .50 (100 × .136) + .35(100 × .134) + .15(100 × .190) = 14.34 g NaOH

Here is how to calculate the amount of water needed:

30% × (total mass of fats + mass of NaOH)

.3 × 114.34 = 34.3 g H_2O = 34.32 ml H_2O

Superfatting

It is wise to subtract 5% of the calculated NaOH. This gives your soap a bit of extra oil/fat and makes sure that all the NaOH is converted. I will discount the lye in the next example.

For this type of soap, use:

50 g coconut = 50/65 = 77%

10 g olive = 10/65 = 15%

5 g beeswax = 5/65 = 8%

65 g total

.77(65 × .19) + .15(65 × .134) + .08(65 × .069) = 9.5 + 1.3 + .35 = 11.17 g NaOH

To discount 5%, compute 11.17 × .95 = 10.6, so only use 10.6 g of NaOH.

The resulting total mass would be 65 g + 10.6 g = 75.6 g.

Thirty percent of that is the amount of water to use:

.30 × 75.6 = 22.68 g H_2O

The Challenge

The challenge for this phase of the lesson is to have students create a unique soap product which meets specifications. See https://steamcrafts.weebly.com/ for student handouts that help to establish the deliverables of this challenge. Perhaps the soap must remove all the fluorescent dye from one's hands. Perhaps the soap must have a nice smell and be in a specific shape. You can pick the specifications!

Evaluate: What Did They Learn?

A form to collect the answers to these questions from your students is provided on our website https://steamcrafts.weebly.com/.

When students engineer their own soap, have them explain the decisions they made. Why did they choose particular oils or particular additives? Answers to these questions can help reveal the physics, chemistry, environmental, and historical lessons learned from this unit.

After making soap, ask your students to write the answers to the following questions to see what else they learned.

1. Soap is made by combining a fat with an alkaline substance. What did the first soapmakers use for these two components?

    ◆ Animal fats and wood ash "tea" were used to make soap.

2. Animal fat or vegetable oil is a triglyceride. The chemical reaction changes the triglyceride into soap molecules. What do these soap molecules look like?

    ◆ They look like little pins with a head and a tail.

3. The soap molecule head is attracted to _____ while the tail is attracted to _____.

    ◆ <u>water</u> while the tail is attracted to <u>dirt, grime, bacteria, and viruses</u>.

4. Fats and oils are triglycerides. Draw a most basic version of a triglyceride molecule.

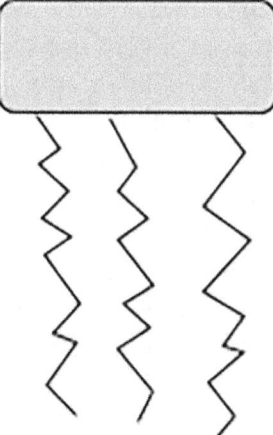

5. What is saponification?

    ◆ The process of triglycerides breaking apart into soap and glycerol.

6. What happens to the triglyceride molecule when it encounters sodium hydroxide (NaOH)?

    ◆ The top part pops off, becoming glycerol, and the three fatty acids float freely as soap molecules.

7. What is the point of "trace"?

    ◆ The point at which you can trace a shape on the surface of a fresh batch of soap is called "trace."

8. A soap molecule has a head and a tail. Which part embeds itself into a greasy stain?

    ◆ The tails are attracted to grease, dirt, and other unwanted particles.

9. What is a micelle?

    ◆ A micelle is a spherical arrangement of soap molecules with the heads out and the tails in.

Summary

Soapmaking is a craft that has changed the course of human civilization. It is a chemical that students will likely use daily, whether after using the restroom, when helping wash the dishes after supper, or during a bath or shower. One can make soap the original way with wood ashes and animal fat, or a modern way with sodium hydroxide and a variety of animal and plant fats. Soapmaking can be demonstrated by the teacher, or in small groups of students if directly supervised. If working with sodium hydroxide or wood ashes is a safety concern, pre-saponified soap base can be melted over low heat, and modified to include colorants, scents, and exfoliants. Making soap is a way for youth to directly apply history, mathematics, biology, engineering, and chemistry. The physical object, soap, can serve as a token of that learning and help youth see how school subjects show up in their daily lives.

Contemporary Soapmakers

Making soap is a popular craft in today's culture, and there are many artisans and craftspeople who excel in this process. For links to examine modern soap artisans, please see our website https://steamcrafts.weebly.com/.

References

Bybee, R. W. (2009). *The BSCS 5E instructional model and 21st century skills*. National Academies Board on Science Education.

Civil, M. (1960). Prescriptions medicales sumeriennes. *Revue d'Assyriologie et d'archéologie Orientale, 54*(2), 57–72.

Davis, R. (2015). The doctor who championed hand washing and briefly saved lives. *NPR*. https://www.npr.org/sections/health-shots/2015/01/12/375663920/the-doctor-who-championed-hand-washing-and-saved-women-s-lives

Dean, K. R., Krauer, F., Walløe, L., Lingjærde, O. C., Bramanti, B., Stenseth, N. C., & Schmid, B. V. (2018). Human ectoparasites and the spread of plague in Europe during the second pandemic. *Proceedings of the National Academy of Sciences, 115*(6), 1304–1309.

Dewey, J. (1938). *Experience and education*. Macmillan.

Jabr, F. (2020). Why soap works. https://www.nytimes.com/2020/03/13/health/soap-coronavirus-handwashing-germs.html

Jiahui, S. (2023). How did ancient Chinese wash their clothes? https://www.theworldofchinese.com/2023/03/how-did-ancient-chinese-wash-their-clothes/

Kadar, N., Romero, R., & Papp, Z. (2018). Ignaz Semmelweis: The "Savior of Mothers": On the 200th anniversary of his birth. *American Journal of Obstetrics & Gynecology, 219*(6), 519–522.

Konkol, K. L., & Rasmussen, S. C. (2015). An ancient cleanser: Soap production and use in antiquity. In: Rasmussen, S. C. (Eds) *Chemical technology in antiquity* (pp. 245–266). American Chemical Society.

Piaget, J. (1955). The construction of reality in the child. *Journal of Consulting Psychology, 19*(1), 77.

Wilson, G. (2023). What plant did Native Americans use for soap? https://storables.com/gardening-and-outdoor/plant-care-and-gardening-tips/what-plant-did-native-americans-use-for-soap/

5

Practical Paper

Introduction

Have you ever made paper? I remember making paper as an elementary school student. The lumpy, blue "paper" is in a trunk in my attic, and I can still remember the awe I felt after creating it, writing on it, and putting it away for safekeeping. You may have a similar memory from your youth. In this chapter, you will learn how to use the craft of papermaking to teach an interdisciplinary STEAM unit to your students. You will learn the science and history of paper and learn how to engage your students in this fascinating, ancient activity. Your students will also learn what paper is made of, what holds it together, how it is created from a slurry of fibers in water, and how it can be easily recycled (Figure 5.1).

Paper History

The Invention of Paper

Do your students know who invented paper or where it originated? Some might think it just "grows on trees." Paper wasps have been making paper from plants for a very long time, long before people ever figured out how to do it. Fossil evidence for paper wasps in Japan is 300,000 years old (Takahashi & Aiba, 2022), and in Florissant, Colorado, a 34-million-year-old fossil of a paper

DOI: 10.4324/9781003428312-5

Figure 5.1 Scooping up paper pulp in a mold and deckle. Image by author Christine Schnittka.

wasp was found by a park ranger (Meyer, 2003). If you look closely at a paper wasp's nest, you will notice the fibers that built it.

These industrious insects get cellulose fibers from plants. They chew up plant matter, spit out the saliva and plant mixture, and wait for it to dry. Similarly, a papermaker crushes plants, mixes the plant matter with water, and spreads out the slurry to dry.

Prior to the invention of paper, people recorded and preserved their ideas by etching on rocks, inscribing on animal skins, writing on birch bark, or carving into bones or turtle shells. The ingenuity of early civilizations manifested in diverse ways to document ideas. In the ancient Chinese capital, Yinxu (pronounced Yeen-shu), over 100,000 bones with writing carved into them were discovered (Xueqin, 2013). There is evidence that in ancient Mesopotamia 5,000 years ago (today's Iran), people wrote on wet clay (in a process called cuneiform) by pressing wedge-shaped lines into it with a tool (Van De Mieroop, 1997).

In Egypt over 2,000 years ago, people would pound stalks of the papyrus plant to flatten them, and layer them orthogonally to make a sheet. Once dry, this sheet could be written on with ink. But, papyrus is not paper.

In the year 105 CE, people in China started making true paper from the inner bark of the mulberry tree (Morgan et al., 2019). Nobody knows where

Figure 5.2 Fossil wasp from Florissant Fossil Beds National Monument, Colorado. Image created by author Christine Schnittka from a photo from the National Park Service in the public domain.

they got the idea from, but perhaps it was from watching paper wasps make their nests (Figure 5.2).

Eastern Papermaking

The story often told is that Ts'ai Lun invented paper in China in 105 CE. This paper (The Chinese character for paper is 紙, pronounced Shee) was made by peeling mulberry bark (*Broussonetia papyrifera*), chopping it, soaking it in water, beating it with a hammer, and then spreading it out flat to dry in the sun (Figure 5.3).

This made a lumpy, thick paper (Bloom, 2017). Paper was used in China for writing, but also for tea bags, sanitation, and paper money. Regardless of who the inventor was, papermaking was a Chinese trade secret for nearly 500 years (Figure 5.4). Eventually this secret spread to Korea, Japan, Tibet, India, the Middle East, Egypt, Spain, France, and finally England in the late 1400s (Hunter, 1978). Papermaking began in the United States in 1690.

> The English word, "library" is derived from the Latin word, "liber" which means "inner bark." The English word, "paper" is derived from the Greek word "papyros" and the Greek word for the inner layer of the papyrus plant is "biblia," which is where the Latin word for library, "biblioteca" comes from.

Figure 5.3 Mulberry tree branch. Image created by author Christine Schnittka.

Figure 5.4 Early Chinese papermaking. Image created by author Christine Schnittka, inspired by an image in the public domain.

In Japan, it is also common to use mulberry bark, which the Japanese call "kozo," but shrubs such as gampi and mitsumata, which have longer fibers, are also used (Bloom, 2017). The Japanese word for handmade paper is 和

紙, pronounced "washi." "Wa" is the word for Japan, and "Shee" is the word for paper. Papermaking started in Japan in the year 610 CE after a Korean Buddhist monk, with his prayers written on paper, brought the tradition there. Japanese papermakers use a screen made from thin strips of bamboo (簀called a "Su") which is set into a hinged frame (桁 called a "Keta"). Usually, a slimy and viscous substance called "neri," made from the roots of a hibiscus or hydrangea plant, is added to the water to help the fibers spread out evenly. Neri slows the water as it drains from the Su. Paper sheets are stacked on top of each other. Once a stack of paper is complete, it is pressed to remove excess water. Then, the pieces of wet paper are peeled off the stack and brushed onto a board to dry in the sun. Before the invention of papermaking machinery in France in 1798, papermaking was a common career in Japan, with 800,000 papermakers busily working. If you have ever seen traditional Japanese fans, umbrellas, or window screens, you have seen washi (Figure 5.5).

Figure 5.5 Early Japanese papermaking: Washi. Image created by author Christine Schnittka, inspired by an image in the public domain.

Western Papermaking

When papermaking reached Europe around the year 1100 CE, it was a craft practiced in a similar way to the Japanese and Chinese styles, however, the dominant fiber used was cotton recycled from old rags. The old rags were ripped, boiled, and beaten until they were nothing but lint. A screen adhered to the top of a rectangular wooden frame (called "the mold") was paired with an empty rectangular frame (called "the deckle"), and these two pieces of equipment were dipped into a watery slurry of fibers. After the water drained away, the deckle was removed and the new piece of paper was pressed onto a stack. All the new pieces of paper were separated from each other with a sheet of fabric, called a "felt."

By the 1800s, papermaking had really taken off in Europe for several reasons. First, the demand for paper and books was growing due to greater access to schooling and increased public literacy. Second, technologies had been invented to speed up the process of papermaking. The Dutch invented a machine (creatively called the "Hollander beater") to mechanize beating the plant pulp. Prior to this invention, the plant pulp had to be beaten by hand or with a very loud stamping mill. This Hollander beater consisted of a large, oval tub and a paddle wheel powered by a windmill. As the wind blew outside and turned the windmill, the paddle wheel would beat the plant material. A Hollander beater could prepare in one day what required eight days with a stamping mill.

In addition to the new beater technology, the continuous papermaking machine was invented in 1800 by the French balloonist Nicholas-Louis Robert. Instead of dipping a screen into the slurry, the slurry continually poured onto a moving screen much like the conveyor belt operated by a grocery store cashier. At the end of the screen/belt was a set of rollers that squeezed the new paper to remove the water. By 1800, the printing press was in use around the world, but early printing presses were operated by hand and produced one sheet at a time. In 1822, Scottish engineer David Napier invented a rotary printing press. This press was speedier than the stationary Gutenberg press. However, when the steam-powered rotary printing press was invented in 1843 by New Yorker Richard Hoe, one machine could print 8,000 sheets of paper each hour. That drove up the demand for paper considerably! Since there weren't enough old cotton rags to go around, Europeans started using wood from trees in 1843, and today most of the paper made in the world is from trees (Figure 5.6).

Meeting the Standards

Teaching this chapter as written focuses on STEAM principles that include: historical elements that influenced technological advancements, engineering principles including iterative design, criteria and constraints, and scientific measurement principles as well as data collection and analysis.

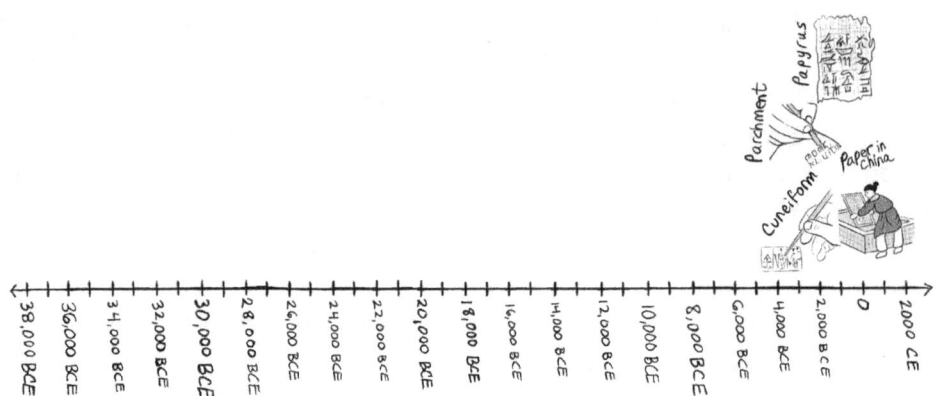

Figure 5.6 Timeline of papermaking history. Image created by author Christine Schnittka.

For more detailed information regarding which specific standards are covered in this unit, please refer to our website: https://steamcrafts.weebly.com/.

 ## Materials

- Assortment of paper samples
- Digital projector display for teacher presentation(s)
- Magnifying lenses
- Scissors (for student use)
- Glue (tacky glue or other liquid craft glue)
- Tape (masking or cellophane are fine)
- Vegetable oil and droppers/pipettes
- Droppers/pipettes for water samples
- Water-based colored ink markers
- Aluminum foil
- Duct tape
- Waxed paper
- Cotton balls
- An electric blender or food processor
- Cutting boards
- Hammers (or wooden mallets)
- Something that has a screen on it, like a picture frame with window screen stapled to it. Acquiring an actual mold and deckle would be ideal.
- A big bowl or dish pan, the bigger the better
- Lots of kitchen towels or cloth dinner napkins

If making paper from plant matter,

- A big pot that you do not cook food in
- A stove or hot plate
- Sodium carbonate or washing soda (from the laundry section in a grocery store)
- A colander or slotted spoon for removing the fibers

Optional materials

- One or many digital microscopes
- Printed copies of handouts found on our website: https://steamcrafts.weebly.com/

Safety

- An electric blender should only be operated by the teacher, plugged into an outlet with GFCI protection, away from a source of water.
- If plant materials are used, never use any that are unknown or likely to cause an allergic response.
- Heating or boiling water should only be done by the teacher with a hotplate plugged into an outlet with GFCI protection, away from a source of water, with potholders available.
- If sodium carbonate is used (washing soda), be careful to wear gloves if reaching into a pot of water containing it.
- When beating plant matter with a wooden hammer, youth should wear goggles to protect their eyes from splashing material or accidental hammer accidents.

The Lesson

> **The BSCS 5E Instructional Model for Paper Making**
>
> The lessons in this book are designed around the BSCS 5E instructional model designed by the Biological Sciences Curriculum Study (Bybee, 2009). Based on Dewey's model of reflective thinking (Dewey, 1938), Piagetian theory (Piaget, 1955), and other learning cycle models that followed, the five phases of this model are: Engage, Explore, Explain, Elaborate, and Evaluate. The purpose and summary for each phase are explained in the sections that follow.

- To find accompanying presentations, student handouts, and more be sure to visit our website: https://steamcrafts.weebly.com/.

Engage: Paper Hunt!

Purpose
The purpose of the Engage phase of this lesson is to build excitement about papermaking, to initiate curiosity about paper and the process of creating something that students know well. It allows the teacher to assess the prior knowledge and experiences of the students in order to build on that knowledge in future phases of the lesson.

Overview
Students bring paper samples to class, classify and sort them, and examine them under microscopes. If available, digital microscopes can be used to examine different paper products. Being able to see these items at 200× magnification is very interesting. Once they see paper close-up, students will be shocked at how different it looks on a microscopic scale versus a macroscopic scale. Encourage students to attempt to draw the patterns that they find.

There is paper all over the place, and certainly all over your school. At home, students have paper in their kitchen cabinets, paper in their desks, paper in their bathroom, in their garbage can, on their bookshelves, and paper in the recycling bin. Encourage students to bring at least six DIFFERENT types of paper to class (Figure 5.7). Try not to give too much information here as you want students to really be looking around thinking "Is this made of paper?" (Whether something is "paper" or not will be explored later, you just want some samples so you can examine, compare, and discuss.)

Figure 5.7 Stack of collected papers. Image created by author Christine Schnittka.

Once students have brought in sufficient paper samples, scramble and sort the entire collection into table groups or station groups. Have students in groups examine them closely to see what makes them similar and what makes them different. If you have a class set of magnifying lenses or microscopes, or one handheld digital microscope, gather that as well so students can look even more closely. Did students find paper that was: Thick? Thin? Colored? Shiny? Rough? See-through? Recycled? Sorting the found paper into categories would be a good way to both investigate the paper and practice the task of classification. Paper might be classified this way to begin, and then into more discrete categories (Figure 5.8).

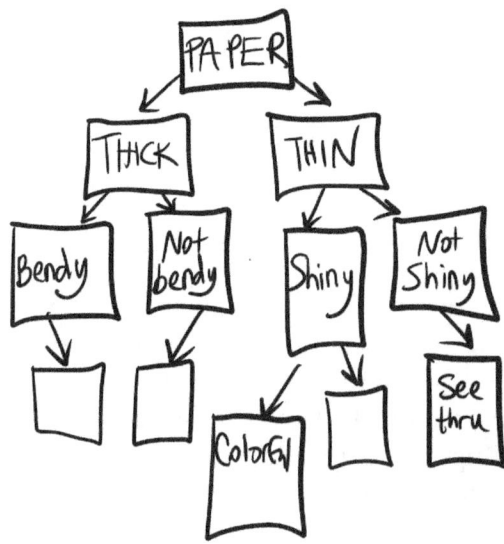

Figure 5.8 Paper classification. Image created by author Christine Schnittka.

Probing Questions to Ask

As students are sorting their found paper samples, you can ask some questions to find out what they know.

What do you think paper is made of?

- ◆ Students may know that paper is made from plants, but most will probably think only of trees.

How do you think paper is made?

- ◆ Students may know that machines make paper, but few will know the details.

Why did you decide to sort these papers this way?

- ◆ Students may sort by color or weight (physical properties) rather than intrinsic differences.

How did you decide that this was paper?

- ◆ Students may include non-paper samples. Answers to this question will help elucidate prior conceptions about what paper is.

- A student handout is provided on our website https://steamcrafts.weebly.com/ that will help students sort different paper samples and group them according to their similarities and differences.

Explore: Paper Experiments

Purpose
The purpose of this phase of this lesson is to allow students to have experiences with the phenomenon prior to learning any new content. Every student has encountered paper. Some may have even had some experience with making it, or learned how it is made. This phase attempts to level that field of knowledge in order to have a more concrete foundation to build further understanding, and even address any misconceptions that students may have about papermaking.

Overview
In this phase of the lesson, your students will continue to explore the properties of paper by modifying samples of paper with water and oil and ink and looking at the samples under a microscope or with a hand lens. But first, they will decide what paper is, so begin this lesson with a discussion.

Probing Questions to Ask
Ask your students, what makes paper, "paper"? Write students' ideas on the board.

Hold up a sample of aluminum foil and ask, "Is this paper? Is being thin a quality of paper?"

- ◆ Students may say that something is paper if it's thin. However, aluminum foil is thin, and it's not paper.

Hold up a sample of something you can write on that is not paper, like a small whiteboard or small chalkboard. Ask, "Is this paper? Is being able to write on it a quality of paper?"

- Students may say that it's paper if it can be written on. A wall can be written on, but it is not paper. So, being written on is not the definition of "paper."

Hold up some cotton balls. They can be actual bolls from a cotton plant or cotton balls for medical and cosmetic purposes. Ask, "Is this paper? Can you make paper from this? Is being made of cotton a quality of paper? Is being made from trees a quality of paper?"

- Students may say that paper is made only from trees. However, some paper is made from cotton, and cotton is not a tree. So, being made from a tree is not the definition of paper.

Hold up some duct tape or masking tape and ask, "Is this paper? Is being bendable a quality of paper?"

- Students may say it's paper if they can bend it. However, duct tape can be bent, and we really don't think of THAT as paper! So, what is paper?

Perhaps taking a close look at paper will help answer this question. Have your students take some of their paper samples and tear them. Construction paper is a good type for this activity, as is toilet paper. Ask, "What does the paper look like where the tear is?"

- Students will notice the frayed edge and may notice small fibers that they can pick off. Pass out hand lenses to allow for better viewing of these fibers (Figure 5.9).

The Water Test

Working in small groups, provide a small dish of water with pipettes. Have students dip or drop water on their paper samples and record the results.

Ask, "Do you notice anything that happens in water that wouldn't happen to aluminum foil, duct tape, or a piece of wood?" "Why do you think some papers break down easily and others do not?" Students may think there is a glue that holds some fibers together. Paper is made of very small fibers that look like threads, and when paper is torn or moistened with water, those fibers can separate from each other. Toilet paper is made from the shortest of these fibers, and because of that, if you put toilet paper in water, the fibers will separate from each other easily and form a slurry. Paper made from longer fibers does not break down as easily.

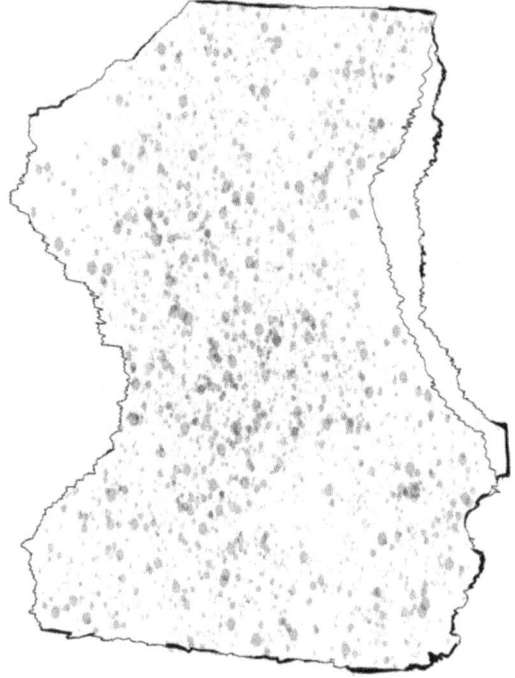

Figure 5.9 Ripped paper. Image created by author Christine Schnittka.

The Ink Test

Provide each group with a sample of water-based markers. Have students write on each paper sample with a marker and record the results. Ask, "Does the ink stay where you put it, or does it spread?" Looking at the ink with a magnifying lens may help students see this more closely. Ask, "What makes some paper react differently to ink than others?"

The Oil Test

Finally, provide each group with a small dish of cooking oil and some paint brushes or pipettes. Ask students to paint or drop a small amount of cooking oil onto the paper and record what happens. Ask, "Why do you think some papers became see-through?" Include thin paper, like newsprint or magazine paper, in this activity, as the paper will appear translucent when held up to light but will not fall apart into fibers. In the past, people who couldn't access glass for their windows would use waxed or oiled paper. In Laura Ingalls Wilder's book, *On the Banks of Plum Creek*, Laura's house had a greased paper window. As people moved across the western frontier of the United States in the 1800s, they often made windows of greased paper since glass was not readily available.

These three tests can be conducted at the same time, and students can tape their samples onto a grid for data collection and analysis.

Explain: The STEAM Concepts

Purpose
The purpose of this phase of the lesson is to allow students to gain new scientific knowledge and understanding of how the paper works in order to make informed design decisions in a later phase. Teachers engage students in discussion and deeper exploration so that students can visualize and comprehend the importance of the science, math, art, and technology of paper when they are later asked to apply their new understanding into their design.

Overview
A presentation found on our website https://steamcrafts.weebly.com/discusses different examples of paper science. In this phase of the lesson, you should first ask your students to explain their new reasonings and understandings. It's very important in this phase of the lesson to find out what students are thinking before teaching them the STEAM concepts of paper. What follows is a discussion of the basics and the details of paper science.

Paper Science: The Basics
Paper is made from fibers that contain the chemical, "cellulose." Students can 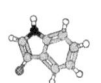 get a good look at plant cellulose by tearing apart a stalk of celery, looking at where the fibers are, and seeing how long they can be. It may be a good idea to pass out pieces of celery for dissection during this explanatory phase.

Water on Paper
What makes paper, "paper" is that it is made from small plant-based fibers that stick together. Water loosens these fibers from each other, so the paper breaks down into a slurry of fibers. The fibers are chemically bound to each other. The shortest of fibers do not have as many bonding sites with nearby fibers, so they separate more easily. The longer fibers, or fibers with more surface area (flattened and fibrillated), have more bonding sites and hold together better. When the fibers get wet, the water molecules tug and pull on them. These tiny forces can add up and overwhelm the chemical forces which keep the fibers stuck together. The fibers will separate if the tugs and pulls from the water are stronger than the chemical forces holding them together. This is why smaller fibers will separate from each more easily than larger ones (Figure 5.10).

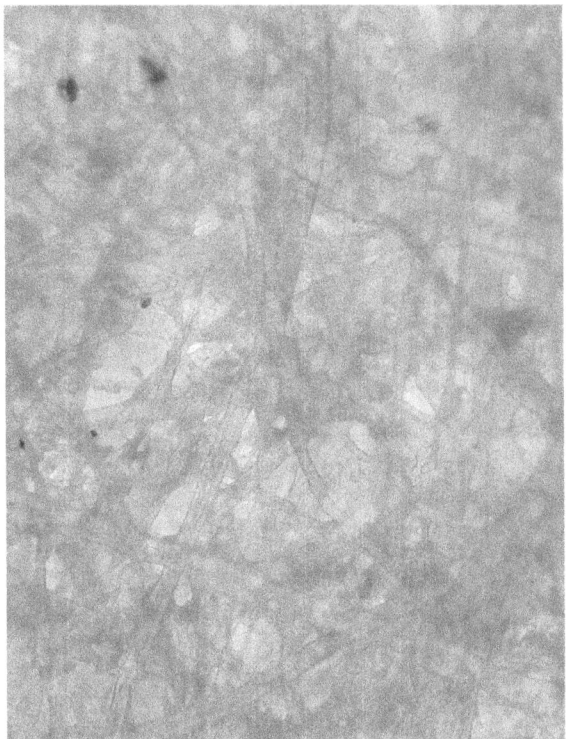

Figure 5.10 "Texture (Paper Macro)" by garreyf is licensed under CC BY 2.0.

Ink on Paper

Ink reacts differently on some paper samples because the paper has been treated with a coating that prevents the ink from even touching the paper fibers. When ink touches the paper's fibers, the ink clings to the fibers and travels along them, spreading out. Capillary action is the phenomenon that makes paper towels absorbent, allows plants to soak up water, and blood to get into your fingers and toes. Water molecules in the ink cling to the fibers, and as more water molecules enter the scene, they bump and push their neighbors further and further along. The water molecules creep along the fibers, and they can do this in any direction regardless of gravity. Astronauts on the International Space Station use capillary action to move liquids around, since there is no gravity to pull them in any particular direction. You can see capillary action by filling up one glass with colored water, and then draping a piece of paper fabric from inside the liquid, over the side or into another glass.

Oil on Paper

When oil is applied to paper, the oil fills in all the holes that had been filled with air. While air is translucent (see-through), it tends to make light scatter. Oil is translucent too, but light goes in a straight line through oil. Normally, most of the light hitting a piece of paper just bounces off it, but some does go through. Imagine you could watch a ray of light as it encounters a piece of paper. To the light ray, the piece of paper would resemble a stack of hay, with piles and piles of cellulose fibers to encounter. Each time the light ray leaves the air and strikes a cellulose fiber, it changes speed and bends. Each time it leaves the cellulose fiber and enters air, it changes speed and bends again. Light strikes so many fibers along the way, bending each time, so that it ends up exiting the paper in a totally different direction from the way it entered. Well, light travels the same speed through oil as it does through cellulose. Scientists would say that oil and cellulose have the same "index of refraction." So, when the gaps are filled with oil, the light does not have to bend each time it leaves a fiber to enter the oil or leaves the oil to enter a fiber. This makes the light ray able to just go straight through the paper. Students can test this by holding a piece of paper up to a light before and after smearing a drop of oil into the paper. Wax and oil have the same index of refraction, so waxed paper is translucent too.

Ask your students,

Have you heard the word, "cellulose"? Do you know anything that is made from cellulose?

- Students may have seen cellulose sponges in the grocery store, but these sponges are not paper and do not fall apart when soaking in water. Even though it is made of cellulose, it lacks the fibers, so it is not paper.

Does the word cellulose remind you of anything?

- Students may recognize the word, "cell." Tell them that plants are made of living cells, and each cell is surrounded by a wall made from cellulose.

What function does a cell wall have in the plant?

- Students may think that a cell wall is for protection or to trap moisture. The cellulose in the cell wall gives the plant structure.

Do you know how water moves around plants?

- ◆ Show students an image of the inside of a plant stem and explain that long xylem cells carry water up from the roots to the leaves. Long phloem cells form the bidirectional tubes that send sugars from the leaves to the rest of the plant. Both xylem cells and phloem cells contain cellulose, and many of these cells are quite long, many centimeters long. They elongate as a plant grows. This is what a plant fiber is. The inner bark contains mostly phloem cells while the woody core of a plant stalk contains xylem cells. If you take one fiber plucked from a piece of paper and look at it with a powerful microscope, you will see that it is made of bundles of these long cells stuck together with pectin, which is a type of plant plastic. Beating the fibers helps loosen the cells from each other and fray the bundle, creating more surface area for bonding sites (Figure 5.11). There is more cellulose in the stalks and stems of plants than in the leaves or roots.

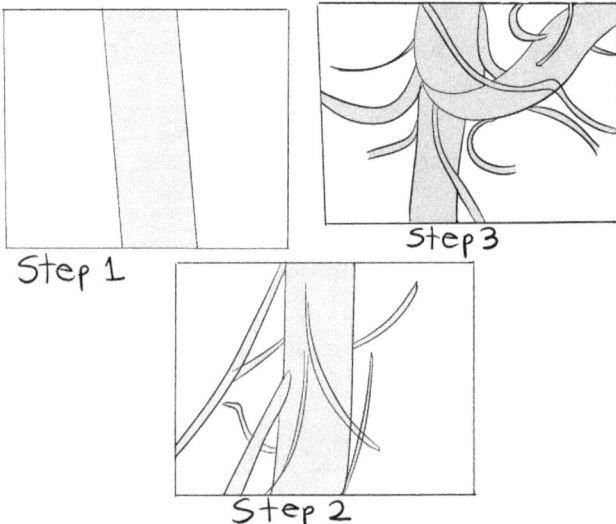

Figure 5.11 Beating plant fibers creates more surface area. Image created by author Christine Schnittka.

Which part of a plant do you think contains the most cellulose?

- ◆ Students may think that leaves have the most cellulose since leaves are flexible like paper. Show students some cotton and tell them that the best place to get cellulose is cotton. Most cellulose in a plant is just underneath the bark (Figure 5.12).

Figure 5.12 Cotton boll and balls. Image created by author Christine Schnittka.

If cellulose lines the tubes that carry water, where do you think most of the water movement happens?

♦ Fluffy cotton is 90% cellulose. Grass leaves are only 30% cellulose. The inner bark of a plant stem is about 50% cellulose, so many papermakers peel the bark off plants and use that as a source of cellulose. There is so much cellulose in the inner bark (called the cambium) because that's where most of the tubes for moving water and sugar are! This picture of the cambium in a plant, taken with a microscope, lets you see all the cell walls and tubes in the cambium layer (Figure 5.13).

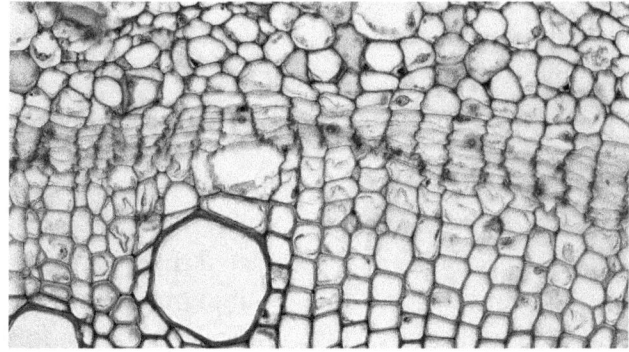

Figure 5.13 "Herbaceous dicot stem: Vascular Cambium in older Richinus" by bccoer is licensed under CC0 1.0.

Has anyone ever told you or anyone in your family to get more fiber in your diet?

- When a doctor tells you to get more fiber in your diet, to eat your vegetables for their fiber, the doctor is talking about cellulose because all plants have it!

Why do you think fiber is good for you?

- Tell students that when we eat cellulose, it just passes right through us! However, just as a cellulose sponge soaks up water, the cellulose in the food we eat helps our digestive system work better by soaking up water too. Water sticks to the cellulose and as the cellulose moves through our digestive system, it carries that water along as our food makes its way through our bodies.

The fact that water sticks to cellulose so well is related to papermaking.

Paper is made from lots and lots of little cellulose strands that stick to each other. No additional chemicals are needed. Imagine dropping a box of uncooked spaghetti noodles onto the floor. They would fly all over and not stick to each other, and you could clean them up one noodle at a time. If you cook spaghetti too much, it gets sticky, and the strands clump together. Cellulose strands stick together well with water and pressure.

Do you think you could turn a cotton ball into a piece of paper? What special papermaking technique would you need to use? If you wet the cotton and then pressed hard enough, you could make the cotton ball turn into paper.

 Paper Science: The Details

Cellulose ($C_6H_{10}O_5$) is a hydrocarbon made from carbon, hydrogen, and oxygen. Plants are like chemical factories because they take carbon from carbon dioxide in the air, hydrogen from water (H_2O), and oxygen from both air and water and make all sorts of things from those simple ingredients—sugar, cellulose, oils, and starches.

The cellulose chemical looks like Figure 5.14. If you could count all the atoms, most of them are hydrogen.

Cellulose has six-sided hexagonal connected rings with arms sticking out. The connected rings could go on and on, making cellulose stretch forever like a rope. Plants can make very long cellulose strands, and they use those strands like you would use lumber to build a house. Cellulose makes a plant stand up straight and strong.

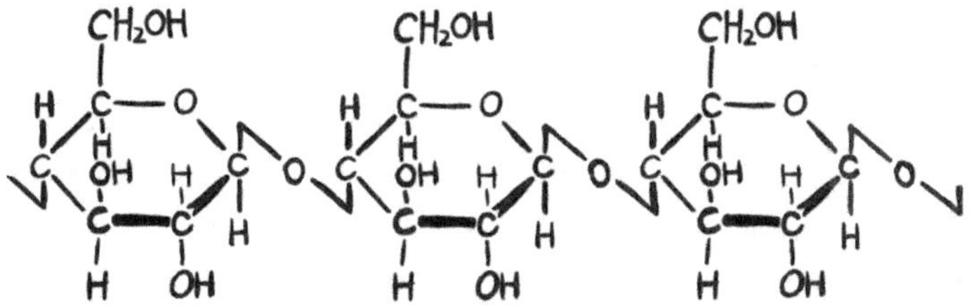

[Cellulose molecule structural diagram]

Figure 5.14 Cellulose molecule. Image created by author Christine Schnittka.

On the tips of the cellulose molecules, there are oxygen atoms and hydrogen atoms. Those hydrogen atoms stick very easily to water. It's called a "hydrogen bond" when two things stick to each other because of the hydrogen atoms. Even though "hydrogen bond" sounds like a bond between two hydrogens, it happens when hydrogen sticks to another type of atom, like oxygen. Hydrogen atoms stick to the oxygen atoms in water for the same reason that a balloon will stick to the wall if you rub it on your hair. It's not a permanent bond, just a force of attraction! In Figure 5.15, you can see the oxygen atoms in water sticking to the hydrogen tips of the cellulose molecule.

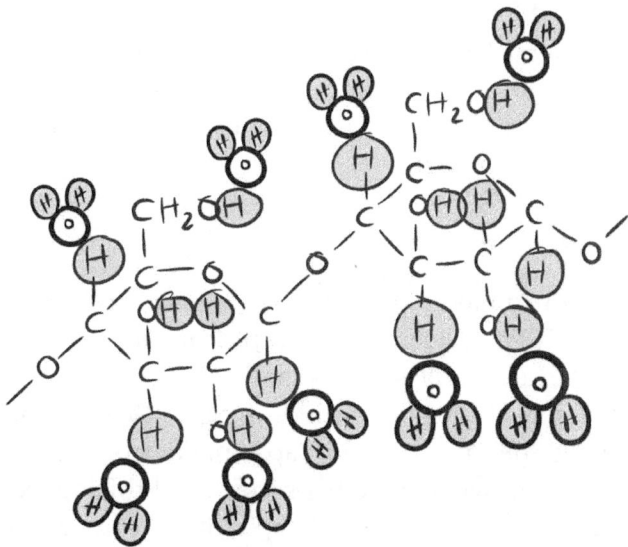

Figure 5.15 How cellulose sponges attract water molecules. Image created by author Christine Schnittka.

There are four different ways that chemicals bond to each other: ionic, covalent, metallic, and hydrogen. Hydrogen bonds are the weakest of the four, but they are vital for papermaking. Hydrogen bonding makes water molecules stick to each other and stick to cellulose fibers, and ultimately, what makes cellulose fibers stick to each other when dry.

All those hydrogen atoms sticking out of a cellulose molecule make it a good material for sponges. Paper cannot be made from hair and fur and wool because the hair is made from keratin instead of cellulose. Keratin has fewer places for hydrogen bonds to help the fibers stick together. That's good news, because imagine if the hair on your head turned to paper after you washed it! There are enough hydrogen atoms on a molecule of keratin to allow your hair to get wet, but not enough to make it a good ingredient for papermaking.

Elaborate: Paper Art, Craft, Technology, and Engineering

Purpose
The purpose of this phase of the lesson is to apply the science of paper to craft, art, technology, and engineering, and have students create paper that meets specific requirements.

Overview
Now that your students have experimented with paper and learned about the science and history of paper, it's time to engineer some paper! After making paper by following some specific instructions, students can engineer paper that solves a particular problem.

The Challenge
The challenge for this phase of the lesson is to have students create a unique paper product. See https://steamcrafts.weebly.com/ for student handouts that help to establish the deliverables of this challenge. To engineer paper, students can start by thinking of particular kind of paper they might need to solve a problem. Perhaps they need a thin paper made from recycled homework for wrapping their sandwich in. Perhaps they need thick paper for making a hardcover book. Or, perhaps they need paper that holds up well when wet, or resists bleeding when drawn on with markers. Have students work in groups to decide how to use the materials and processes they have explored to design and create a special type of paper that solves a real-world problem. Have students think about what they might use paper for. Would they use it for artwork? For homework? To make a lampshade or umbrella? To fold into a box? Have students think about the properties needed for each use. To make a lampshade, thin paper is needed. To make a box, strong paper is needed. How might students vary their paper ingredients for different results and for different uses?

Making Paper From Plants
Step 1: Acquire Plant Matter
To make paper from plants, you can pick the plants yourself or purchase some dried or cooked paper mulberry bark (kozo). Several papermaking supply stores, like Carriage House Paper, carry kozo. Dried kozo will need to be soaked and cooked prior to use, but pre-cooked fiber is shipped damp, and only needs hand beating.

If your students want to pick plants for making paper, have them choose dried grasses or leaves. While these contain less cellulose, they also contain less lignin, the polymer that glues fibers together, so they are easier to process. If students pick fresh, green leaves, they need to dry them first and that takes time! If they don't dry them first, they will have green paper that looks like a seaweed chip. Remind your students not to collect roots, and not to collect parts of any poisonous plants. If you use a lawnmower to cut your grass at home, you can save those clippings and bring them to school for papermaking. Some people like to make paper from dry, fallen leaves. Others like to use the dried, long leaves of the iris plant.

Step 2: Cooking Plant Matter
The next task is to cook the plant material so that the cellulose fibers separate from each other, and this is a bit of a challenge. If you use pre-cooked fibers, you can skip this step. But if you are using raw plant material, some cooking is needed. Soaking the dried plant material for 24 hours helps a bit but cooking it for an hour in a large pot with some washing soda is even better. For every fist full of grass clippings, add a teaspoon of washing soda. It will probably smell funny to cook grass clippings on the stove, and it may take an hour or more for the fibers to separate from each other. The teacher could start this at home and finish it up at school on a hotplate.

The washing soda dissolves the lignans that hold the plant together, so you will see the plants turn mushy and the water turn a dark color. After cooking for about one hour, strain the plant material in a colander and rinse it well with fresh water.

Washing soda is made from the chemical sodium carbonate (Na_2CO_3). It's called "soda" because of the "sodium" in it.

Washing soda is similar to baking soda, but baking soda's chemical formula is $NaHCO_3$. You can turn baking soda into washing soda by putting it in the oven at 200°F on a baking sheet. As the baking soda gets hot, it changes into washing soda + water + carbon dioxide. Here is the chemical equation:

$NaHCO_3 \rightarrow Na_2CO_3 + H_2O + CO_2$

When baking soda gets hot, it produces water and carbon dioxide. That's why it makes cookies and cakes rise!

Step 3: Beating Plant Matter

After cooking, rinsing, and cooling, put the plant material on a cutting board and beat it with a hammer or a rolling pin. Students enjoy doing this, but it does make a mess! This helps separate the fibers from each other. Wooden mallets, the kind used in seafood restaurants for cracking crabs, work well. Scrap wood can be used instead of cutting boards. Students should wear safety goggles to protect their eyes from accidents (Figure 5.16).

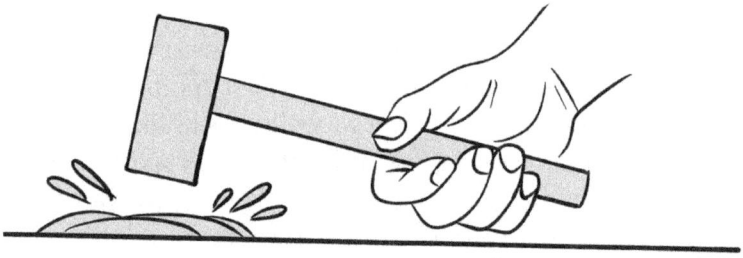

Figure 5.16 Mallet squishing plant matter. Image created by author Christine Schnittka.

After beating the plant matter, it can be blended in a food processor or blender with a lot of water for additional processing, but it is not necessary if the pulp was well beaten.

Place the beaten and/or blended plant matter in the refrigerator or freezer if you aren't using it right away to keep it from rotting.

Making Paper From Existing Paper

If you want to avoid picking leaves, drying them, cooking them, beating them, and blending them to get a papermaking slurry, your students could recycle some paper they no longer need, like newspaper and notebook paper. Have them cut it or tear it up into bits, soak it in water, and then put it in a blender with a lot of water for a couple seconds. Save this blended paper in a jar and put it in the refrigerator if you aren't using it right away. Skip to Step 4.

Making Paper From Cotton Rags and Clothing

Yes, you can make paper from cotton rags, jeans, and t-shirts. Start with clean fabric and cut it up into small squares—the smaller the better. Traditionally, papermakers cook rags made from cotton or linen in washing soda and then beat the rags to separate the fibers. You can try this, or you can put a small amount of cut up squares in a blender with a lot of water and blend until smooth. With a standard kitchen blender, it takes a long time for just a few squares of fabric to get blended. Cooking prior to blending is preferable. Save this blended cotton in the refrigerator if you aren't using it right away. Skip to Step 4.

Making Paper From Dryer Lint

Making paper from dryer lint is a tricky process since dryer lint usually contains fibers from many different kinds of fabric: wool, polyester, cotton, ramie, linen, nylon, etc. Remember, animal fibers are not suited for papermaking since the keratin molecule does not have enough hydrogen bonding sites, so your wool sweater lint might be great for making felt, but not so great for making paper. However, if you dry a load of cotton towels and collect that lint, it can be used for papermaking just like any other plant. Skip to Step 4.

Step 4: Making Paper

This step is messy, so it may be best to do outside, and depending on the number of students, several stations might need to be set up. For each station, take a big wash tub (a vat) and fill it with water. Ideally, the vat is shallow but wide. Vats can be purchased from papermaking supply stores like Carriage House Paper, or wash tubs can be repurposed for papermaking. Add the slurry of plant, paper, or clothing pulp and mix it well by hand. There needs to be enough pulp so that it's concentrated enough to make a sheet of paper, but not too concentrated that the paper is too thick. Ideally, students would use a mold and deckle purchased from a papermaking supply store or fabricated by stapling some window screen to the bottom of a picture frame to make the mold and using a second picture frame for the deckle. A mold and deckle can also be 3D printed (Figure 5.17).

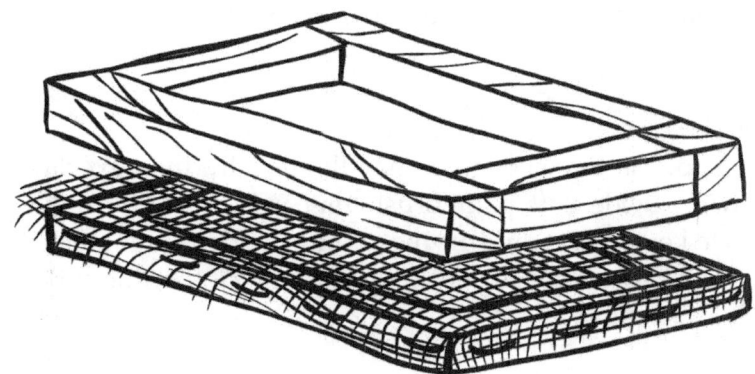

Figure 5.17 Mold and deckle with window screen. Image created by author Christine Schnittka.

Use the mold and deckle together to scoop up some of the watery mix. After the water drains, remove the deckle and turn the mold upside down to release the wet piece of paper from the screen onto a damp cloth, like a dishcloth or fabric napkin. Place another cloth on top. A stack of inexpensive polyester fabric napkins works well for these separating cloths. Papermakers traditionally use wool felt.

When I have my class do papermaking, the students come up to the vat in small groups. I provide a stepping stool for younger students. These are the steps:

1. Stir the vat with your hand.
2. Use the mold and deckle to scoop up pulp. Use a sponge to mop up excess water underneath the mesh on the mold after the water drains.
3. Remove the deckle.
4. "Couch" the sheet of new paper onto a cloth by putting the mold upside down on a damp cloth. Sponge off any water on the screen, and remove the mold. Place another cloth on top. Blot away any excess water on the top cloth with a sponge.

While waiting for a turn at the vat, students can prepare more fibers by hammering them on wooden boards with crab mallets, or by viewing some videos about papermaking around the world. See the papermaking section on our website, https://steamcrafts.weebly.com/, for a collection of videos.

Step 5: Pressing the Stack
After the class has created a stack of paper, press it between two cutting boards and put something heavy on top for a while or clamp the two boards together with clamps.

Step 6: Drying the Paper
When the paper is dry enough to handle, usually the next day, it can be brushed (with a wide, soft, paint brush) onto a flat surface like a window or countertop to keep it flat while drying, or hung to dry while stuck to the cloth (it will curl a bit if you use this technique). Use a clothesline and clothespins to hang the drying paper.

Step 7: Testing the Paper
When the paper is ready to handle, have students test it. Have them tear it, write on it, and fold it. Strength can be tested by punching a hole in bottom of the paper and hanging weights from that hole with a string or paper clip. Ink bleeding on the paper can be tested with a variety of ink pens by pressing the pens onto the paper for five seconds then writing the name of the pen next to the dot. The dots can be compared with each other.

Evaluate: What Did They Learn?

After making paper, ask your students to write the answers to the following questions to see what they learned. A form to collect the answers to these questions from your students is provided on our website https://steamcrafts.weebly.com/.

1. Who made the first piece of paper?

    ◆ Nobody knows for sure, but perhaps China's Ts'ai Lun invented paper in 105 CE.

2. How did the technology of papermaking spread throughout the world?

    ◆ Buddhist monks in China traveled to Korea, bringing paper with prayers written on them. Once Koreans knew how to make paper, the knowledge spread to Japan, India, Iran, and eventually Europe and the rest of the world.

3. What is paper made from?

    ◆ Paper is made from plant fibers. These fibers give plants structure, and they are made from cellulose. The walls of all plant cells are made from cellulose.

4. What makes the fibers stick to each other when you make paper?

    ◆ The hydrogen atoms that stick out from the cellulose molecule hold onto water, and after the water evaporates, the cellulose molecules bond directly to each other. This "bond" is not strong, which is why you can easily tear paper, separating the fibers from each other. But, with enough small fibers sticking to each other throughout the paper, there is a strong enough web of connections between the fibers.

5. Why do we beat the fibers?

    ◆ The more you beat the fibers, the more "fibrillated" they become. They rip and tear and split apart, which increases the surface area and the number of OH groups on the surface. Highly fibrillated fibers will stick better to one another because of the abundance of OH groups for hydrogen bonding.

6. What are some properties of paper?

   ◆ Paper can be thick or thin, translucent or opaque, strong like cardboard or weak like toilet paper. All paper will break apart into fibers if soaked in water long enough, and all paper gets weaker when wet. All paper, unless it is treated with a chemical, is absorbent.

7. What can you make paper from?

   ◆ Paper can be made from plant materials, fabric derived from plant materials, and other paper. Papermakers combine different raw materials to make special papers with the properties they need.

8. What can you DO with the paper you make?

   ◆ Paper can be used for writing and painting, wrapping presents, filtering tea and coffee, cleaning up spills, protecting fragile things, boxes and envelopes for packages, packaging for cereal and crackers, and so much more! It's a material that is used in every room of your home, and in every facet of your life.

Summary

Papermaking is an activity that students will remember for a very long time, and some of your students may save their handmade paper for 50 years like I did! Teaching STEAM content and practices in the context of the art of papermaking has the potential to make a lasting impact. It's so very practical to recycle paper, and the reward is great. Go ahead and teach some chemistry, physics, biology, technology, mathematics, and engineering through this ancient craft!

Contemporary Paper Artists

Papermaking is still a relevant art and craft today. Artists and craftspeople around the world make paper, and do fascinating things with what they make.

- For links to examine modern papermaking artists, please see our website https://steamcrafts.weebly.com/.

References

Bloom, J. M. (2017). Papermaking: The historical diffusion of an ancient technique. In: Jöns, H., Meusburger, P., & Heffernan, M. (Eds) *Mobilities of knowledge. Knowledge and space* (p. 10). Springer.

Bybee, R. W. (2009). *The BSCS 5E instructional model and 21st century skills*. National Academies Board on Science Education.

Dewey, J. (1938). *Experience and education*. Macmillan.

Hunter, D. (1978). *Papermaking: The history and technique of an ancient craft*. Courier Corporation.

Meyer, H. W. (2003). *Fossils of Florissant*. Smithsonian Books.

Morgan, E. C., Overholt, W. A., & Sellers, B. (2019). *Wildland weeds: Paper mulberry, Broussonetia Papyrifera*. https://edis.ifas.ufl.edu/publication/IN498

Piaget, J. (1955). The construction of reality in the child. *Journal of Consulting Psychology, 19*(1), 77.

Takahashi, Y., & Aiba, H. (2022). A fossil paper wasp (Vespidae: Polistinae) from the Chibanian (Middle Pleistocene) Shiobara group in Tochigi Prefecture, Japan. *Paleontological Research, 27*(2), 205–210.

Van De Mieroop, M. (1997). Why did they write on clay? *Klio, 79*(1), 7–18.

Xueqin, L. (2013). Zhou (1046 BCE-256 BCE) oracle bones excavated from Yinxu, ruins of Yin (1300 BCE-1046 BCE). *Contemporary Chinese Thought, 44*(3), 27–33.

6

Brilliant Beeswax

Introduction

When I was a child, there was magic in the house when the power went out and we would light all the candles. We would listen to the storm outside or cuddle up under blankets. The glow of a candle can create good feelings. While candles are used to celebrate birthdays, to symbolize prayers, or to set a mood, there was a time when candles were a necessity that allowed people to read or work at night and to make their way safely through a dark house.

In fourth grade, I made a green candle colored with crayons in a paper cup. The smell of that crayon-scented candle, and the memory of peeling back the paper cup to reveal what I made is still with me over 50 years later. There is so much to learn from a candle! In 1848, the British scientist Michael Faraday gave a series of lectures and wrote a book called *The Chemical History of a Candle*. He wrote about the science of the wax, the science of combustion, the science of the wick, and the shape of the flame (Emden & Gerwig, 2020). Faraday said in his first lecture that thinking about the science of a candle is "an open door by which you can enter into the study of natural philosophy" (Faraday, 1886). Faraday's book, which is an easy and entertaining read, is published online for free by The Project Gutenberg. In this chapter, you will learn about candle history, candle science, and candle technology, and read a lesson you can use to guide your students in creating candles safely from wax "sand" or sheets of beeswax (Figure 6.1).

DOI: 10.4324/9781003428312-6

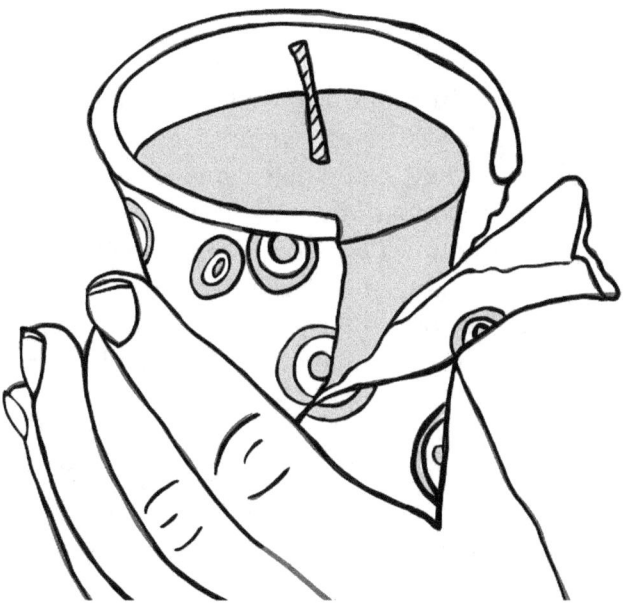

Figure 6.1 Candle in a paper cup. Image created by author Christine Schnittka.

Candle History

The very first candles were made over 3,000 years ago. Around the world, people used different kinds of fats and waxes to make them. What makes a candle special is its portability. Burning liquid oil requires some sort of container for the oil, which, if spilled, can spread quickly and create large fires. A candle can be put in a rucksack and taken on a trip, and if it falls over, it is less likely to cause a large fire than liquid fuel. Both plants and animals make fats and waxes, so there are plenty of options for extracting this solid fuel and making candles, and people have been doing so for a very long time.

Romans

The Romans used the fat from cows or sheep, called tallow, to make their candles about 3,000 years ago. These candles probably smelled like food when they were freshly made, but as the candles aged and spoiled, they most likely stunk when burned! Fat cut away from pieces of animal meat would be cooked to remove the solid bits, and then the liquid grease would cool and solidify. When you fry up some hamburger meat in a skillet, and you drain the fat off into an empty can rescued from the trash can, the solid fat that you can remove from the cooled can is tallow. Next time you make tacos, save this solid fat in a little container in your freezer. When you have enough to make a proper candle, melt it and pour it into a container and put a wick in it!

China

In ancient China, around 200 BCE, people made scented candles from whale fat or beeswax, molded in paper tubes. The wicks were made from tightly rolled paper, not cotton string. The Chinese would use these candles not only for light but also to tell time. They would determine how long it took for a standard candle to burn and then mark the candles by the hour so that one could keep track of the passage of time (Whitrow, 1989). Sometimes they would make a candle so that the scent changed each hour! Imagine being a child in China 2,200 years ago and being told to do your chores until the one-hour candle mark was achieved, and the scent changed from lavender to rose!

Native Americans

Native Americans living in the Pacific northwest would catch a fish called the eulachon, a type of smelt, put it on a stick, and dry it. The eulachon was a fatty fish about 8 inches long and would actually burn like a candle after it was dried. There is a video linked on our website, https://www.steamcrafts.weebly.com/ which shows you how to catch a eulachon, and ten minutes into the video, you can see how to turn it into a candle fish. One fish does not stay alight for very long, however. The candle fish is more like a torch fish (Figure 6.2).

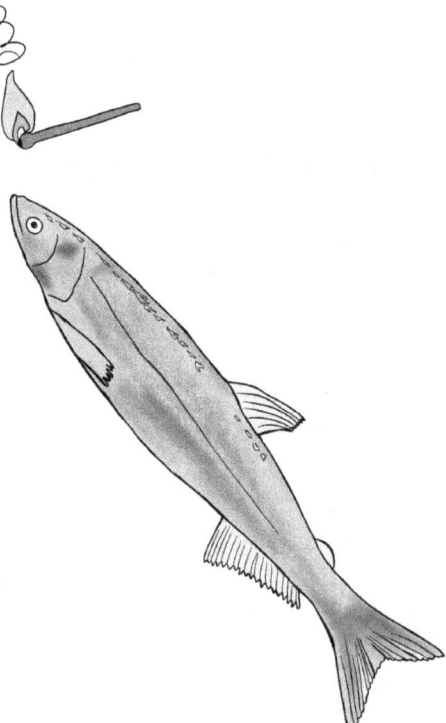

Figure 6.2 Candle fish. Image created by author Christine Schnittka.

Tibet

In Tibet, candles were made as early as 600 BCE from yak butter, and butter candles are still made and used there today. They are lit in Buddhist temples, and it is considered a good deed to bring yak butter to the temples as an offering, where monks will melt the butter for making candles. While I have never smelled a yak butter candle, I'd probably prefer it to a candle fish!

Greeks and Egyptians

The ancient Greeks and Egyptians used beeswax for their candles, often importing this expensive wax from far and wide. Beeswax can be removed from beehives after honey has been extracted. Since wax is present throughout the honeycomb, the entire thing is boiled in water. As the wax melts, it floats to the surface of the water and can be skimmed off. Perhaps it's a cultural preference to prefer the smell of beeswax over yak or fish oil, but I think that the smell of a beeswax candle is warm and soothing!

India

In India, people would boil cinnamon branches and berries to extract the wax from them. Can you imagine the smell of a cinnamon fruit candle? Cinnamon berries are small, and the dried buds look just like the cloves you might have in your spice drawer Figure 6.3. There are many species of berries that have wax coatings, such as bayberries and wax myrtle berries, and when boiled

Figure 6.3 *Cinnamonium cassia.* Image created by author Christine Schnittka from Michał Boym's "Briefve Relation de la Chine" (Paris, 1654).

in water, this wax melts and then floats to the surface of the water. When the water cools, it can be removed (Gode, 1951).

Europe and North America

In the 1700s, people started catching and killing sperm whales in large numbers, and using a white, waxy substance in their heads to make candles. One whale has around 1900 liters (500 gallons) of this semi-solid wax in its head. The process of removing the oil and the wax from the whale's head was terribly difficult (Irwin, 2012). Of course, this was very bad for the whales. By the middle of the 1800s, a candle making machine had been invented, and this made these whale wax candles more affordable, but required more and more whales to be killed (Figure 6.4).

Figure 6.4 Sperm whale candles. Image created by author Christine Schnittka from a photograph of an object in the Whanganui Regional Museum in New Zealand.

Killing all those whales was terrible for the whales and for the ocean ecosystems. In the 1800s, humans hunted and killed around 300,000 whales. From the year 1900 to 2000, almost 3 million whales were killed, and their population was decimated to only 20% of what it had been. These whales were not killed for food… but for their lipids—their wax, oil, and fat. Eventually we didn't need as many candles to light dark rooms at night because electricity was being produced and wired into homes, so people turned this great supply of whale oil into soap and margarine. Since the whale oil was colorless, people would add yellow food coloring to the whale oil to make margarine. Eventually, people figured out how to pump oil from the ground and make wax from that. People also started using machinery to take oil from crops like coconuts and cotton seeds and turn it into wax by adding hydrogen.

Throughout history, people have desired an indoor and portable source for light at night. Light gives us comfort, safety, and allows for productivity past sunset. However, the human quest for sources of wax to make candles, from whales to bees, has at times been a destructive one. Wax is a natural material, but it is a highly concentrated energy source which is solid at room temperature. In this chapter, you will learn how to teach your students about the history of candles, the science of candles, as well as the engineering and craft of candle making (Figure 6.5).

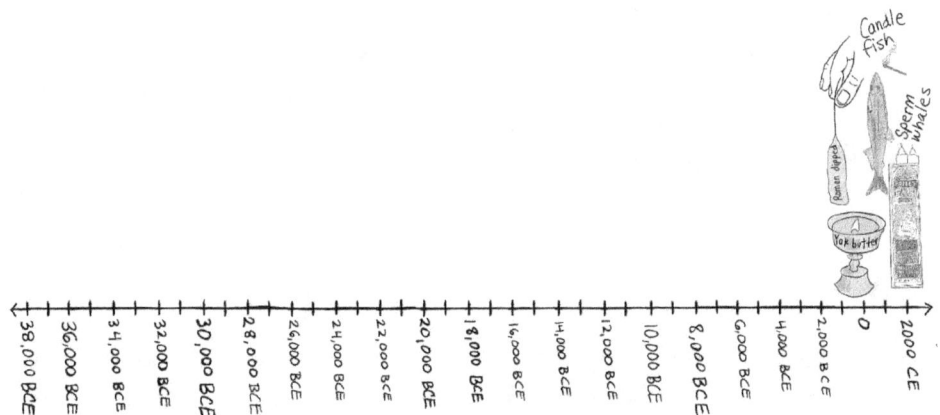

Figure 6.5 Candle timeline. Image created by author Christine Schnittka.

Meeting the Standards

Teaching this chapter as written focuses on STEAM principles that include: historical elements that influenced technological advancements, engineering principles including iterative design, criteria and constraints, and scientific measurement principles as well as data collection and analysis. For more detailed information regarding which specific standards are covered in this unit, please refer to our website: https://steamcrafts.weebly.com/.

Materials

- Secure a variety of materials which contain wax: dental floss, lipstick, floor wax, candles, crayons, wax-coated cheese, etc.
- Beeswax pellets (check to make sure they are high quality)
- A chunk of beeswax, perhaps a candle with the wick removed
- Aluminum foil to catch melted wax
- Candle sand in various colors (a type of ground wax that pours like sand)
- Beeswax sheets
- Crayons for crushing and melting
- Old candle stubs for crushing and melting
- Cotton string or prepared cotton candle wicks
- Soy wax pellets
- Ziploc bags
- Hammers or wooden mallets for crushing wax
- Non-flammable containers such as recycled glass jelly or yogurt jars, coffee cups gleaned from a second-hand store, or other non-metal, non-flammable containers for candles
- Electric coffee cup warmers that have a visible temperature setting

Safety

- Tie back loose hair and have a source of water or a fire extinguisher available when using a lit candle. Place some aluminum foil underneath the candle.
- While candles are burning, they should always be monitored by an adult.
- Never leave a burning candle unattended.
- If any students have asthma or other respiratory issues, do not burn candles in the classroom.

- Make sure that burning candles are not near flammable materials. Make sure that nothing flammable is within 30 cm (12") of a burning candle.
- Make sure the burning candles cannot be accidentally knocked over.
- If multiple candles are burning, keep them at least 3 inches away from each other.
- Have a well-maintained fire extinguisher nearby, within arm's reach when burning candles.
- Do not exceed the melting temperature of the wax you are using. If using a coffee cup warmer for wax melting, set the warmer to the desired temperature.

  - Soy wax melts at 82°C (180°F)
  - Beeswax melts at 68°C (155°F)
  - Coconut wax melts at 54°C (130°F)
  - Crayons melt at 49°C (120°F)
  - Paraffin wax melts at 43°C (110°F)

The Lesson

> **The BSCS 5E Instructional Model for Candle Making**
> The lessons in this book are designed around the BSCS 5E instructional model designed by the Biological Sciences Curriculum Study (Bybee, 2009). Based on Dewey's model of reflective thinking (Dewey, 1938), Piagetian theory (Piaget, 1955), and other learning cycle models that followed, the five phases of this model are: Engage, Explore, Explain, Elaborate, and Evaluate. The purpose and summary for each phase are explained in the sections that follow.

- To find accompanying presentations, student handouts, and more be sure to visit our website: https://steamcrafts.weebly.com/.

Engage: Experience Wax!

Purpose
The purpose of this phase of the lesson is to build excitement about candles, and to initiate curiosity about them and how they are made. Students can see

how wax is prevalent in their daily lives. It's also a chance for the teacher to find out students' prior experiences with candles and the science and history of candles.

Overview

Students explore various objects made with wax, including beeswax pellets. The teacher demonstrates the importance of a wick in a candle.

Probing Questions to Ask

Hold up the objects and ask students what they might have in common (Figure 6.6):

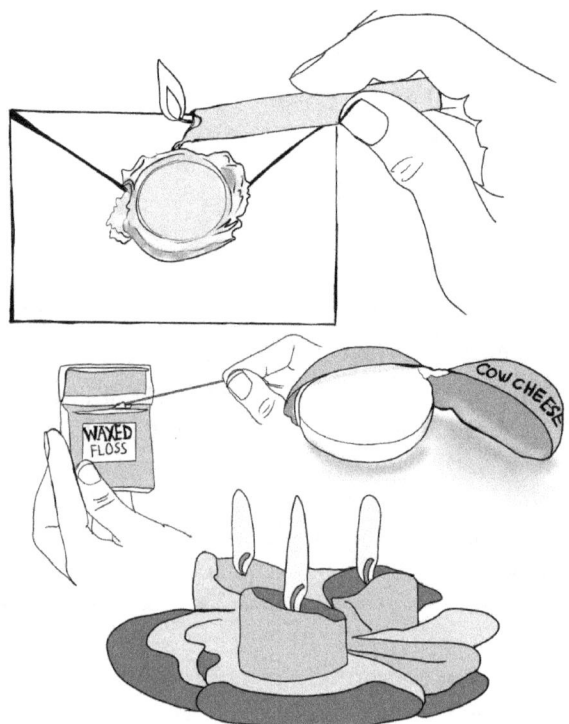

Figure 6.6 Various uses for wax. Image created by author Christine Schnittka.

- a small wheel of cheese coated in red wax
- a spool of wax-coated dental floss
- a small birthday cake candle
- a crayon
- a tube of chapstick

Ask, what is wax?

- Wax is a substance, solid at room temperature, which contains hydrocarbons.

What are some properties of wax?

- It's slippery and shiny
- It melts
- It's soft enough to dig a fingernail into

Pass out beeswax pellets to students. These can be purchased in a craft supply store for candle making. Be aware that some imported beeswax is cut with petroleum products, so look for beeswax produced locally. Ask students to warm the pellet in their hands, and then work it into different shapes. Have them smell it, and even take a tiny taste of it. Beeswax is edible!

As a demonstration, take a chunk of beeswax and hold it in one hand while attempting to light it on fire with the other hand (holding a lit candle, lighter, or match). The beeswax will drip onto the aluminum foil, but it will not light on fire.

Ask, why do you think this wax will not burn when candles do indeed burn?

- Students may say that the wax needs a wick.

Ask, why do you think candles need a wick?

- Students may think that the fire needs something to attach to.

Now, grasp a small piece (less than 2 cm long) of candle wick with tongs in one hand, and light the wick on fire with the other hand. Be sure to have a bucket of water nearby in case you need it. The wick will burn for a short time, and then extinguish, leaving behind black soot.

Why do you think the wick doesn't burn up when it's in a candle, but it burns up when there is no candle?

- This will stump the students, but by the end of this lesson they will know the answer!

- Student handouts and instructions for this activity can be found on our website https://steamcrafts.weebly.com/

Explore: Weaving with Purpose

Purpose
The purpose of this phase of the lesson is to allow students to all have experiences with the phenomenon prior to learning any new content. Some students have different levels of experience with candles. This phase attempts to level that field of knowledge so all students will have a more concrete foundation upon which to build further understanding.

Overview
Students explore the properties of wax by dripping water on waxed paper, drawing with crayon on paper and then painting over it, making prints with waxed paper, and more. Finally, students safely observe a burning candle which is inside of a glass hurricane vase.

Probing Questions to Ask
What do people use wax for other than for candles?

- A long time ago, people used to drip melted wax onto envelopes to seal the letter inside. This was called sealing wax. You can still purchase sealing wax in some stationary stores.
- Wax is used to make crayons!
- It is common for produce processors to coat some fruits and vegetables with a thin layer of wax to seal the moisture inside. If you have a cucumber, you can even scratch the wax off.
- Have you ever seen cheese coated with red wax? The wax protects the cheese.
- Some people use waxed paper to wrap up sandwiches.
- If you like Gummi Bears, guess what? They contain wax!
- Many cosmetics contain wax, particularly lipsticks.
- Dental floss? Much of it is coated in wax.
- If you have a sewing basket with needles and thread, you might find a small block of beeswax nestled in there. Wax is used to coat the thread so it's easier to work with.
- Wax is used to polish furniture and floors.

Ask students:
Where do you think we could find wax in nature?

- Plants make wax, and it can be found coating the leaves or fruit. Sometimes, if you scratch the surface of a leaf, you will get some wax under your fingernail.

- Honeybees excrete wax and use it to build their hives with.
- Some insects, like the Beech Blight Aphid, make wax that they decorate their bodies with!

Wax Explorations

The following explorations can be used to help students become familiar with wax properties. These explorations could be set up as stations around the classroom with instructions printed out at each.

Water Beading on Waxed Paper

Drop some water on a piece of waxed paper. Keep adding water to your drop. How big can you make one drop? Notice the shape that the drop takes. Why do you think that the water has that shape? Take a toothpick and stab your drop (Figure 6.7). Does it pop? Can you drag one drop into another drop with a toothpick?

Figure 6.7 Water droplets on waxed paper. Image created by author Christine Schnittka.

Draw with a White Crayon on Paper, Then Paint It with Watercolors

Take a white crayon and make a drawing on a piece of white paper. Now, paint on top of that with watercolor paint of any color. What do you see? Why do you think the paint behaves the way it does?

Waxed Paper Transfer

Prepare pieces of waxed paper so they are the size of a regular piece of printer paper and put them in an inkjet printer. Print a colored picture onto the piece of waxed paper and cut it into squares for students to work with. Have students place the waxed print upside down on a piece of white printer paper, and rub it with a stiff piece of plastic, like a credit card. The image will transfer to the printer paper. Why do you think it's so easy to transfer an image from the waxed paper to the printer paper?

Dental Wax

You can buy dental wax in a pharmacy. It's a very soft wax that people with braces use to cover up sharp edges and keep their mouths from hurting. This soft wax can easily be formed into shapes. Have students take a small piece and see what it can do. Can they flatten it? Stretch it? Twist it? Roll it?

Melted Crayons

Crayons are made of colored wax. Put a piece of aluminum foil in an electric skillet on LOW. Peel the paper off some crayons and break them up into small bits. Place them on the aluminum foil and watch them melt into each other! Have students take turns putting crayon pieces onto the foil. After all students have had a chance, turn the skillet off and wait for it to cool. When it's cool, you can take it out, peel off the foil, and display your class's colored wax art (Figure 6.8).

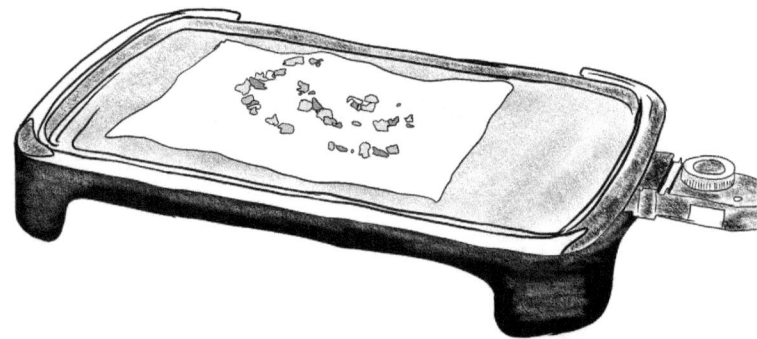

Figure 6.8 Wax melting on hot paper. Image created by author Christine Schnittka.

Candle Observations

Try to have a lit candlestick in a sturdy candlestick holder placed inside of a hurricane lamp (for safety) for students to observe. If a lit candle is not possible, videos of lit candles can be used instead. We have found many online

Figure 6.9 Candle in a hurricane vase for safety. Image created by author Christine Schnittka.

by searching "closeup video of candle burning." Have students take a good look at the candle flame and draw what they see. Prompt them to look for different colors in the flame. Ask them to notice the way that the wick looks. Have them notice the way the melted wax and solidified wax on the outside of the candle look (Figure 6.9).

- Student handouts and instructions for this activity can be found on our website https://steamcrafts.weebly.com/.

Explain: The STEAM Concepts

Purpose
The purpose of this phase of the lesson is to allow students to gain new scientific knowledge and understanding of how candles work so that they can make informed design decisions in a later phase.

Overview
A presentation found on our website https://steamcrafts.weebly.com/discusses different examples of candle science. Students learn about different sources of wax, particularly how bees make it. Students learn what makes a candle burn, and the physics of flames.

Candle Science: The Basics

Sesto and García-Rodeja (2021) interviewed 22 children who were five to six years old as they observed a burning candle which was then covered with an inverted glass. The children predicted that the candle would go out, but for various reasons. Some said it would go out because the glass was cold. Others said it would go out because it couldn't get any air. When the children saw condensation on the inside of the glass, some said it was because the fire stained the glass, or because water droplets came out of the fire. However creative these explanations were, the researchers found that all the children had natural explanations for the phenomena and concluded that five- or six-year-old children have the capacity to make observations and predictions and formulate explanations for scientific phenomena. Keep that in mind as you teach this unit!

Wax
What is wax? There are many kinds of wax, but what they all have in common is that wax is a chemical made from hydrogen, carbon, and oxygen.

Waxes are in the chemical category, "lipid." Other lipids are butter, oil, vegetable shortening, lard, and fats of all kinds. Unlike oil, fats and waxes are solid at room temperature, and melt easily. Like other lipids, wax does not dissolve in water, and it burns. A piece of wax can bend easily when warmed a bit. Animals and plants make waxes naturally, and people can make wax from oil, but not easily. Wax can be separated from oil, which is what happens when crude oil is pumped from the ground—the wax is separated out. In the mid-1800s, James Young figured out how to distill coal to make paraffin wax.

Soy

Making wax from soybeans is better for the environment than making wax from crude oil pumped from the ground but making wax from soybeans uses a lot of electricity. The beans are heated and pressed. Water evaporates from the beans because of the heat. The pressing squeezes the oil from the beans. All that oil is collected, and then put into a machine that heats it, pressurizes it, and adds hydrogen. It takes 6 pounds of beans to make 1 pound of wax, and a lot of electricity to heat and pressurize the beans. Most candles you see for sale today are made of paraffin wax, but you will see some made from soy wax, beeswax, or palm wax.

Palm

Palm wax comes from palm oil, and palm oil comes from the fruit of the oil palm tree (*Elaeis guineensis*). The palm fruits are treated just like the soy beans—heated and pressed, then pressurized to add hydrogen. You have seen soybean fields on the side of the road before—soy grows all over the United States. But, have you seen a palm tree farm? Probably not. Most palm tree farms are in parts of the world near the equator, parts that are warm and lush with a year-long growing season. The problem with palm tree farms is that they take up a lot of room, and the farms usually replace natural habitat, like rainforests. The farmers will burn down natural areas to plant these palm trees. I have seen this devastation firsthand in my travels, and thus I try to avoid purchasing candles and food that contain palm oil.

Wax Myrtle

Another difficult way to make a candle is with the berries of the Wax Myrtle plant, also called bayberries, which have a waxy coating. People boil the berries in water, and the waxy coating melts and float on top of the hot water. After the water cools, the wax becomes solid again. It takes 15 pounds of bayberries to yield one pound of wax.

Burning

Burning happens when oxygen combines with something. You burn food when oxygen breaks it up. You burn gasoline in your lawnmower when oxygen mixes with it. A wooden log burns when oxygen combines with cellulose and changes it into a black soot, water vapor, and carbon dioxide gas. Solid wax does not burn! Try lighting a candle on the end without the wick. It just melts! Liquid wax will not burn either. If you touch a lit match to a pool of liquid wax, nothing happens. The secret is that wax must be vaporized to burn. Wax is a hydrocarbon, meaning it contains hydrogen and carbon. Hydrogen is what makes wax solid—it stiffens up the molecule, and wax vapor burns because oxygen can more easily combine with the hydrogen atoms in wax vapor. This burning creates water when oxygen combines with hydrogen, and it creates carbon dioxide or carbon monoxide when oxygen combines with the carbon atoms in wax vapor. When you burn wax vapor, water and carbon dioxide or carbon monoxide are released as the long hydrocarbon molecule is broken up into smaller and smaller pieces by the oxygen coming and grabbing the hydrogens and carbons.

Animal Wax

Honeybees are one animal that makes wax. Young honeybees have slits on their bellies where they excrete thin wafers of wax, which they chew up and spit out to build their honeycombs (Figure 6.10).

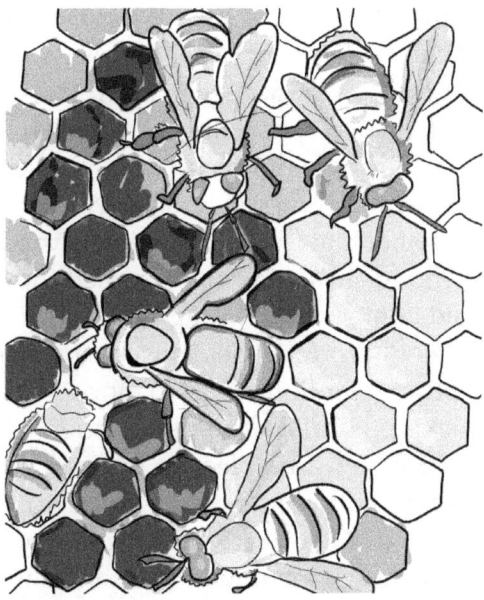

Figure 6.10 Bees on a hive. Image created by author Christine Schnittka from a photograph by Max Westby licensed under CC-BY-NC-SA 2.0 Used with permission.

Only very young bees, between one and three weeks old, make wax. After they are 21 days old, the wax production stops, and the bees leave the hive to go collect nectar and pollen from flowers. While the young bees are making wax, they are eating honey made by the older bees in the hive. The older bees collect flower nectar, put it into wax-lined cells in the hive, and fan the liquid to evaporate the water. The young bees eat that high-calorie food, and since they don't need all those calories to live, they can convert it into wax. If a baby bee eats eight grams of honey, it will make one gram of wax. What an unusual thing! Is the wax really their poop, and they are being creative with poop? Nope.... Bees do poop, and their poop is yellow, but it's not wax. Wax comes out of tiny glands underneath their skin that contain special fat cells. Compare this to your pet dog or cat. If you feed your cat or dog too much food, they store all those extra calories as fat in their bodies. Their skin stretches, so the cat or dog can get really plump! But a bee is an insect, so a bee's skin is hard and crunchy. Insects don't have bones, so their skin must be strong and tough. If a baby bee eats too much food, like honey, the food turns to fat, but it can't plump up like a chubby baby kitten can. Baby bees are born from wax-lined rooms in the hive, eat honey in wax-lined cells, turn that extra nutrition into wax and squirt it out from little oval-shaped openings in their hard skin. It's such a wonderful thing.

Wicks

A candle is made of wax and a wick. The wick can be a piece of string or even a piece of wood or tightly rolled up paper. What makes a wick work is the fact that it "wicks." Have you heard of paper towels wicking up water? When water touches a paper towel, you can see it move through that paper towel "quick as a wick." Well, melted wax will wick through string or wood. The melted wax at the top of a candle moves up through the wick just like water will move through a plant stalk or a paper towel. When the liquid wax gets to the top of the wick it's so hot that it evaporates into a vapor. It's the vapor that burns on a candle. If you made a wick out of something solid, like a piece of metal, liquid wax could not move up through it and then evaporate into a vapor. A metal wick just won't work. A wick must be made of a fibrous material. It must have spaces within it for liquid wax to move.

The science of wicking is called "capillary action." You have tiny veins in your body called capillaries. In a piece of wood or a piece of yarn, there are tiny spaces also—tiny pathways for wax to flow into. Now, you might find a piece of metal wire inside of a wick. This piece of metal is not helping the melted wax flow upward; it's conducting heat from the flame down into the wax to melt it more. A wick with metal in it will cause a candle to burn up faster. You may be thinking, why doesn't the wick just burn up and go away when a flame is on it? The wick DOES burn up, but some carbon is left behind like a carbon chimney that still has tiny spaces for melted wax to move through. If you take a used birthday candle and smush the wick in between your fingers, you can see that it is made of dusty carbon stuck together in a waxy glue.

When you try to light a candle, sometimes it takes a while for the wick to catch on fire. That's because the match flame has to melt the wax in the wick and then vaporize it, so that the wax vapor burns on its own. Once the wick is on fire, the heat from the flame melts the wax at the top of the candle, and capillary action allows the wax to wick up the wick, evaporate, and keep the flame going.

Guess what? If you blow out a candle, you can see white smoke. That is wax vapor! If you put a lit match near this wax vapor, it will ignite.

If you look closely at a candle wick, you will notice that most are braided. While you can make a wick from simply twisted cotton yarn, a braided wick is nifty because will bend and curl downward as it burns. This keeps the wick short and the flame close to the surface of the candle.

Candle Science: The Details
Wax Chemistry
What makes wax solid?

Each molecule of wax is a long, thin string of carbon atoms with two hydrogen atoms bonded to each carbon atom, and some oxygen atoms attached as well, and these strings slide past each other, making wax sort of soft, but still solid.

The more hydrogen atoms there are on each hydrocarbon molecule, the more difficult it is for the molecule to bend, and the more solid it becomes. Vegetable shortening is a cooking fat that is solid and white, almost like a wax, made by adding hydrogen to the oil molecules, which is why it's called a hydrogenated fat. If even more hydrogen was added to vegetable shortening, it would become totally solid, and we could say it is "wax." This is not something you can do at home. Chemists need special equipment to force hydrogen atoms to bond with an oil molecule. However, vegetable shortening is enough of a wax to actually burn like a candle. Just stick a wick down into a jar of vegetable shortening and light it! (Figure 6.11).

Why doesn't wax dissolve in water?

The molecule, H_2O, water, is polar. That means that one side of a water molecule has a positive electric charge and the other side has a negative electric charge. Why is it called "polar"? On a magnet, the pole is a point where the magnetic field is the strongest. On the water molecule, the pole is the point where the electric charge is the strongest.

Figure 6.11 A shortening candle. Image created by author Christine Schnittka.

The hydrogen atoms on the water molecule are positively charged and the oxygen atom is negatively charged. The negative side of one water molecule will be attracted to the positive side of another water molecule. The polarity of water makes it "sticky." Water sticks to other polar molecules also, just like two magnets will stick together at their poles. Water will stick to all sorts of polar molecules and all these little sticky water molecules can dissolve things by tearing them apart. If you put a grain of salt into water, the sticky water molecules will pull all the salt molecules apart. But wax is not a polar molecule. There is no section of the long wax molecule that has a positive or negative charge, so water molecules will not stick to it. If you put a little bead of wax into a cup of water, you can stir and shake that cup of water all day long, and the wax bead will not break up into smaller bits. The polarity of water is an important feature, and it makes some things dissolve in water (polar things), and other things have nothing to do with the water at all (non-polar things). When you drop water onto a piece of waxed paper, on the surface of a waxed car, or onto a waxed kitchen floor, that water beads up into a little mound. All the polar water molecules are clinging to each other, but not the wax.

Flame Physics

The shape of a candle flame is like a long, pointed oval. If you were to light a candle in a microgravity environment like the International Space Station (ISS), it would not be a long, pointed oval; it would be a sphere. As air heats up around the candle flame, it rises. But, warm air does not just magically rise, it has to be pushed up. Cold air is denser than warm air, and it falls due to gravity. This cooler air replaces the warmed air and pushes it up. While warm air is being pushed up, it creates a draft. This draft of air is what causes the long oval shape of the candle flame. On the ISS, there is not enough gravity to pull down the cooler air, so the warmer air is not forced up. The warmer air just goes everywhere, and so there is not a concentrated stream of air to create a long oval flame (Figure 6.12).

Figure 6.12 Flame convection. Image created by author Christine Schnittka from an image by NASA.

Elaborate: Candle Art, Craft, Technology, and Engineering

Purpose

The purpose of the Elaborate phase of this lesson is to apply the science of combustion to craft, art, technology, and engineering. Now that your students have experimented with wax and candles and learned about the science of them, it's time to engineer some candles! After making them by following some specific instructions, students can engineer their own to meet certain specifications.

Overview

Students are given a challenge to design and construct a candle which meets certain specifications. Perhaps the candle needs to burn for a specific period of time or fit into a specific candle holder. Students design their candle, manufacture it, and then test it under adult supervision.

The Challenge

The challenge for this phase of the lesson is to have students design and make a candle of their choosing which meets certain criteria set by the teacher. There are many ways to make candles. Some people pour melted wax into a container that contains a wick, and then wait for it to cool and harden. The wick can be secured by a stick or pencil resting on top of the container (Figure 6.13).

Figure 6.13 A poured candle in a jelly jar. Image created by author Christine Schnittka.

Some people dip a wick into melted wax over and over again, building up the candle layer by layer (Figure 6.14).

However, a safe and fun way to make a candle is to roll up a sheet of beeswax around a wick. These beeswax sheets can be purchased or made. To make them, melt some beeswax and pour it onto a piece of waxed paper. Cover with another piece of waxed paper, and once it cools a bit, start rolling it out with a rolling pin. If it has been worked like this, it will not be brittle and will not break easily when cool. Then, place a wick at one end and start rolling the wax up tightly into a cylinder around the wick. Beeswax works well for these rolled candles because it is soft after it's rolled with a rolling pin (Figure 6.15).

Figure 6.14 Making taper candles. Image created by author Christine Schnittka from "Candle Making at The Homeplace 1850s Farm" licensed under CC PDM 1.0.

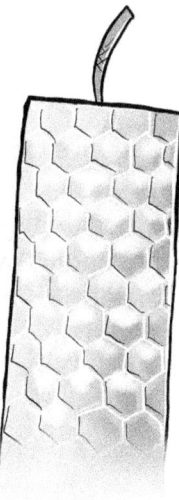

Figure 6.15 A beeswax candle. Image created by author Christine Schnittka.

Another way to prepare wax for candle making is to fill a Ziploc bag full of wax pieces (crayons, soy wax pellets, used birthday candles, candle sand, etc.), seal it, and then hammer it on a cutting board until pulverized. Pour the pulverized wax into a container and add a wick. No melting needed! A product of pulverized wax, often called candle sand, can be purchased from craft stores or online. This candle sand can be mixed in with other types of pounded and crushed wax.

Depending on the safety requirements for your classroom, choose a method or methods for students to use. Hammering wax in a plastic bag with a wooden mallet is fun for youth, and can result in some creative candles when the wax debris is poured into clear jars.

After students have made their candles, test them safely one at a time in a hurricane vase! Light the wick and observe it safely. Does it burn well? Does the thickness of the candle impact the burn time? Does the melted wax stay where it belongs, or does it drip?

Evaluate: What Did They Learn?

When students engineer their own candles, have them explain the decisions they made. Why did they choose a particular material for a wick? Why did they choose a particular material for a wax? Answers to these questions can help reveal the physics, chemistry, environmental, and historical lessons learned from this unit. A form to collect the answers to these questions from your students is provided on our website https://steamcrafts.weebly.com/.

After making candles, ask your students to write the answers to the following questions to see what else they learned.

1. The ancient Chinese used candles to keep track of time. How did they do this?
   - They would determine how long it took for a standard candle to burn and then mark the candles by the hour.
2. What is a tallow candle made from, and what does it smell like?
   - It is made from beef fat and might smell rancid after a while.
3. In Tibet, what is often used for candles today?
   - Yak butter!
4. How is the wax removed from a beehive?
   - The hive is boiled in water, the wax melts and floats to the top, and then when the water cools, solid wax is removed.

5. How were sperm whales used to make candles?
   - Sperm whales were hunted nearly to extinction for the waxy substance inside their heads.
6. What is wax?
   - Wax is a substance, solid at room temperature, which contains hydrocarbons.
7. What are some uses for wax other than candle making?
   - Wax is used to seal cheeses, beverage containers, and when coated on paper, to wrap up food. Wax is used for sealing envelopes and when coated on string, for flossing teeth. It is used to make cars and floors shiny. Wax has so many uses.
8. Where can wax be found in nature?
   - Plants make wax, and it can be found coating leaves or fruit. Sometimes, if you scratch the surface of a leaf, you will get some wax under your fingernail. Honeybees excrete wax and use it to build their hives with. Some insects, like the Beech Blight Aphid, make wax that they decorate their bodies with!
9. What makes wax flammable?
   - Wax itself is not flammable, wax vapor is. Once a wick is lit, the heat from the flame vaporizes the wax and keeps the flame burning. The reason it often takes a while to light a candle is that you must hold the match or lighter on the wick long enough for wax to vaporize.
10. What are the properties of a candle wick?
    - A candle wick must be made of a material that allows capillary action to draw liquid wax up toward the flame. A wick cannot be solid, it must have tiny spaces inside it, which is why braided or twisted cotton is often used.
11. Why not use a non-flammable material for a wick, as long as it has the ability to encourage capillary action?
    - A non-flammable material will work at first, but as the wax is consumed through combustion, the candle will get smaller and the wick will be too long for liquid wax to travel to the top of the wick. A flammable wick, one made of cotton or wood, will shorten as the candle is consumed.
12. Why is a candle flame oval shaped?
    - As hot air rises, it creates a draft which pulls the flame upward. Hot air rises because cooler air falls and pushes it up.

13. Why is a candle flame spherical on the International Space Station?
    - On the International Space Station, there is not enough gravity to pull cooler air downward, so warm air does not rise. A candle flame is spherical because there is no draft to pull it into an oval shape.

Summary

Candle making can be a safe craft to teach to youth when it is properly monitored and planned. For many many generations, our ancestors around the world relied on candlelight at night to move about the house, prepare and eat meals, care for the elderly and young, read, sew, mend their fishing nets, and simply carry on being productive after sunset. Candle making is an ancient part of world cultures and can provide youth with a connection to their ancestral roots. Candles are useful products that bring joy and warmth to our homes and are used in many religious traditions. All young people have seen candles in some form, and understanding the science behind candle making and candle combustion provides a real-world connection to many of the physics and chemistry concepts learned in school. Through candle making, teachers can also help youth understand fire safety, a vitally important topic.

Contemporary Candle Artists

Candle artisans and craftspeople are still working to make the world a brighter place today. For links to examine modern candle artists, please see our website: https://steamcrafts.weebly.com/.

References

Bybee, R. W. (2009). *The BSCS 5E instructional model and 21st century skills*. National Academies Board on Science Education.

Dewey, J. (1938). *Experience and education*. Macmillan.

Emden, M., & Gerwig, M. (2020). Can Faraday's *The Chemical History of a Candle* inform the teaching of experimentation? An hermeneutic approach for teaching scientific inquiry from a proven historical exemplar. *Science & Education, 29*(3), 589–616.

Faraday, M. (1886). *The chemical history of a candle: A course of lectures delivered before a juvenile audience at the Royal Institution*. Chatto & Windus.

Gode, P. K. (1951). History of wax candles in India (AD 1500–1900). *Annals of the Bhandarkar Oriental Research Institute, 32*(1/4), 146–165.

Irwin, E. (2012). The spermaceti candle and the American whaling industry. *Historia, 21*, 45–53.

Piaget, J. (1955). The construction of reality in the child. *Journal of Consulting Psychology, 19*(1), 77.

Sesto, V., & García-Rodeja, I. (2021). How do five-to six-year-old children interpret a burning candle? *Education Sciences, 11*(5), 213.

Whitrow, G. J. (1989). *Time in history: Views of time from prehistory to the present day.* Oxford University Press.

7

Plant Pigments

Introduction

When I was a child, my mother would get angry if I spilled grape juice on my shirt or got red clay or grass stains on the knees of my pants from playing outside. However, throughout history, different plants and minerals were used *on purpose* to make fabrics colorful. In this chapter, you will learn how to use the craft of natural dyeing to teach an interdisciplinary STEAM unit to your students. You will learn the science and history of natural dyeing and learn how to engage your students in this fascinating, ancient activity. Your students will learn what dyes are made from, which substrates are ideal for natural dyes, and learn about contemporary artists who work with natural dyes.

Dye History

In the past, natural dyes were difficult to obtain, and therefore expensive. This influenced cultures around the world. People with more wealth could afford to purchase cloth dyed with bright colors. People with less wealth wore clothes that were the colors of natural fibers—brown and white. The wealthy could dye their clothes purple and bright red. You could tell who had more resources by the colors of their clothes (Figure 7.1).

DOI: 10.4324/9781003428312-7

Figure 7.1 Clothes on hangers. Image drawn by author Christine Schnittka from photo by Kazuhiko Maeda which is licensed under CC BY 2.0.

Red Madder

When people started dyeing their yarn, thread, or cloth, they used plants or minerals from the ground, or animals like insects and sea creatures. The oldest colored cloth anyone has ever found was dyed red with the roots of the madder plant, which grows all throughout warm parts of southern Europe, Asia, Africa, and the Americas. Red madder-dyed cloth was found in King Tut's tomb in Egypt from 1323 BCE and in the archaeological excavations from Mohenjo-daro, an ancient city in modern Pakistan from 2500 BCE. The common madder plant (*Rubia tinctorum*) has yellow flowers and dark red berries, but it's the roots which have been used for dyeing for thousands of years. The red coats worn by the British during the Revolutionary War were dyed with madder root. Today we know that madder root contains harmful chemicals that can cause cancer and birth defects, so it's not wise to use madder for dyeing (Figure 7.2).

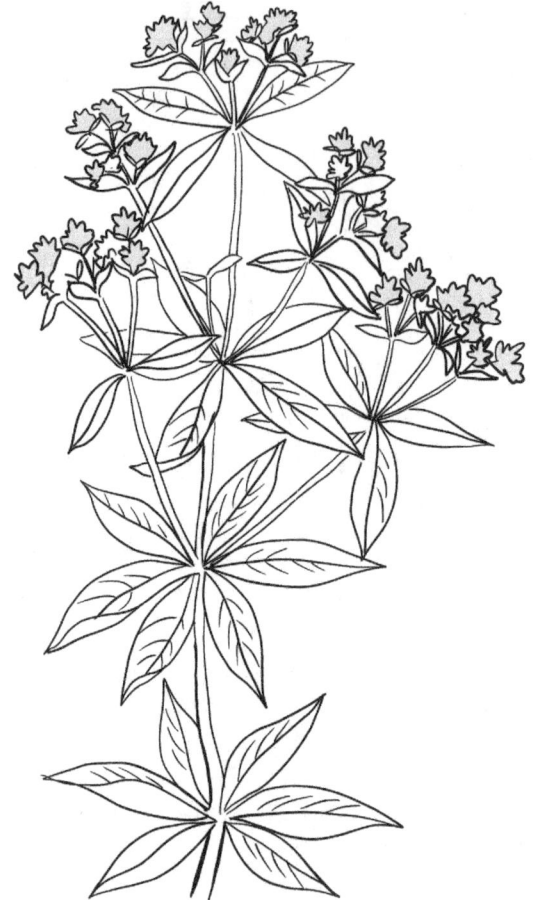

Figure 7.2 Madder plant. Image by author Christine Schnittka.

Murex Snails

Other ancient garments were dyed purple, and that purple dye was made by opening up a sea creature commonly called murex, and taking out a little gland. "Murex" is a genus of snails in the *Muricidae* family, but the many "murex" snails used for dyeing are in the *Bolinus* genus and the *Hexaplex* genus of the *Muricidae* family.

Bolinus brandaris, pictured (Figure 7.3), is a Mediterranean Sea snail. The dye from this snail was called Tyrian purple or Phoenician red by the ancient sea-faring Phoenicians who lived around Tyre, Lebanon, in 1200 BCE. We call these people "Phoenicians" because that's what the ancient Greeks called them, but we don't know what they called themselves. The word, "Phoenician" is derived from the Greek word, "φοινός" pronounced "phoinos," which means blood-red. Today, we remember the

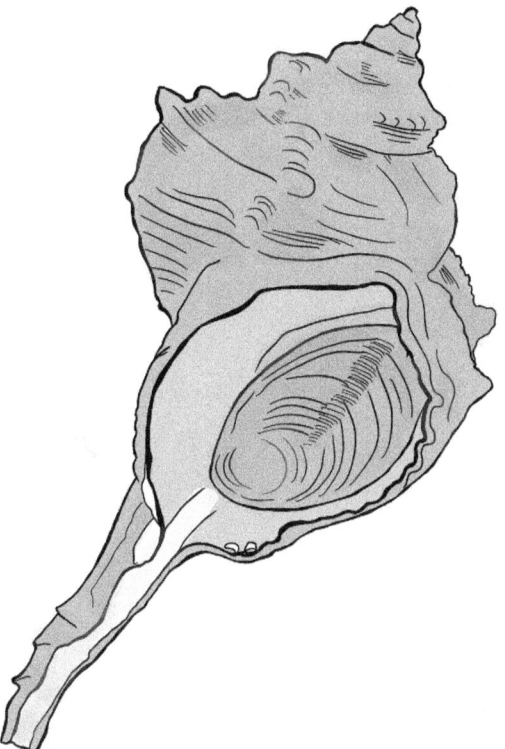

Figure 7.3 Murex snail. Image by author Christine Schnittka.

Phoenicians best for having developed the first alphabet. They created written characters to represent sounds instead of entire words and spread this new alphabet all over the Mediterranean region. As they spread their alphabet, they also sold and traded their red or purple dye, which was quite expensive. At times, dye derived from the murex snail was worth more than its weight in gold!

Another murex snail used for dye is the *Hexaplex trunculus*, which produces a pale blue color. This creature makes a mucus that contains a chemical very similar to the chemical used to dye blue jeans: indigo. In ancient Jewish tradition, the threads of the fringes of special prayer shawls were probably dyed with the mucus of this snail. The highly valued blue dye was called תכלת (pronounced tekelet), and the oral tradition is that the sea creature called "hillazon" found near Tyre made this color blue. The coastal Mediterranean people who dyed with *Hexaplex trunculus* most likely crushed the snails to access and remove the gland containing the dye. It would take smashing thousands of smelly little sea creatures in order to dye one garment (Figure 7.4).

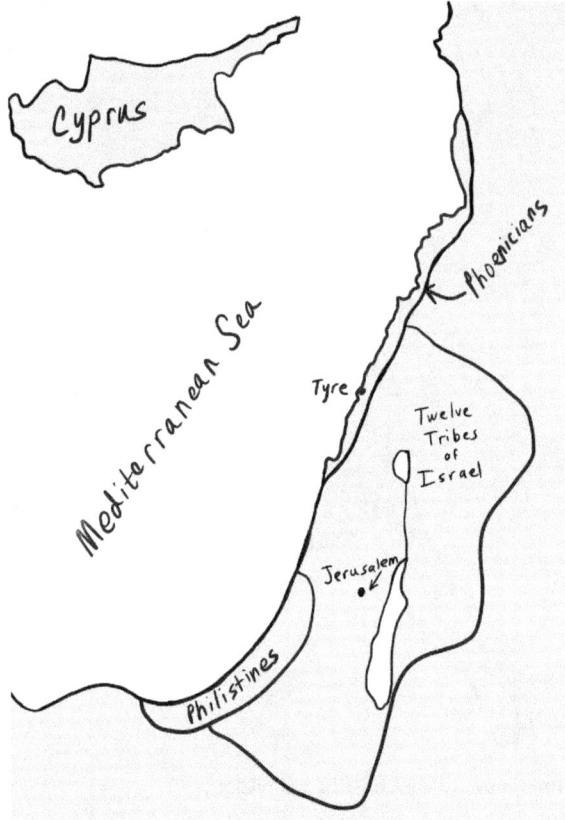

Figure 7.4 Historic Mediterranean Sea countries. Image by author Christine Schnittka.

Cochineal

If madder root was not available to dye something red, another possibility was to use bugs! A type of little red bug called cochineal (*Dactylopius coccus*) was crushed, and is still crushed today, to make the red dye, "carmine" (Figure 7.5). If you have ever used a red dye to stain a microscopic specimen

Figure 7.5 *Dactylopius coccus* cochineal bug. Image by author Christine Schnittka.

for viewing under a microscope, you used acetocarmine, a combination of vinegar and carmine. A little background on the words cochineal and carmine: the word, cochineal, comes from the Latin word, *"coccinus,"* which means scarlet-colored. And the word, carmine, comes from the Persian word, *"carmir"* which means red.

These little red insects feed off the moisture of the prickly pear cactus which is native to the Americas, particularly Mexico, and farmers brush the bugs off the cactus leaves to harvest them (Figure 7.6). The Aztec, Maya, and Peruvians used cochineal bugs to dye cotton and wool clothing. The prickly pear cactus and its buggy friends have since spread to all parts of the world where they are not particularly wanted. Australia was so overrun with prickly pears 100 years ago that the government had to create a "Prickly Pear Board" to figure out how to get rid of the invasive cactus and the cochineal bugs. However, cochineal bugs thrive best in South America.

In Mexico and the southeastern region of the United States, prickly pear fruit and leaves, once peeled, are eaten as a special treat, but not the cochineal bugs! Although some birds and rats seem to enjoy munching on them, they contain carminic acid which is not too palatable to humans. However, you

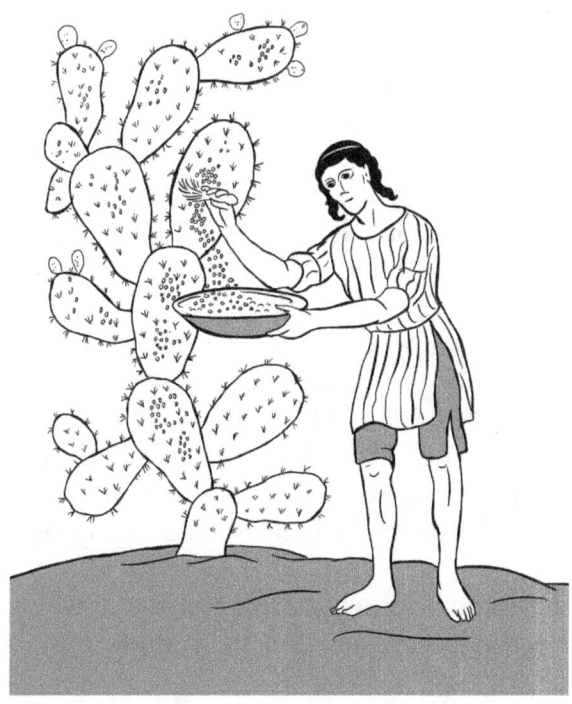

Figure 7.6 Collecting cochineal from the prickly pear cactus. Image adapted by author Christine Schnittka from "Mesoamerican Collecting Cochineal" in the public domain.

have most likely eaten cochineal bugs mixed with sugar many many times in your life, as the bugs are used to color many sweet foods. Next time you enjoy a red candy, yogurt, or drink, check the ingredients label for "carmine." If you see it there, you now know where it came from!

Indigo

If murex snails were not available or affordable for blue dye, indigo was the preferred alternative. There are a variety of plants that produce the blue indigo pigment, and while many grow well in tropical regions, indigo-producing plants grow all over the world. There is archeological evidence that indigo-producing plants were used to dye fibers 6,000 years ago in Peru. Plants that produce indigo were also grown in India, East Asia, China, and Africa. An indigo-dyed garment from 2500 BCE was found in Thebes, Greece, during an excavation. King Tut was buried in 1300 BCE with a small indigo blue linen scarf. There is a tablet from 700 BCE in Mesopotamia that gives a recipe for dyeing wool blue.

Indigo is thought to have originated in India, where it was used for dyeing and for medicine, and spread via trade routes from there. On the western coast of India, the Sanskrit word for the plants that produced this dye is नीळी pronounced "nye-lee." Nye-lee was used for indigo dye and as treatment for common ailments such as gas, fevers, and intestinal worms. There are dozens of species of indigo in the Indigofera genus that grow in India. *Indigofera suffruticosa* grows in the north, *Indigofera longiracemosa* grows in the south, and *Indigofera tinctoria* grows all over India (Figure 7.7).

In Asia and Eastern Europe, the plant, *Persicaria tinctoria* is the one traditionally used for extracting indigo. While Indigofera is a legume (a bean plant), *Persicaria* is in the knotweed family. It has been grown and used for dye, and for medicinal purposes, in China and Japan since 1000 BCE. It's been called Japanese indigo, Chinese indigo, and Dyer's Knotweed. The Chinese name for it is 青黛, pronounced "ching dai".

In South America, Mayans used *Indigofera suffruticosa*, which they called xiquilite (pronounced "chickie-light"), for blue dye. The blue dye derived from this plant was called "anil" by the Europeans who went there. The town Santiago Niltepec in southwestern Mexico is named after the blue dye. The chemical "aniline" is named for the blue dye because it was first derived from indigo.

While the people from India called this blue dye "nye-lee," the Europeans who imported it called it "indigo" after the country they imported it from, India.

The plant *Isatis tinctoria*, commonly called "woad," produces a pale blue color, and it was often used in England. When the English first encountered

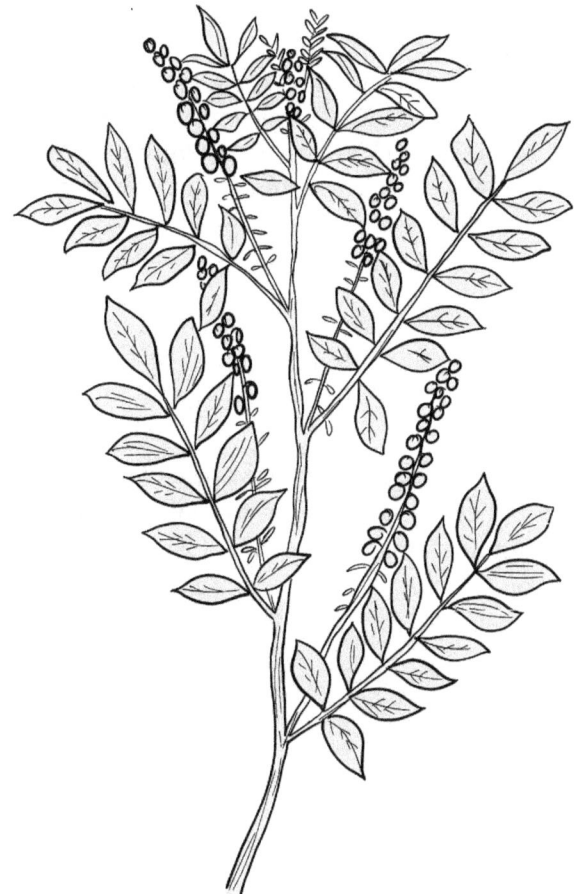

Figure 7.7 *Indigofera tinctoria*. Image by author Christine Schnittka.

indigo from India in the 15th century, they were determined to make it themselves. Europeans started establishing plantations to grow indigo in the colonies they ruled over. There is a dark history of the production of indigo by enslaved people in North and South America, particularly in South Carolina. The common story is that a teenage girl living in South Carolina named Eliza Lucas first grew it in 1730 after her father sent her some seeds from his travels in the Caribbean. However, Eliza did not know how to extract the blue dye from the plants. People from indigo-rich countries were brought in (against their will) to do that work and share that expertise. The marriage of indigo and misery also took place in India, where British colonists forced farmers to grow it instead of food for their families. Growing indigo, as well as growing cotton, dominated the southern United States for many years, until synthetic indigo was produced in 1878 by the German chemist, Adolf von Baeyer.

> Are you wearing something dyed with indigo? Most jeans are now dyed with synthetic dyes. The blue in the first American flag was dyed with indigo. Have you heard of blue-collar workers? They wore indigo-dyed shirts. Jeans were often called dungarees when I was a child. This thick, blue cotton fabric was named for Dongari Kapar, a village in India, where they used indigo to dye cotton cloth.

Dyeing with indigo is a complex process not entirely conducive to elementary and middle school classrooms. However, it is such an ancient and important dye that we have a link to instructions on our website: https://steamcrafts.weebly.com/.

What natural dyes accidentally stain your clothes today? Juice? Ketchup? Mustard? Perhaps we can find out how to make fabric dyes from everyday materials, just like our ancestors thousands of years ago did (Figure 7.8). In the following lesson, you will find out!

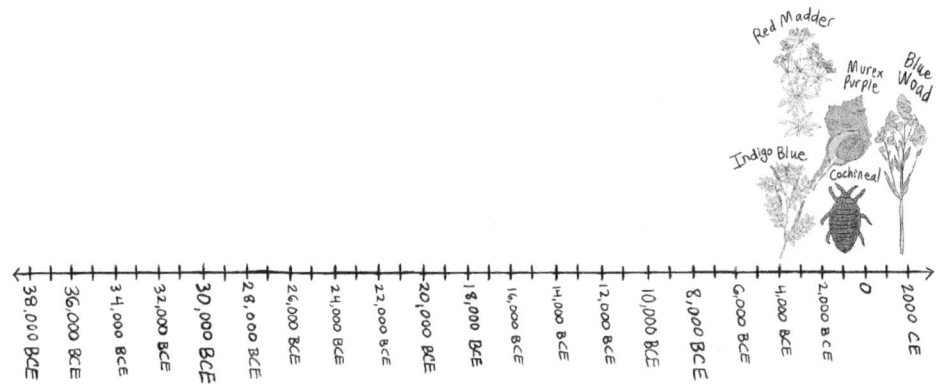

Figure 7.8 Timeline of dyeing history. Image created by author Christine Schnittka

Meeting the Standards

Teaching this chapter as written focuses on STEAM principles that include: historical elements that influenced technological advancements, engineering principles including iterative design, criteria and constraints, and scientific measurement principles as well as data collection and analysis. For more detailed information regarding which specific standards are covered in this unit, please refer to our website: https://steamcrafts.weebly.com/.

Materials

- Foods that can be used for dyes
- Cochineal bugs
- Magnifying lenses
- Small cups of warm water
- Plastic or metal spoons for crushing the cochineal bugs
- Any sort of paper for containing the crushed bug dust
- Wooden craft sticks
- Two electric slow cookers
- Hot pads
- Tongs for removing fabric from hot liquid
- Clothes pins, string, and rubber bands for Shibori
- Alum
- Iron nails or pennies
- Baking soda
- Vinegar
- Plastic plates or trays
- Plenty of paper toweling or washable washcloths
- Squares of 100% cotton fabric that have been washed in washing soda and dried: nine per group
- Goggles
- Plastic bowls for holding the dye
- Hot water kettle (electric, plug in)
- Clothes pins (wooden or plastic) for holding the fabric for dipping
- Plastic baggies for containing the food stuff
- Rubber bands
- String
- Optional: Clothesline tied up outside or somewhere in the classroom
- Optional: Wooden mallets and plywood squares

Safety

- Only use natural dyes with children that are safe to use.
- Do not use madder root, given its toxic properties.
- Have students wear goggles and an apron to protect eyes and skin from the pigments. Caution children about heat sources, and do not use water that is over 60°C (140°F) with youth.

The Lesson

> **The BSCS 5E Instructional Model for Making Using Natural Dyeing**
> The lessons in this book are designed around the BSCS 5E instructional model designed by the Biological Sciences Curriculum Study (Bybee, 2009). Based on Dewey's model of reflective thinking (Dewey, 1938), Piagetian theory (Piaget, 1955), and other learning cycle models that followed, the five phases of this model are: Engage, Explore, Explain, Elaborate, and Evaluate. The purpose and summary for each phase are explained in the sections that follow.

- To find accompanying presentations, student handouts, and more be sure to visit our website: https://steamcrafts.weebly.com/.

Engage: You Can Use That for What?

Purpose
The purpose of the Engage phase of this lesson is to build excitement about natural dyes, to initiate curiosity about what can be used for natural dyeing and the process of creating and using a natural dye.

Overview
Students bring foods from a list to class and try to determine what they will be used for. Next, students examine cochineal bugs, crush them, and add the dust to water. Students examine all the foods and decide which ones to make dyes from.

Note to Teachers: To prepare for this lesson, there are a few different approaches. One option is to look through your kitchen for some of the items listed below which can be used to make dyes for fabric. Think about what might stain your hands or clothes. Take a look around your kitchen pantry, refrigerator, and spice rack. Every item is not needed, but see if you can find at least one item from each color family. Also, locate some cochineal bugs. You may have to order them and wait a few days for them to arrive. They can be purchased from dye shops, Etsy, or even Amazon.com. One purchase of an ounce of these little bugs will provide you with enough bugs to teach this multiple times, and it will provide your students with an unforgettable experience!

Another way to acquire the food items is to have students look at the list provided (perhaps a day or two before the lesson) and go on a scavenger hunt at their house to find some examples—this might be advisable if you have large classes or if you would like to try many different dyes. Some natural dyes are more vibrant than others.

Here is a list of some kitchen/household ingredients that might work for different colors (Figure 7.9; Table 7.1):

Figure 7.9 Kitchen dyes. Image by author Christine Schnittka.

Table 7.1 Some kitchen dyes

Red/Pink Dyes	Brown Dyes	Yellow Dyes	Green Dyes
Cherries	Coffee grounds	Yellow Onions	Artichokes
Roses	Black Tea	Turmeric	Spinach
Raspberries	Beets	Saffron	Chamomile
Pomegranates	Onion Peels	Celery Leaves	Tea
Strawberries	Acorns	Dandelion Flowers	Grass
Avocado skins	Walnuts	Curry Powder	Parsley
Avocado pits		Lemon	
Cranberries		Mint	
Tomatoes		Pecans	
Blue Dyes	Purple Dyes	Orange Dyes	
Red Cabbage	Blackberries	Oranges	
Black Beans	Grapes	Paprika	
Plum Skins	Blueberries	Carrots	
	Elderberries	Chili Powder	

In addition to collecting the dye ingredients, the teacher should prepare some small cotton fabric swatches. Cut enough 2–3 inch squares out of an old white cotton t-shirt or a cotton white sheet so that each student has three swatches.

When class starts, reveal the items (except the cochineal bugs) that have been gathered and ask students to predict what they will be using the items for. They will likely think they are going to be making something edible, not dyeing fabric.

Next, prepare students by saying that you are going to add one more item to the collection, and this item also shares the same characteristic or trait that the others do. Bring out a bowl full of dried cochineal bugs!

Pass the bugs around and let students, in small groups, examine them with magnifying lenses. They will recognize that these little dried things are dead bugs, but reassure them that they are not poisonous and will not harm them (Figure 7.10).

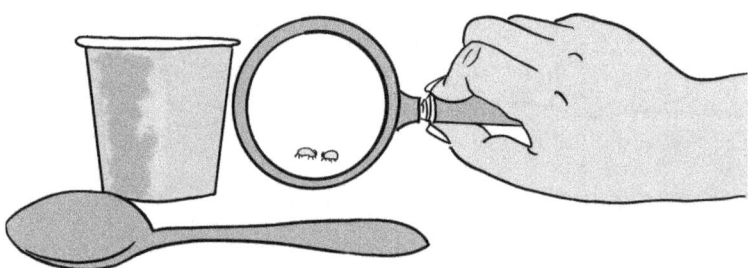

Figure 7.10 Exploring cochineal bugs. Image by author Christine Schnittka.

Have each group place a few bugs between two pieces of paper and crush them. They can crush them with a pencil eraser or the back of a spoon, or roll the pencil over the paper/bug sandwich until the bug is dust.

Pass out small cups of warm, almost hot water and instruct students to put their bug dust in the water and stir with a wooden craft stick. The water will turn a fuchsia pink color.

While students are still engaged with the squashed bugs, it is a good time to probe for their prior knowledge and understanding. You can also help to guide the discussion in a direction that gets them thinking about where the lesson might be headed.

Probing Questions to Ask

As students are exploring their cochineal bugs and examining the foodstuffs that can be used for dyeing, you can ask some questions to find out what they already know.

What do all these items, including the bugs, have in common?

- ◆ At this point, students will be able to infer that all the items will release a color when put in water.

What color do you think this item (hold up a food item) could release?

- ◆ Obvious colors, like green from spinach, will be easy to predict, but black beans, red cabbage, and other food items might not be so easy to guess!

Why do plants and some animals have colors? Why aren't carrots white like other plant roots?

- ◆ Some students will know that plants use color to attract pollinators. Most will not know about artificial selection and the scientific reasons that pigments are present.

How do you think your blue jeans got their color?

- ◆ While most jeans are dyed with synthetic dyes today, they were once dyed with indigo.

How do you think the red and blue in the US flag got its color back in the 1700s?

- ◆ After having been exposed to cochineal, students may guess that the red stripes of the US flag were originally colored with bug juice.

What do you think gives color to your clothing and sheets and towels today?

- ◆ Most likely, students will guess "chemicals" but have no further understanding.

Ask students to predict the color that each food item will release into water (Table 7.2).

Ask students what they might want to do with colored water they extract from plants or bugs. Give students a hint if they are stumped. Many of them have seen or participated in tie dyeing. They can dye things with these plants and bugs!

Table 7.2 Example colors

Item	Color
Turmeric	Yellow
Red Cabbage	Purple
Black Beans	Blue
Avocado pits and skins	Pink

Before the lesson ends, have students choose one item per group that they want to investigate further.

Note to Teachers: Commercial fabrics are treated with a starch or a sizing to make them stiffer, which will need to be removed prior to dyeing. Even well washed fabric will benefit from a deeper scouring to remove oils that might prevent dyes from adhering. To do this, obtain a new or old white sheet, old white t-shirts, or new muslin fabric from a fabric store. Just make sure it's 100% cotton, as synthetic fabrics like polyester and nylon will not work well with natural dyes. Wash the fabric with sodium carbonate, commonly called washing soda (not baking soda). You can purchase washing soda from a grocery store, and it's usually marketed as a laundry booster. Either boil the fabric on the stove in a large washing (not cooking) kettle with some washing soda added (follow the directions on the box), or use a washing machine with hot water. After washing and drying the fabric, cut it into squares of 5-8 cm (2–3″) in size. You will need enough for each group to have three swatches per dye they have prepared, so approximately nine swatches per group. Also, it might not be a bad idea to cut some extras for future dye experiments in later lessons.

Many kitchen items can become a natural dye without much processing. However, some dyes are best prepared ahead of time on a kitchen stove. Avocado skins and pits, acorns, black beans, and red cabbage need to be boiled for about an hour in a large pot of water to give vibrant results, which you can accomplish utilizing a crock-pot overnight or an instant pot. After the water is the color that you want, strain off the food stuff, and test the dye with a sample of fabric. Either boil a small piece of cloth in the dye, or let it steep for several hours. Different food items will need more time steeping in order for the dye to stick. In our experiments, we found purple/black grapes, wild blueberries, turmeric, black tea, coffee, onion skins, black beans, paprika, and strawberries to be the easiest foods, with minimal steeping. After dyeing, rinse the fabric and let the fabric dry naturally (Table 7.3).

Table 7.3 Steeping times

Steeping instructions for small cotton swatches: Add 300 ml (10 oz) of boiling hot water to a heat-safe cup, and then add dye ingredients to each cup individually. Allow each item below to steep for a minimum of 15 minutes in the hot water, then either remove the dye ingredients with a strainer or spoon or leave them in with the fabric swatches. Allow all fabric to remain submerged in the dye bath overnight.		
Black Tea One large tea bag per cup; produces an orangey brown dye.	**Coffee** One heaping tablespoon of coffee grounds; produces a light brown/tan dye.	**Paprika** One heaping tablespoon of ground paprika powder; produces a light orange dye.
Strawberry Slice/squash 3–5 large strawberries; produces a light pink dye.	**Black Beans** Two heaping tablespoons of canned black beans with juice–crush into smaller pieces; produces a tan dye.	**Grapes** Slice/squash 8–10 dark colored grapes; produces a light purple or pink dye.
Wild Blueberries Two heaping tablespoons of fresh or frozen wild blueberries; produces a deep purple dye.	**Turmeric** One heaping tablespoon of ground turmeric powder; produces bright yellow dye.	**Onion Skins** Entire outside of one onion (red or yellow), sliced into smaller pieces; produces light yellow or an orangey dye.

Explore: Kitchen Chemistry Experiments

Purpose

The purpose of this phase of this lesson is to allow students to experience dyeing fabric with dyes they prepare themselves. This hands-on experience helps them practice experimental methods and experience something they can relate to in a tangible way.

Overview

In the previous section, students examined a variety of plant and animal dye sources and chose, in groups, which ones to investigate further. In the Explore phase of the lesson, the objective is to allow students to do just that. They will decide, in groups, which foods to crush and turn into a dye, and then use it on cotton swatches.

In small groups, challenge students to crush the food item that they chose to work with. They can use a mortar and pestle, the back of a spoon, or even a pencil rolled over the item. You can hand out wooden mallets, the kind used for cracking crabs and lobsters, and small pieces of plywood. The food item could be placed in a plastic baggie to keep it from splattering.

The teacher should then walk around and add some hot water to each group's crushed food item in a beaker or other sort of bowl. Students can stir the food "tea" and then test their dye with the fabric squares clipped with a clothespin. The fabric can be used without modifying it, or it can be folded or twisted before being clipped, or tied up with rubber bands. Those types of modifications will create patterned areas of dye.

Have students collect data on the time each fabric sample is immersed in the dye, the type of food item used for the dye, and the color achieved.

Probing Questions to Ask

As students are exploring (crushing) their potential dye source, or waiting for the dye to soak into their swatch, ask:

Did you see the dye pigment before you crushed the food item?

- ◆ Some foods, like spinach, will be green before crushing, so there is no guesswork involved.

Where do you think the dye particles are? Are they inside the plant cells? Outside of the plant cells?

- ◆ Students may think that if they do not see the color, it does not exist.

What chemical do you think is making the color that you see?

- ◆ Students will likely not know this answer. They may think that that item contains paint.

Why do you think plants contain these colored chemicals?

- ◆ It is likely that students will know that plants use color to attract animals.

Which plant part do you think contains the most color?

◆ Students may know that flowers, berries, and leaves all contain colors.

What do you think is making the color stick to your fabric?

◆ Students may think that the colors get absorbed into the fibers of the fabric. It is not likely that they know that the pigments adhere to the fibers and can be rubbed off.

After students have dyed their fabric squares and documented their data, have them use the clothespins to hang the fabric on the clothesline to dry. Alternatively, they can simply place their dyed fabric samples on some paper toweling.

• Student handouts are available on our website https://steamcrafts.weebly.com/ to help students think about what items they might bring from home to test as fabric dye.

Explain: The STEAM Concepts

Purpose
The purpose of this phase of the lesson is to allow students to gain new scientific knowledge and understanding of how natural dyes work in order to make informed design decisions in a later phase. The teacher should engage students in discussion and deeper exploration so that they can visualize and comprehend the importance of the science, math, art, and technology of natural dyes when they are later asked to apply their new understanding.

Overview
A presentation and an accompanying student note-taking sheet can be found on our website https://steamcrafts.weebly.com/ which discusses different examples of dye science. In this phase of the lesson, you should first ask your students to explain their new reasonings and understandings. It's very important in this phase of the lesson to find out what students are thinking before teaching them the STEAM concepts of dyes. What follows is a discussion of the basics and the details of dye science.

Dye Science: The Basics

Both plants and animals are used for dyeing, and they have different mechanisms for producing color. Plants contain pigments with chemical structures and chemical names. Leaves are usually green; flowers can be red or yellow or purple. Berries and other fruits can be red or purple or blue. Some pigments are: chlorophyll, carotene, flavonoid, curcumin, anthocyanin, and betalain. The pigments in plants are there for a reason. They can help shield plants from UV damage, attract pollinators, and protect the plant from disease.

Plant Pigments

The green pigment in leaves, chlorophyll, helps the plant absorb sunlight and convert the light into the sugar glucose. The plant uses glucose for many things. The plant "burns" the sugar, combining it with oxygen and breaking it down into carbon dioxide, water, and chemical energy. Plants also use sugar to build healthy tissues, such as cell walls, new leaves, and seeds. Chlorophyll can be damaged by UV light, so other pigments are in leaves to shield the chlorophyll. In the fall, when the chlorophyll degrades, you can see those other pigments.

The orange pigment in carrots is called carotene. Carotene is usually found in leaves, which is why leaves turn orange in the fall. This orange pigment actually helps the plant absorb sunlight, but you don't see it with all the

Figure 7.11 Orange carrots. Image by author Christine Schnittka.

green pigment there. So why is carotene in roots like a carrot? It seems that **people** put the carotene into the carrot. Long ago, carrots were white, just like other roots you pull from the ground. Sometimes the roots would store a bit of carotene. Because the carotene makes the root taste better, people started growing carrots from the seeds of carrot plants that had slightly orange roots. Then, they grew carrots the next year from the seeds of carrot plants that were even more orange. Eventually, this artificial selection process made all carrot roots orange (Figure 7.11).

The red, blue, white, or yellow pigment in plants comes from flavonoids. Flavonoids help plants reproduce by attracting insects and other animals. Those animals either eat the berries and poop out the seeds, or suck nectar from the flowers, and in doing so, spread pollen around to help the plants make seeds.

Some plants have the pigment, betalain, which can be purple or yellow. Beet roots are red because of this pigment. Betalain helps protect the plant from pathogens (Sadowska-Bartosz & Bartosz, 2021).

The yellow pigment, curcumin, is found in the rhizomes of the plant *Curcuma longa*, commonly called turmeric. The turmeric plant has yellowish rhizomes which are usually boiled and then dried and ground up for a spice added to food. Before people could buy makeup in stores, some would rub curcumin rhizomes on their cheeks to give them a healthy color.

When a fabric is dyed with plant pigments, molecules of the pigment get stuck to the fibers of the cloth. Acids and bases can change the properties of plant-based pigments, it is fun to paint vinegar (an acid) or liquid soap (a base) onto a plant-based dyed cloth to see it change color.

Animal Pigments

Some animal products are also used for dyeing. The cochineal insect is used for creating a red dye, cow urine is used for producing a yellow dye, the lac insect is used for a red or violet dye, the Murex snail is used for producing a purple dye, and octopi are used for a brown dye.

Cochineal bugs and *Kerria lacca* (the insects that are used to make shellac) contain carminic acid, $C_{22}H_{20}O_{13}$ which deters predators, but gives the bugs their red hue (Eisner et al., 1980). Carminic acid is also called E120 or natural red #4 when put into food products.

In the village of Mirzapur on the Ganges River in India, cow urine was traditionally used for producing a yellow dye. The cows would be fed a diet of mango leaves, and their urine was collected. After evaporating the water in the urine, a yellow powder remained. This craft was banned in 1908, as the cows suffered greatly from malnutrition and kidney stones (Grovier, 2018).

Fibers

Wool is actually a really good fiber for dyeing. The dye particles do not rub off easily because they get trapped under the little scales on the wool fiber. This is what some fibers look like under a microscope (Figure 7.12).

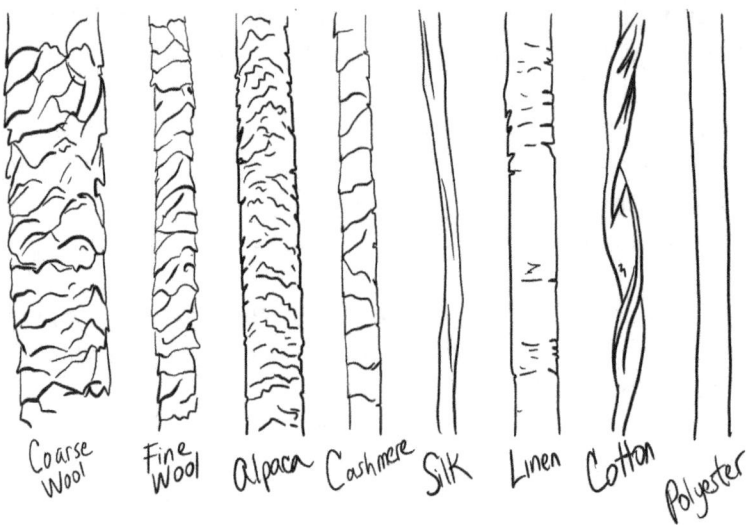

Figure 7.12 Microscopic fibers. Image by author Christine Schnittka.

 Dye Science: The Details

There are four main categories of plant pigments: chlorophylls, flavonoids (anthocyanin and curcumin are flavonoids), carotenoids, and betalains.

Some pigments in plants are fat soluble because they are located in the chloroplasts, the organelles that are responsible for photosynthesis (Humphrey, 2004). Some pigments are water soluble, and these are found in the plant's sap.

Chlorophyll

Chlorophyll, the fat-soluble pigment found in the chloroplasts of plant cells, has been around for 2.6 billion years (Humphrey, 2004). It is made of magnesium, nitrogen, carbon, hydrogen, and oxygen with a chemical formula of $C_{55}H_{70}O_6N_4Mg$. The magnesium atom in each molecule of chlorophyll makes the molecule vulnerable to acids, and so a bright green spinach leaf will turn a dull olive color when exposed to even a slightly acidic environment (Indrasti et al., 2018).

Anthocyanins

Anthocyanins are flavonoids. They are the red and blue water-soluble pigments found in the vacuoles of plant cells. There are over 600 different types of anthocyanins, with various combinations of carbon, hydrogen, and oxygen. They give color to black beans, red cabbage, berries, grapes, and even red onions. For example, the chemical formula for one of the anthocyanins, aurantinidin, which gives the petals of the impatiens flower their color, is $C_{15}H_{11}O_6$. Anthocyanins are very reactive to pH and can be used as an acid-base indicator. Purple cabbage juice will be green in a basic environment, and bright pink in an acidic environment. The beautiful hydrangea blooms you see in various shades of blue, purple, and pink, have anthocyanins which are modified with the pH of the soil that the plant grows in (Schreiber, 2014).

Curcumin
Curcumin is a fat-soluble flavonoid, a yellow pigment you see in curry powder. The chemical name for curcumin is diferuloylmethane and the formula is $C_{21}H_{20}O_6$. Sugar is also made from carbon, hydrogen, and oxygen, but the numbers of each element are different in sugar. Change the numbers of atoms of carbon, hydrogen, and oxygen in a molecule, and you get a different chemical entirely.

Carotenoids
Carotenoids are fat-soluble pigments found in carrots, sweet potatoes, tomatoes, pumpkins, and oranges. They are also found in lobsters, egg yolks, flamingoes, and canaries! There are over 1,000 different types of carotenoid molecules, but each type has a long chain of 40 carbon atoms. The formula for α- carotene, the kind of carotenoid found in carrots, is $C_{40}H_{56}$. The formula for lutein, the carotenoid found in egg yolks, is $C_{40}H_{56}O_2$.

Betalains
Betalains are water-soluble pigments which contain nitrogen. Their chemical formula is $C_{24}H_{26}N_2O_{13}$. They are found in beets, but also in pokeberries, the purple berries I played with as a child, making purple potions, and staining my clothes.

Elaborate: Dye Art, Craft, Technology, and Engineering

Purpose
The purpose of the Elaborate phase of this lesson is to apply the science of natural dyes to craft, art, technology, and engineering. Now that your students have experimented with dyes and learned about the science and history of dyes, it's time to engineer some dyed items!

Overview

After dyeing by following some specific instructions, students can dye in a way that solves a particular problem. They will use their food-sourced dye, but modify it with an acid or a base, and treat the fabric with one of several mordants to achieve a dye that withstands washing as well as being in the sun. They will also use Shibori techniques to produce a pattern that they design.

The Challenge

The challenge for this phase of the lesson is to have students create a unique dye product. See https://steamcrafts.weebly.com/ for student handouts that help to establish the deliverables of this challenge. Your students have the skills to make dyes from household spices and foods, but now it's time to teach them about modifying their result with Shibori and mordants, and task them with developing a naturally dyed patterned cloth that holds up to the sun and the washing machine.

The first dye that was not made from a plant, animal, or mineral source was mauve, a sort of pinkish purple. In 1856, William Henry Perkin, only 18 years old, made this dye while on vacation from college trying to make the drug quinine, which was used to treat malaria. Accidentally, he made a purple color, which was later called mauveine. After this time, many dyes were chemically engineered, and natural dyes fell out of favor. Perkin's story is an inspiring one, as he was still a teenager when he developed this important dye (Figure 7.13).

Figure 7.13 William Henry Perkin. Image drawn by author Christine Schnittka from a self-portrait in the public domain.

Shibori

Shibori is a Japanese technique for blocking dye with folds and creases, or blocking dye by binding fabric with string or rubber bands, or sewing patterns in fabric, and then gathering the fabric by pulling on the thread. Shibori has been practiced for 1,300 years, and originated in China. It was originally a way that poor people could make their hemp clothes look more expensive (the poor were forbidden from wearing silk). Eventually, the wealthy started decorating their silk with shibori. People in India were dyeing their cloth 6,000 years ago with a technique called "bandhani." This involved tying and pinching fabric before dyeing. It's where we get the word, "bandana" from. Shibori traditionally used stitches to gather fabric, while bandhani used wrapping/binding.

There are six main techniques used in Shibori.

Kumo Shibori uses objects. Tie fabric around these objects.

Miura (mee-youra) Shibori uses string to bind the fabric.

Kanoko Shibori uses elastic bands to bind the fabric.

Arashi Shibori uses a pole. Wrap the cloth around the pole then scrunch it down.

Nui Shibori uses hand stitching to gather portions of fabric.

Itajime (eet-a-jeemie) Shibori uses wooden or plastic shapes clamped on the fabric to create patterns.

Challenge students to use a Shibori technique with a dye they created.

Mordant Chemistry

If pigments do not attach to fibers easily, or if they get washed away easily, another chemical, called a mordant, is used as a sort of glue. The mordant sticks to the fiber, and the pigment attaches to the mordant. Mordants contain a metal, usually aluminum or iron. It works best to cook the fabric in water (using a pot you do not use for food) with the mordant added for about 30 minutes. As the fibers cool after cooking, the mordant sticks to them. I once used a cooking pot for this task, and my pot now has a permanent film inside it that I can't seem to remove. So, dedicate a pot to these non-food tasks.

Some kitchen chemicals are good mordants: Cream of Tartar is one possibility. Cream of Tartar, with the chemical name potassium hydrogen tartrate, $KC_4H_5O_6$, contains the metal, potassium.

Alum, or potassium aluminum sulfate, is a fantastic mordant, and since it's used to make pickles and can be found at many grocery stores.

Iron is also a good mordant. If you boil old nails in water, atoms of iron come off the nails and float in the water. You can then boil your fabric in the iron water (in your non-food cooking pot).

Copper is a good mordant too! If you boil some pennies in water, you will get a copper mordant solution. But copper is not good to eat, so be sure never to use a cooking pot that you will use for food later on.

Using an electric slow cooker or two, make a couple of mordant solutions in the classroom and boil some of the undyed fabric squares in them for at least 30 minutes. Label these fabric squares with the name of the mordant used. After the squares dry, students can dye them with the kitchen dyes they made.

The challenge for students in this phase of the lesson is to combine a kitchen-based dye with a mordant and a Shibori technique to make a patterned, dyed fabric square which does not fade in the sunlight and does not fade in the washing machine. Perhaps this fabric could be used for an umbrella at the beach! Acids (vinegar) and bases (baking soda) can also be used to modify the results, as many natural dyes change colors with pH. Students will need to keep track of their trials and photograph their results. When they have finally engineered a dye that is color fast (does not fade), they have succeeded as generations before did, in the quest for colorful cloth (Figure 7.14).

A possible table for data collection follows (Table 7.4).

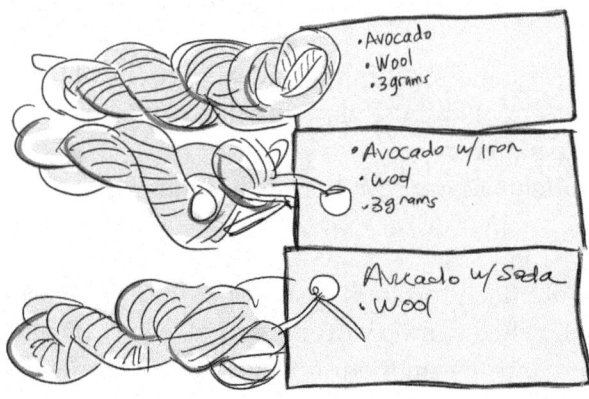

Figure 7.14 Natural dye data. Image by author Christine Schnittka.

Table 7.4 Possible data collection configuration

Natural dye source	Acid or base added	Mordant	Shibori technique	Before sun	After sun	After washing
Blueberries	Acid (vinegar)	Alum	Clamp with clothes pin	(insert picture)	(insert picture)	(insert picture)

Evaluate: What Did They Learn?

After making natural dyes and using them, ask your students the following questions to see what they learned.

1. What were some of the very first dyes ever used to color cloth? Where did they originate?

    ◆ The oldest colored cloth anyone has ever found was dyed red with the roots of the madder plant, which grows all throughout warm parts of southern Europe, Asia, Africa, and the Americas. Red madder-dyed cloth was found in King Tut's tomb in Egypt from 1323 BCE and in the archaeological excavations from Mohenjo-daro, a city built around 2500 BCE, located in modern Pakistan. The common madder plant (*Rubia tinctorum*) has yellow flowers and dark red berries, but the roots have been used for dyeing for thousands of years.

2. How were dyes used to show off how much wealth one had?

    ◆ People could dye their clothes with materials they had available nearby, but only people with extra wealth could afford to purchase dyes from other countries. If you lived in India, having blue clothing was not a big deal, but if you lived in England, and you could afford to buy indigo from India, you could display your wealth.

3. What are some animals that are used to make natural dyes?

    ◆ *Bolinus brandaris*, a Mediterranean Sea snail produces a dye called Tyrian purple or Phoenician red. Another snail, *Hexaplex trunculus*, which produces a pale blue color, is used to dye the fringes on some Jewish prayer shawls. *Dactylopius coccus,* or cochineal bugs, can be crushed to make a red dye, "carmine." The urine from cows which were fed only mango leaves can be used for a yellow dye.

4. What are some plants that are used to make natural dyes?

    ◆ Indigo is a common plant-based dye. In addition to indigo, which is created with a chemical reaction, there are four main categories of plant pigments: chlorophylls, the flavonoids anthocyanin and curcumin, carotenoids, and betalains. Beets, grapes, turmeric, black beans, and avocados can easily be used for dyeing.

5. Why do plants contain colorful pigments and chemicals?

- These colors attract pollinators and seed spreaders. Plants with no color do a poor job of attracting pollinators and seed spreaders, so their genes do not multiply as much. The more colorful and attractive the flower or fruit, the better chance it has of passing on its genes to the next generation. In addition, these pigments help shade and protect the plant's DNA from harmful radiation from the Sun. Sometimes, the pigment tasted bad, and keeps a predator from killing it. These colors help plants survive and thrive.

Summary

Natural dyeing is an activity that students will remember for a very long time, and it's very practical. Once students learn how, they can design and dye their own clothing. When you teach STEAM content and practices in the context of the art of natural dyeing, it has the potential to make a lasting impact. Go ahead and teach some chemistry, physics, biology, technology, mathematics, and engineering through this ancient craft! Inspire your students to get their hands stained today!

Contemporary Dye Artists

Dyeing is still a relevant art and craft today. Artists and craftspeople around the world are still creating and using natural dyes and doing fascinating things with them. For links to learn about modern natural dye artists, please see our website: https://steamcrafts.weebly.com/.

References

Bybee, R. W. (2009). *The BSCS 5E instructional model and 21st century skills*. National Academies Board on Science Education.

Dewey, J. (1938). *Experience and education*. Macmillan.

Eisner, T., Nowicki, S., Goetz, M., & Meinwald, J. (1980). Red cochineal dye (carminic acid): Its role in nature. *Science*, *208*(4447), 1039–1042.

Grovier, K. (2018). The murky history of the colour yellow. https://www.bbc.com/culture/article/20180906-did-animal-cruelty-create-indian-yellow

Humphrey, A. M. (2004). Chlorophyll as a color and functional ingredient. *Journal of Food Science*, *69*(5), C422–C425.

Indrasti, D., Andarwulan, N., Purnomo, E. H., & Wulandari, N. (2018). Stability of chlorophyll as natural colorant: A review for suji (Dracaena Angustifolia Roxb.) leaves' case. *Current Research in Nutrition and Food Science Journal*, *6*(3), 609–625.

Piaget, J. (1955). The construction of reality in the child. *Journal of Consulting Psychology*, *19*(1), 77.

Sadowska-Bartosz, I., & Bartosz, G. (2021). Biological properties and applications of betalains. *Molecules*, *26*(9), 2520.

Schreiber, H. (2014). Curious chemistry guides hydrangea colors. https://www.americanscientist.org/article/curious-chemistry-guides-hydrangea-colors

8

Milk Metamorphosis

Introduction

When I was a young girl, I would look forward to going over to my great aunt's house because she always kept a special cheese in her fridge that I thought was the best cheese in the world! I would look forward to the salty and savory taste, which was unlike anything I had ever had. There are countless times throughout my life when I have learned of another type of cheese, or something related to cheese and thought to myself, "All of this comes from milk?!" It is interesting to think that just from one source—milk—we could get the variety of different products that we enjoy all around the world today! (Figure 8.1).

How did we discover the different methods of cheese making? How was butter first created? What made people look at cows or goats (or other ruminants) and think—we shouldn't just butcher them for meat—we should harvest their milk and turn it into a shelf-stable delicacy? In this chapter, take a walk through early human history to discover the leaps and bounds of human technological advancement and ingenuity that had to occur before you could ever ask for extra parmesan on your favorite soup. Examine the physical and chemical changes that are required to create the variety of dairy products we eat today. Experiment with different variables to create a unique product that has all the properties and savory textures that you prefer.

DOI: 10.4324/9781003428312-8

Figure 8.1 Young Amanda looking in the fridge. Drawn by author Christine Schnittka.

Cheese and Butter History

Before people could begin making cheese and butter, a number of things had to occur. First, people had to develop agriculture, so that they were living in a specific place for a long period of time. This didn't occur until after the Earth began to warm up after the last Ice Age. As the Earth began to slowly warm, there were places on Earth that had more stable and reliable climates and other factors that influenced agricultural success. Around 9000 BCE, the Mediterranean region had developed hot, dry summers and cool, wet winters which allowed people to begin growing cereals (such as bran, rye, oat, wheat, etc.) and create farmland (Kindstedt, 2012). According to archaeological evidence, people became successful agricultural farmers around 9000 to 8500 BCE; this opened the door to turning their attention to protein sources and securing a stable supply of meat and animal products (Kindstedt, 2012; Figure 8.2).

The first herding and domestication of goats and sheep occurred in the Taurus Mountains. Goats and sheep were suited for domestication

Figure 8.2 Early farming. Drawn by author Christine Schnittka from a mural painted in Egypt in 1200 BCE.

(Kindstedt, 2012). The Taurus Mountains are located in what is known as the Fertile Crescent which is near present day Iran. Domestication of cattle reportedly did not begin until around 7000 BCE in central Anatolia (which is present day Turkey) as animal husbandry practices spread throughout the region due to the drastic uptick in the human population and the need to feed a larger number of people (Kindstedt, 2012).

Once people began harvesting crops and practicing animal husbandry in a more widespread and traditional manner, the next step was for people to begin to think about animals as more than a meat source. We can reasonably assume that people probably first began using animals for milk in order to feed their own children. As some human mothers either were not available for nursing or were not successful in providing a human source for milk, it is easy to imagine the idea of using animal milk as a substitute to ensure children's prosperity and health. This also required people to have a container of some kind to collect the milk from the animals in order to provide it to children in need. While humankind had been using containers of some kind (baskets, nets, pots, etc.) since around 28,000 BCE, there is no exact timestamp on the first containers that could have been used for milk-collecting purposes (Suddendorf et al., 2020). Early flasks or containers were likely made of either animal skins or organs as well as clay pots, which have been in use by humans since the neolithic era (7000 to 1700 BCE). The first record of milk collection and supposed cheese or butter creation is from 6500 BCE from clay shards found in Anatolia (modern day Turkey) that were lined with milkfat residues (Kindstedt, 2012, p. 9). Archaeologists have even found early baby "bottles" made from clay, with little spouts for the babies to suck on. One early baby botle, in the shape of a mouse, was found on the Italian peninsula and has been dated to 500 BCE, but much earlier ones have been discovered (Figure 8.3).

The final achievement in the history of using milk for butter and cheese would be engineering how to churn and curdle it. There is an old, widely known (and slightly varied) myth that cheese was first invented by a traveler

Figure 8.3 Baby bottle made from clay. Drawn by author Christine Schnittka from a photograph of an item at the Metropolitan Museum of Art from the 5th century BCE.

who lived in Arabian lands, who likely traveled via camel, and the story goes that he had a flask of milk on his journey in the hot sun, and the milk was heated and jostled around against him or his camel. When he arrived at his destination, and he opened his flask for refreshment, the milk had separated into a watery substance and a chunky portion. Because he was so parched, he drank the sweet liquid, which was surprisingly refreshing, and he also ate the chunky pieces as he had worked up an appetite along the way. This is the origin story that has been passed down through generations about the beginning of cheese and butter making, although there are slight variations to the tale depending on the region (Figure 8.4).

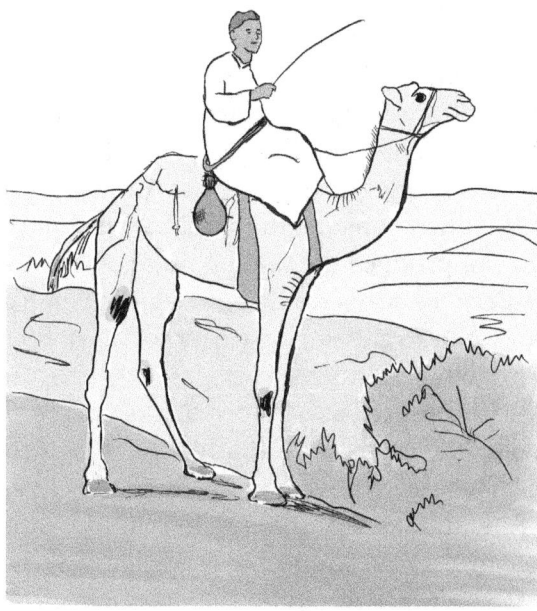

Figure 8.4 Cheese and camels. Drawn by author Christine Schnittka from a photograph by D-Stanley, licensed under CC BY 2.0.

The myth, while plausible, is flawed in that it presupposes that people would be drinking milk. What we know about those who were first to domesticate these ruminant animals is that they were profoundly lactose intolerant. Today, several millennia later, most adult mammals (including humans) are still lactose intolerant. The adults who are able to process lactose today are probably descendants of these ancient cheesemakers. In order to digest milk, which contains a sugar called lactose, the digestive system has to have the ability to break down that sugar into simpler sugars which are easily absorbed. To do this, the digestive tract has to produce lactase, which is an enzyme that helps to break down lactose into glucose and galactose. Young mammals have stomachs that are lined with folds that secrete lactase, making milk drinking possible. As the individual ages, and presumably stops drinking milk, the body naturally stops producing lactase, making it difficult to continue a milk-heavy diet as an adult, as the enzyme lactase is no longer there to break up the lactose, which often results in painful digestion. Lactase persistence for adults, according to geneticists, was not likely to be a widespread occurrence until 5500 BCE (Kindstedt, 2012). Lactose malabsorption is the technical description of the small bowel's inability to digest lactose due to lactase deficiency. Two-thirds of the world's population exhibit lactose malabsorption (Storhaug et al., 2017).

According to Itan et al. (2009), there is a strong coevolutionary relationship between lactose persistence (the ability of one to continue to produce lactose into adulthood) and dairying. As people continued to raise animals more for dairy than for meat, these populations had an increasing ability to digest lactose products into adulthood. This was the requirement that had to be reached to allow dairy products to be widespread. Furthermore, people could create fire around 6500 to 7000 BCE, and pottery was more commonplace, resulting in more opportunities to store milk (Kindstedt, 2012). Once people started collecting milk and storing it, it was only a matter of time before they started seeing it curdle, as raw milk has all the ingredients to ferment by itself. When consumed, people would have noticed that the eating of curds did not produce the same pain and swelling in their belly as did drinking milk. Because curds result from lactose being converted to lactic acid, curds (the precursor to cheese) are easier to digest for those with lactose malabsorption or intolerance.

Butter was likely discovered as a by-product of cheese making. The liquid portion left over after the curds have solidified can be used to make butter. Butter has been used for everything from medicine (by Byzantine physicians) to sculptures (by Tibetan Buddhist monks), to religious offerings by the Celts who planted butter underground in bogs in order to receive favor from the gods (Khosrova, 2016). People throughout history have churned butter with their hands, inside of animal skins, with the "plunger" type churner, and eventually with a churn with a handle, gears, and a paddle. Today, with just a pint of heavy cream and a whisk on a standing mixer, one could churn out fresh butter within minutes.

The first cheeses were likely some of the easiest to create: soft cheeses made by utilizing heat and the addition of acids. Preservation and eventual ripening of cheeses likely resulted later as seen in present day Turkey—where curds are placed inside animal skins and hung to ripen and harden.

Rennet, which is used in the production of cheeses worldwide, is a product originally derived from the stomachs of juvenile ruminants where an enzyme called chymosin is excreted. The exact point in history where this was discovered as a way to curdle milk into cheese is unknown, but agricultural historians theorize that it would have been rather early on in the production of cheese as people who slaughtered animals for meat would have noticed the curdling of the milk in the stomachs of the slain animals. In more modern times, rennet production from animal sources could not keep up with the demand for cheese products, therefore, other sources of rennet were developed. Now, people can purchase rennet produced by plants or microbes. This allows for mass production of cheeses, as microbial rennet is much easier to synthesize and collect than animal rennet (Figure 8.5).

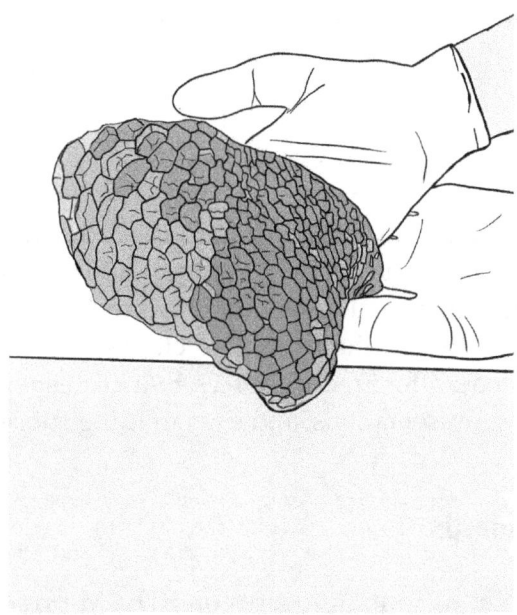

Figure 8.5 Inside ruminant stomach, folds where rennet originates. Image drawn by author Christine Schnittka from photo by Wolfemanwm licensed under CC BY-SA 3.0.

The taste of both cheese and butter is so varied because every single aspect of making these products incorporates variables. The grasses or grains fed to the animal is the first variable, followed by the type of animal from which the milk is collected, the way the milk is extracted and stored, in addition to the way the milk itself is processed—all of these introduce variables in the production process that slightly alter the taste. There are historical records of precise measurements and recipes to produce reliably similar products. Changing even one part of the recipe can have a measurable impact on the resulting product. In today's world where most dairy products are created in an industrialized and standardized approach, we have become accustomed to certain tastes. Our ability to have this dependable expectation of what our cheese or butter will taste like is the result of an immeasurable amount of time, happenstance, trial and error, and human ingenuity over the course of several thousand years (Figure 8.6).

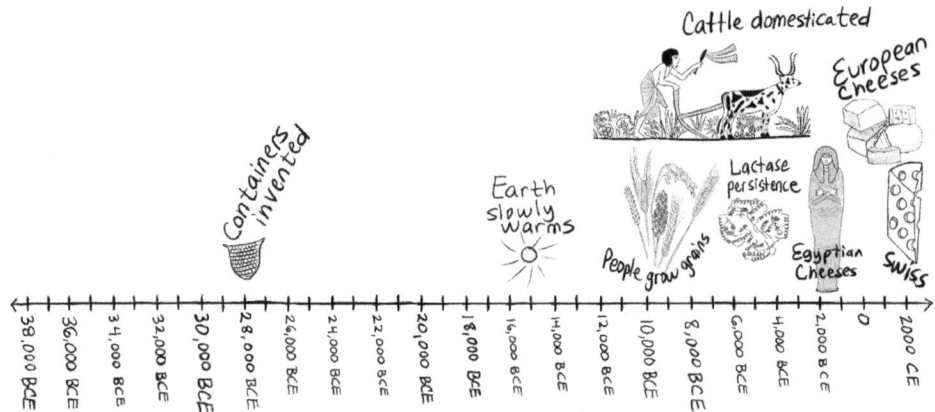

Figure 8.6 Timeline of cheese history. Image created by author Christine Schnittka.

In this unit, students will alter different variables in the cheese-making process to produce a unique cheese, and they will add a flavor-enhancing product to butter to make it a unique product as well.

To teach students about the history of cheese and butter, visit https://steamcrafts.weebly.com/ for free resources that correspond to this chapter, including handouts, presentations, and even grading rubrics.

Meeting the Standards

Teaching this chapter as written focuses on STEAM principles that include: historical elements that influenced technological advancements, engineering principles including iterative design, criteria and constraints, and scientific measurement principles as well as data collection and analysis. For more detailed information regarding which specific standards are covered in this unit, please refer to our website: https://steamcrafts.weebly.com/.

Materials

- 2–3 32 liter or quart sized containers of heavy whipping cream (depending on how many students)
- Standing mixer (hand mixer can be used also) with a whisk attachment
- Medium-sized mixing bowl
- Small bowl
- Sugar
- Sea salt
- Quart-size resealable plastic bags
- Several strainers or colanders with small holes
- Multiple 350 ml (12 oz) containers with lids
- Food grade gloves
- 7–11 liters (2–3 gallons) of whole milk (NOT ultra pasteurized)
- Large pot/cooking container and hot plate OR a slow cooker or instant pot could be used instead.
- Thermometer (thoroughly sanitized)
- Slotted spoon
- Microwave
- Microwavable bowl
- White vinegar
- Spices (garlic, salt, pepper, onion powder, or simply a Greek seasoning)
- Lemon juice
- Citric acid powder
- Disposable cups for hot liquid (such as Styrofoam or paper coffee cups)
- Popsicle sticks or plastic spoons for stirring and mixing
- Easy access to a refrigerator or a cooler with ice to preserve milk products prior to making cheese and butter and student products
- Rennet liquid or tablets (microbial preferred, but animal or vegetable may also be used)

Safety

- Check for any food allergies or sensitivities prior to this unit.
- Thoroughly clean all tools and equipment prior to use and afterward to prevent the growth of bacteria or the spread of allergens.

- Caution children about heat sources, and do not use anything that is over 60°C (140°F) with youth.
- Take caution when heating liquids not to overheat or boil over.
- Heating or boiling milk should only be done by the teacher with a hotplate plugged into an outlet with GFCI protection, away from a source of water, with potholders available.
- If students will be consuming cheese or butter, it is advisable to wear food grade gloves to handle the material that will be consumed.
- The operation of the mixer should be carefully controlled to minimize sloshing and prevent spilling.
- Care should be given when handling the cheese as it is being pressed, especially after heating or reheating, to prevent burns on hands.
- All appliances should be plugged into an outlet with GFCI protection, away from a source of water.
- Do not use expired milk products to make butter or cheese.
- Do not consume butter or cheese products that have not been properly refrigerated or that are older than three days as these homemade products do not contain the preservatives of those products found on the grocery store shelves.
- Extreme caution should be used if students operate a blender. Teachers should be intentional about providing a utensil to use to scrape the inside of the blender to prevent youth from putting their hands near the blades. Youth should not clean blenders and should be taught about the dangers of this tool prior to use.

The Lesson

> **The BSCS 5E Instructional Model for Cheese Making**
>
> The lessons in this book are designed around the BSCS 5E instructional model designed by the Biological Sciences Curriculum Study (Bybee, 2009). Based on Dewey's model of reflective thinking (Dewey, 1938), Piagetian theory (Piaget, 1955), and other learning cycle models that followed, the five phases of this model are: Engage, Explore, Explain, Elaborate, and Evaluate. The purpose and summary for each phase are explained in the sections that follow.

- To find accompanying presentations, student handouts, and more be sure to visit our website: https://steamcrafts.weebly.com/.

Engage: Grandma's Famous Cheese and Butter

Purpose
The purpose of the Engage phase of this lesson is to build excitement about cheese and butter, to initiate curiosity about how butter and cheese differ, and to practice observational skills. Students should leave this phase curious, motivated, and ready to learn more about butter and cheese creation.

Overview
In this section of the unit, students listen to a story and observe as the teacher makes two favorite recipes for butter and cheese. Students begin to question the teacher when the butter looks like cheese and the cheese looks like butter. The section ends with a taste test!

When food is involved, students usually ask, "Can we eat it?!" While some teachers have lab safety rules about not eating in the classroom, others don't mind students partaking in activities involving food. Regardless, food usually gets students' attention. To add to the mystique and intrigue, for this first lesson, teachers can engage in a slightly nefarious activity where students are told that they will be making two different recipes. One is Grandma's cheese recipe, and the other is her butter recipe. The teacher performs the actions described in the recipes exactly as they are written, assuring students that both recipes must turn out perfectly—they're Grandma's after all!

Unbeknownst to the students, the recipes have been mistitled. The cheese is actually butter. The butter is actually cheese.

After giving the students the lab sheet with the recipes on them, and maybe a juicy backstory about how delicious you remember this being when you were a kid, proceed to make both cheese and butter as a whole-class demonstration where students are invited to observe and help you follow the recipe exactly.

The teacher happily proceeds through the recipe and students may follow along at first as they witness the cheese and butter forming, but when the two substances solidify and their properties change, so do students' opinions. Seeing that the "cheese" is yellow and greasy, and the "butter" is white and chunky further convinces students that something is amiss.

While continuing the ruse, the teacher starts to become more uncertain. The teacher skims the ingredients and directions again and states that they need more convincing evidence to believe that the recipe is wrong. The students begin to describe their understanding of cheese and butter and explain that their prior knowledge about butter and cheese does not align with what they are witnessing. The teacher asks for more descriptive observations besides, "butter is yellow and cheese is white"! The students double-down on their claims, trying to convince the teacher of their error.

It's up to the teacher to admit whether there is a mistake. If the students don't provide very convincing evidence, the teacher could withhold information about the ruse, and leave the students guessing until later in the unit. If the students are wildly outraged and adamant that the teacher is mistaken, perhaps the teacher could grin and admit the ruse.

When we performed this lab, we decided to reveal the truth because we didn't want to allow the misinformation to persist. When the students answered the reflection questions on the lab sheet, we preferred that they were answering them with the correct understanding of which product was cheese and which was butter.

Grandma's Cheese Recipe

For the "cheese," pour 2 liters (a half-gallon) of heavy whipping cream into the mixing bowl and begin mixing with the whisk on medium high heat (Figure 8.7). If you are using a hand-held mixer, have a helper hold the mixer. After a few minutes of mixing, the "cheese" will change from a liquid to a fluffy white substance. After a couple of additional minutes of mixing, the consistency of the "cheese" will approach something akin to cake icing, and finally, it will separate into a liquid and a solidified mass that will stick to the whisk. This

Figure 8.7 Grandma's cheese recipe. Image drawn by author Christine Schnittka.

is when the mixer will need to be turned down slightly, because it will slosh the liquid out, making a mess. Remove the solidified mass of "cheese" and put the lump in a strainer, allowing the liquid to drip back into the mixing bowl. Once the liquid stops dripping, put the glob of "cheese" into the small bowl.

After it has drained, take the chunk of "cheese" and add a small bit of salt. Knead the mass with gloved hands, working the salt into the "cheese" and the milky liquid out of it. Once the liquid is removed, you may pour this liquid into a container with a lid (save that buttermilk!), and keep it to be used in the kitchen, if you prefer. (If you have no use for buttermilk, you can pour it down the drain.)

Grandma's Butter Recipe

For the "butter," more care and attention must be taken to ensure that the milk does not overheat. Pour the milk into a cooking container and turn the temperature of the heating apparatus (whether you are using a hot plate, slow cooker, or other kind of small appliance) to medium high while continuing to stir with the slotted spoon. Continually check the temperature of the milk and remove from the heat when the milk reaches 46°C (115°F). At this point, add the vinegar, and gently stir for 30 seconds. The milk will immediately begin separating. Allow the milk and vinegar to sit for 15 minutes without stirring or jostling (Figure 8.8).

Figure 8.8 Grandma's butter recipe. Image drawn by author Christine Schnittka.

After the 15 minutes have elapsed, use the slotted spoon to remove the solidified chunks, and transfer them to the strainer or colander dedicated to the "butter" recipe (Figure 8.9). *Don't use the same strainer for both cheese and butter without thoroughly cleaning them with soap and water first. Continue to remove the solidified pieces and allow the liquid to drip back into the pot.

Put the chunks of "butter" into the small bowl. Add a sprinkle of salt to the solid mass (Figure 8.10). Using gloved hands, work the solid by squishing

Figure 8.9 Stirring the pot. Image created by author Christine Schnittka.

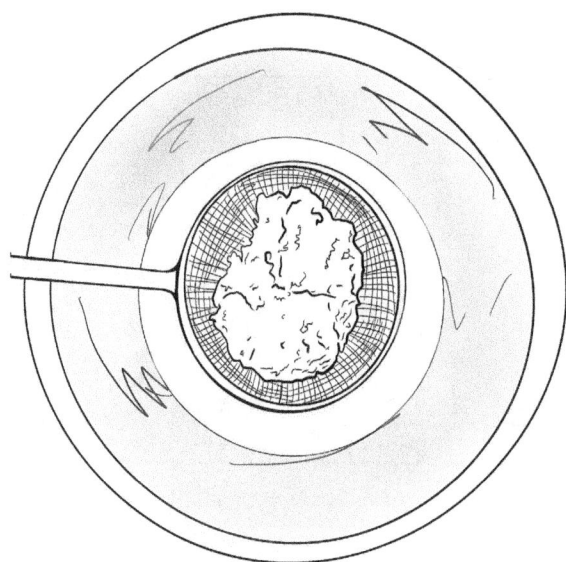

Figure 8.10 Straining the cheese. Image created by author Christine Schnittka.

and squeezing—you may have to use the strainer to help remove more moisture. Once you have squished and squeezed the "butter" for a minute or two, microwave the mass in the microwavable bowl for about 20 seconds or dip it back into the hot liquid in the pot.

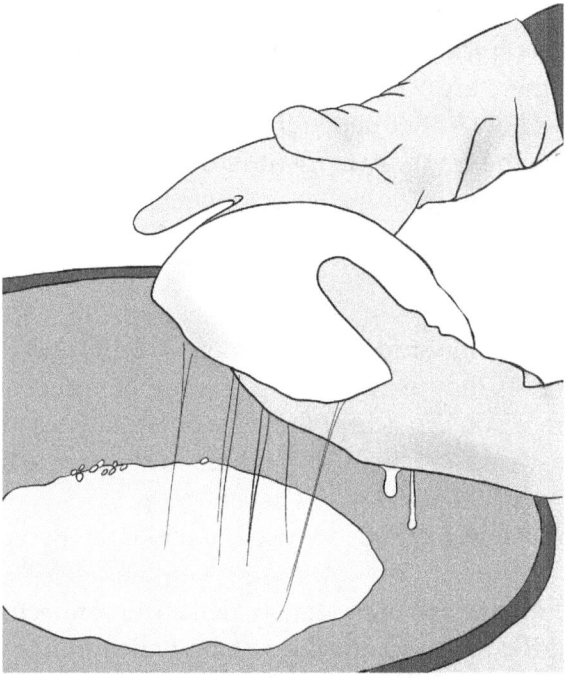

Figure 8.11 Kneading soft cheese. Image created by author Christine Schnittka.

Being careful not to burn yourself, continue to remove the cheese and knead it (Figure 8.11). You can repeat this heating and squishing process two more times, until the mass is smooth and stretchy. You can add some herbs or Greek seasoning to help mask the vinegar taste. The more liquid you remove, the less vinegar you will be able to taste.

At the discretion of the teacher, the students can enjoy the butter and cheese with crackers or even some nice bread!

Probing Questions to Ask

Does this look like the butter and cheese you eat at home?

- ◆ Students will probably have very little knowledge about the process of making cheese or butter, so they may not have any reference until the substances begin to solidify.

Once solidification begins, students will likely be intrigued at the milk's rapid clumping and the butter's separation. This is where students start having trouble accepting that the cheese is "butter" and the butter is "cheese."

Why do you think this is butter? Why do you think this is cheese?

- ♦ Students will be quick to point out the differences in the colors. While they typically associate butter with being yellow and cheese as white, there are certainly yellow cheeses and varying shades of whitish/yellow butter depending on the fat content. Therefore, color may not be the best way to identify the substances.

What about this "cheese" makes you think it is butter? What about this "butter" makes you think it is cheese?

- ♦ Attempt to get the students to be more specific and descriptive with the properties they are observing. Insist that you need adequate proof before you can accept that you potentially made a mistake. Their insistence will likely drive them to be more articulate.

What were the different methods we used to make the two products?

- ♦ Not all students will immediately make the connection that one process included heat and one did not. Not all students will register that one was a physical change, while the other was a chemical change.

- Student handouts and instructions for this activity can be found on our website https://steamcrafts.weebly.com/.

Explore: Cheese and Butter Stations

Purpose
The purpose of the Explore phase of this lesson is to let students try some different methods of making butter and cheese. Using different ingredients and tools, have them observe the variations that can occur. Without introducing any new vocabulary or concepts, allow students to ask questions and express their curiosity and see first-hand how cheese and butter behave. You want to make sure all learners leave this phase with enough hands-on, concrete experiences on which to build new concepts.

For this part of the lesson, students may work through different stations of butter and cheese making. The handouts and instructions for students are located on https://steamcrafts.weebly.com/ for you to access and edit as needed.

Overview
This phase of the unit has students going to different stations around the room to try different ingredients and processes for making butter and cheese.

Afterward, students reflect on the similarities and differences between these products.

Before this lesson, gather and organize all the materials. The butter stations will require access to a power source. A method of heating the milk will need to be determined, and the teacher will need to regularly check the temperature of the milk to ensure it does not surpass 46°C (115°F), which will result in a poor cheese product. Also, determine a way to heat up water for mixing with citric acid.

Teachers should set up each station with the appropriate materials and tools to perform the tasks. Teachers should ask students to follow instructions for each lab station. While the lab activity is happening, the teacher should be monitoring the area where the milk and water are being heated to ensure that they are reaching the exact temperatures and not becoming overheated, while the students should be reading the instructions at the lab stations and recording their observations.

Station 1: Butter Using a Blender
Students will add heavy whipping cream to the blender and allow it to agitate the cream until the solid butter forms. They may add salt to taste and store in a resealable bag or plastic container with an airtight lid. Be sure to monitor this station so students do not put their hands into the blender while it is on.

Station 2: Butter Using a Jar
Students will put heavy whipping cream inside of a jar with a tightly sealed lid and shake the contents for several minutes until the solid butter forms. They may add salt to taste and store in a resealable bag or plastic container with an airtight lid. Use a non-breakable jar for this step.

Station 3: Butter Using a Mixer
Students will put heavy whipping cream inside a mixing bowl, and using a standing mixer or a hand mixer, they will agitate the cream until the solid butter forms. On a small scale, they could even use a hand-held milk foamer, the kind used in coffee shops. Students may add salt to taste and store in a resealable bag or plastic container with an airtight lid.

Station 4: Cheese Using Citric Acid
The teacher will heat up whole milk to approximately 46°C (115°F).

Separately, the teacher will mix citric acid powder into warm water. Use 7 ml (1.5 tsp) of citric acid powder for every 118ml (4 oz) of warm water. Stir until dissolved.

Students will receive a cup with approximately 118ml (4 oz)of warmed milk. Then, they will add 29 ml (2 tbsp) of the citric liquid to the cup of warm milk. The students will stir briefly and then allow the mixture to sit for 10 to 15 minutes. Then, students will remove the curds, strain the liquid, and place the curds inside a plastic bag. They will continue to work the curds, adding a small dash of salt, and remove the liquid as it exits the cheese curd. The resulting product will resemble something akin to a soft mozzarella cheese.

Station 5: Cheese Using Lemon Juice

The teacher will heat up whole milk to approximately 46°C (115°F). Students will receive a cup with approximately 118ml (4 oz) of warmed milk. Then, 29 ml (2 tbsp)of the lemon juice will be added to the cup of warm milk. The student will stir briefly and then allow the mixture to sit for 10 to 15 minutes. Then, students will remove the curds, strain the liquid, and place the curds inside a plastic bag. They will continue to work the curds, adding a small dash of salt, and remove the liquid as it exits the cheese curd. The resulting product will resemble something akin to a soft grainy type cheese.

Station 6: Cheese Using Vinegar

The teacher will heat up whole milk to approximately 46°C (115°F). Students will receive a cup with approximately 118ml (4 oz) of warmed milk. Then, 29 ml (2 tbsp) of the vinegar will be added to the cup of warm milk. The student will stir briefly and then allow the mixture to sit for 10 to 15 minutes. Then, students will remove the curds, strain the liquid, and place the curds inside a plastic bag. They will continue to work the curds, adding a small dash of salt, and remove the liquid as it exits the cheese curd. The resulting product will resemble something akin to a soft semi-solid cheese.

Once the students have made their way through the lab stations and have attempted multiple ways to create butter and cheese, they can begin to reflect on the similarities and differences between cheese and butter making.

Probing Questions to Ask

How were the ingredients for butter and cheese different?

- Students may not understand that the starting materials: heavy whipping cream and milk are actually quite different. The fat content inside of heavy whipping cream is between 36% and 40% while the fat content of the whole milk is usually 3.25%.

Why would milk with a higher fat content be preferable for making butter?

- Butter is 80% fat. It is produced by combining the fat globules in cream together into a greasy, moldable chunk.

- Cheese is higher in protein and lower in fat than butter.

You used different methods to produce butter and cheese. How did your results vary? Was the butter the same at each butter station? Was the cheese similar at each station?

- The results for butter will vary, but students will likely be able to produce the best butter with the jar method. The small amount of cream in the mixer will likely have a difficult time getting mixed evenly. The small amount of cream in the blender can get over agitated, resulting in the butter getting warmed.
- The results for cheese will vary, but there should be a difference in the tastes and the textures of the cheeses. Vinegar will produce a cheese that is more pungent and may require more of the Greek seasoning to be tasty. Citric acid will produce the finest curds and will be the most difficult to strain and clump, but will probably taste the most mild. The lemon juice cheese will probably be the one that clumps easiest, but does not have the pungent taste as much as the vinegar one.

How do the processes of making cheese and butter differ from each other?

- Some students may be able to figure out that cheese uses heat and the addition of an acidic agent to clump the pieces, while butter uses movement or agitation to create solidified pieces.

What is the liquid portion of the cheese called? What is the liquid portion of the butter called?

- The leftover liquid from making butter is called buttermilk. Some students may not know this and be surprised to discover that they unknowingly made buttermilk.
- The leftover liquid from cheese making is whey. Students might recall the story of "Little Miss Muffet" eating her curds and whey—which actually referred to fresh cottage cheese. They may even recognize whey protein as a product in many foods. Whey protein is separated from the cheese-making process and processed and dried to be included as a *"whey"* to make foods filled with more protein.

- Student handouts and instructions for this activity can be found on our website https://steamcrafts.weebly.com/.

Explain: The STEAM Concepts

Purpose
The purpose of the Explain phase of this lesson is to allow students to gain new scientific knowledge and understanding of how butter and cheese are created in order to make informed design decisions about their unique cheese and butter products in a later phase.

Overview
Referring back to the two previous phases of the lesson, ask students to provide their explanations of the phenomena they experienced. Then, it's time to introduce new vocabulary and new concepts in a way that students understand them. Be sure to relate all new concepts back to the experiences students had in the Engage and Explore phases. Teach about the physical properties of cheese and butter. Explain the difference between the chemical change that occurs in cheese making and how that differs from the physical change that occurs in butter creation.

Cheese Science: The Basics
Butter and cheese are both milk products created from the milk of a variety of animals. This variety changes the composition, the texture, and the taste of the resultant dairy products.

While all mammals produce milk for their young, we primarily use ruminants for commercial cheese and butter production. Ruminants are herbivorous mammals like cows, goats, and sheep, which have four chambered stomachs. Globally, cows provide 81% of milk for human consumption, while 15% comes from buffaloes, 2% from goats, 1% from sheep, 0.5% from camels, and the remaining percentage comes from yaks and horses. However, 25% of the milk produced in the United Arab Emirates is from camels, whereas, in Tibet, they use primarily yak milk. People in Sweden milk reindeer to create a special cheese that helps bring in seasonal income.

Female ruminants begin to produce milk after they have given birth (Figure 8.12). On dairy farms, farmers encourage the new mammal mothers to produce more milk than they need to feed their young. The yak mother needs her baby to be nearby in order to start the flow, so the young yak suckles briefly before the farmer pushes it aside to retrieve the rest. Camel mothers will stop producing milk if their young are not nearby. However, cows are different in that they will continue to produce milk even if their calf is not physically present, as long as they are milked regularly. This makes cows ideal for dairy farms.

Figure 8.12 Milking of the reindeer. Image created by author Christine Schnittka by altering an image drawn by Sly and Wilson in 1835, now in the New York Public Library digital collections.

Processing Milk

Once milk is collected on a farm, it is often reviewed under a microscope to check for microbes. Then it is refrigerated and transferred to a dairy where the raw milk is separated into cream and skimmed milk. The cream is heavy in fat, less dense than water, and rises to the top. Skimmed milk, which has been skimmed of the cream, falls underneath the cream. The skimmed milk and cream (40+% fat) are then mixed in different proportions to achieve the desired milkfat. This is how whole milk (3.25% fat), reduced fat (2% fat), lowfat (1% milk), and nonfat/fat free/skim milk (0% fat) are created. Half-and-half is around 10.5% fat.

Once the cream and skimmed milk are recombined at the dairy, the milk is typically homogenized to break the fat globules into smaller pieces. This disperses the fat throughout the milk and prevents a layer of fat from rising to the top.

Some people drink raw milk which has not been heat-treated, but this is generally not advisable. When milk is heated up to a designated temperature at a rapid pace and then cooled, it is called pasteurization. This kills most of the microbes within the milk, making it safer to consume. A UHT (ultra high temperature) pasteurization is sometimes used and the milk is heated to a higher temperature, resulting in milk that is more or less sterilized and it lasts much longer, as even microbe spores are destroyed. Milk that has been UHT pasteurized is not useful for making cheeses, as it loses its ability to curdle or clump together.

Making Cheese

Making cheese usually starts by adding bacteria to the milk to digest the lactose, the milk sugar. The bacteria also make the milk sour, or acidic, which aids in curdling. Afterward, rennet is added, which is an enzyme that helps to speed up the process of curdling (it helps the fat particles stick together). Next, the curdled milk is cut into slices which helps to release the liquid whey. Sometimes salt is added. Eventually, the cheese is strained using a cheesecloth and allowed to drain before it is pressed to remove additional whey. Once enough whey is removed from pressing and shaping, it is salted and air dried and ripened to the desired consistency.

Making Butter

Most commercial butters are made from homogenized and pasteurized cream from cows. The cream is put into a giant churn where it is further separated into fat and buttermilk. Once it is separated, the solid fat clumps are rinsed and salted and packaged.

There are limitless variations to the above steps (animal, process, and method of separation) which results in a wide variety of butters and cheeses (Figure 8.13).

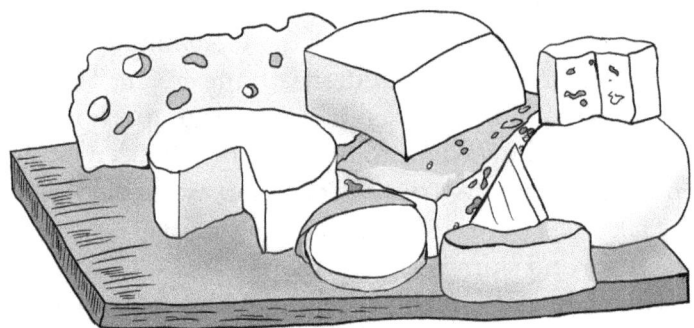

Figure 8.13 Plate of various cheeses. Image created by author Christine Schnittka.

 ### Cheese Science: The Details
Cheese Details

When making cheese with cow's milk, different starter cultures of bacteria are added. The most common are *Lactococcus lactis lactis* and *Lactococcus lactis cremoris*, which are used to make Cheddar, Monterey Jack, Stilton, Edam, Gouda, Muenster, Blue, and Colby cheeses. The cultures *Streptococcus thermophilus, Lactobacillus helveticus, and Lactobacillus delbrueckii lactis* are used to make cheeses such as Mozzarella, Parmesan, Provolone, Romano, Swiss, Gruyere, and other Italian cheeses. These cultures of bacteria break the lactose sugar down into lactic acid, which lowers the milk's pH just like vinegar or citric acid or lemon juice would.

After the starter culture of bacteria is added, rennet is added to help separate the curds from the whey. Clumping of curds occurs when the casein proteins in the milk come together to form large globs. For soft cheeses, an acid such as lactic acid or vinegar or lemon juice will provide enough of a trigger to encourage coagulation, but for harder cheeses, rennet is usually added to speed up the process. It does this by altering the casein proteins which repel each other because they are covered in negatively charged particles. Once altered, casein particles can stick together.

Rennet can be purchased online. Microbial rennet is typically used, but animal rennet and vegetable/plant rennet can also be used. Rennet will significantly affect the milk's cheese yield, as it creates more clumps or curds that would not form without it.

The cheese curds are removed from the liquid whey and are squeezed, salted, and aged according to the recipe for the desired cheese.

Butter Details

For making butter from cow's milk, the fat content of the cream will have a significant impact on the quality and taste of the butter produced. For instance, heavy cream in the United States is typically 36% or more milkfat, whereas in Ireland, double cream is almost 40% milkfat, which is why Irish butter is considered by many to be the most delectable on the market. Some butter is cultured, which means it is provided with beneficial bacteria cultures which make the butter slightly acidic. The color of butter can vary. Sometimes it is white, and sometimes it is a nice buttery yellow. Butter is yellow when the animal consumes carotenoid pigments.

Once the butter is separated from the buttermilk, it is rinsed, and further worked until it reaches the desired consistency and then it is seasoned and packaged for human consumption.

One of the biggest takeaways for students from this unit is to understand that making butter results in a physical change, while making cheese results in a chemical change. Butter *could* be combined with buttermilk, and cream would be reconstituted because the chemicals do not change. Conversely, because cheese is created using a chemical change, cheese can never be reversed back into milk. The addition of the bacteria as well as the heat and acid chemically alter the composition of the milk. This is an important science concept that can be emphasized throughout the unit.

Elaborate: Butter and Cheese Art, Craft, Technology, and Engineering

Purpose
The purpose of the Elaborate phase of this lesson is to apply the science, art, and technology of milk to the engineering of butter and/or cheese.

Overview
Now that your students have experimented with butter and cheese, and learned the science behind both, it's time to engineer some unique butter and cheese! After making butter and/or cheese by following some specific instructions, students can engineer their own to meet certain specifications.

The Challenge
Students will use the desired pasteurized and homogenized milk (cow, goat, etc.) to create their own unique cheese and/or butter recipe. See https://steamcrafts.weebly.com/ for student handouts that help to establish the deliverables of this challenge.

Make sure students consider all the variables:

1. Milk source
2. Culture
3. Rennet
4. Type of acid
5. Ripening time (age)
6. Pressing
7. Additional ingredients to enhance flavor (adding garlic or parmesan to a soft cheese, or mixing honey with butter, or even combining homemade butter and cheese to make a nice alfredo sauce!)

Evaluate: What Did They Learn?

After making cheese, ask your students to write the answers to the following questions to see what they learned. A form to collect the answers to these questions from your students is provided on our website https://steamcrafts.weebly.com/.

1. What obstacles to dairy production did humans have to overcome in order to produce cheese and butter?

    ◆ People first had to become farmers and grow crops. Then, they had to start herding animals. Eventually, they had to attempt to drink milk produced by these animals and make containers to collect the milk, and then lastly, understand the processes that are required to make cheese or butter.

2. When did people make cheese and butter?

    ◆ Nobody knows for sure, but based on archaeological evidence, people probably started consuming milk products around 6500 BCE.

3. What were the likely first containers for butter and cheese?

    ◆ Early containers were likely made of animal skins or organs or clay pottery.

4. Why are so many people lactose intolerant?

    ◆ Lactose is a sugar found in milk. Young mammals produce an enzyme in their stomachs to help break this lactose down into lactic acid and make it digestible. Once people age, they can stop producing this enzyme, making it difficult and often painful to digest lactose-heavy foods. Lactose was not consumed worldwide until relatively recently. Only certain people are descended from the first butter and cheese makers, and those individuals are more likely to have lactase persistence (the continuation of lactose being produced in the stomach after maturity), and therefore are more likely to be able to tolerate lactose in their diets.

5. Why is rennet used in cheese production?

    ◆ Rennet is used to speed up the process of casein coagulation in cheese. It makes the surfaces of the casein proteins lose the negatively charged "tails" and makes it easier for them to stick to each other, significantly increasing the ability of the milk to clump.

6. Can you make cheese without rennet?

    ◆ Yes, but cheese without rennet is usually soft. Additionally, because of the lack of rennet, a significant amount of acid is used to prompt the clumping of the casein, which can make the flavor of the resulting cheese rather sour tasting.

7. What is the significant difference between butter and cheese making?

    - Butter is made via physical changes, while cheese is made via chemical changes.

8. Why are most cheeses and butters made with cow's milk?

    - Cows are ideal for large-scale production because they make the most milk per animal, they produce milk even when their young are no longer present, and the milk is considered nutritious with lower fat than other milk sources. It is also a valuable source of vitamins and protein.

9. Why is milk often homogenized?

    - Milk is usually homogenized to break the fat globs into more uniform sizes, which helps to prevent separation of the fat from the liquid.

10. Why is the process of pasteurization so important?

    - Pasteurization is the rapid heating and cooling of the milk which kills off a designated level of microbes and makes milk safe for human consumption.

11. Why wouldn't ultra homogenized milk or UHT milk work for cheese making?

    - Ultra homogenization reduces the size of the fat molecules which interferes with clumping. UHT heats up the milk and destroys not only more microbes, but also makes the milk will lose its ability to clump.

Summary

Cheese and butter crafts have been entwined with human history for thousands of years. Without this skill, several generations of human populations may not have survived, as it provided a stable protein source during tough times. Butter adds flavor to our food, while cheeses have added an incredible compliment to dishes around the world! While our tastes for different cheeses have differentiated depending on the region we live in, one thing remains for sure—cheese makes a delicious addition to almost any meal, adding nutrition and protein that our lives would be incomplete without!

Contemporary Cheese and Butter Makers

Butter and cheese making is still a relevant art and craft today. Dairies and chefs create new cheeses and make delicacies around the world with their signature recipes.

For links to see some world-renowned cheese and butter makers, please see our website: https://steamcrafts.weebly.com/.

References

Bybee, R. W. (2009). *The BSCS 5E instructional model and 21st century skills*. National Academies Board on Science Education.

Dewey, J. (1938). *Experience and education*. Macmillan.

Itan, Y., Powell, A., Beaumont, M. A., Burger, J., & Thomas, M. G. (2009). The origins of lactase persistence in Europe. *PLOS Computational Biology, 5*(8), e1000491.

Khosrova, E. (2016). *Butter: A rich history*. Random House.

Kindstedt, P. (2012). *Cheese and culture: A history of cheese and its place in western civilization*. Chelsea Green Publishing.

Piaget, J. (1955). The construction of reality in the child. *Journal of Consulting Psychology, 19*(1), 77.

Storhaug, C. L., Fosse, S. K., & Fadnes, L. T. (2017). Country, regional, and global estimates for lactose malabsorption in adults: A systematic review and meta-analysis. *The Lancet Gastroenterology and Hepatology, 2*(10), 738–746.

Suddendorf, T., Kirkland, K., Bulley, A., Redshaw, J., & Langley, M. C. (2020). It's in the bag: Mobile containers in human evolution and child development. *Evolutionary Human Sciences, 2*, e48.

9

Fungal Food

Introduction

To me, the smell of fresh baked bread evokes feelings of warmth and security. I grew up with loaves of fresh baguettes every night at dinner, sliced at a specific angle with a specific thickness. Mom was, and still is, particular about her bread slicing. A poignant memory as an 11 year old was finding just the right brick outside in a field for my mom to use in the oven to create steam for making the perfect baguette (Figure 9.1).

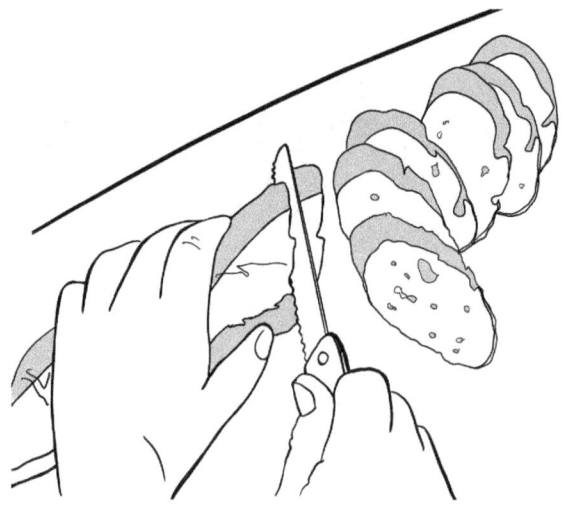

Figure 9.1 Slicing baguette. Image by author Christine Schnittka.

DOI: 10.4324/9781003428312-9

The science of bread and brick-made steam evaded me, but I enjoyed the results nevertheless. Of course, my sisters and I did not like to eat the crust, just the soft stretchy interior, slathered with butter. These memories and emotions associated with bread are not universal, as you will read in this chapter. Bread, as I experienced it as a child, requires wheat, and wheat is not a staple in every culture. However, every nation and culture in the world has developed its own *version* of bread from one grain or another. From lavash in Iran, mantou in China, tortillas in Mexico, sopaipillas in Chile, naan in India, injera in Africa, baguettes in France, to biscuits and cornbread in the United States, you can find some sort of cooked grain paste all over the world. Cooked grain paste? Yes! Read on!

Bread History

What is bread? It's a cooked paste (we call this paste, "dough") made by mixing water with a crushed grain. Grains like wheat, corn, barley, teff, and rye can be eaten raw, but are much tastier and healthier when cooked. Cooking kills any bacteria residing on the grain that might make one sick, but cooking also makes the nutrients easier to digest.

There is evidence that people were making bread 4,000 years ago in Africa from a grass called sorghum. Sorghum grains look like millet with tight clusters of seeds filling up the stalk. This ancient grain was used to make flatbreads and the innovation spread from Africa to Asia and India. However, there is evidence of 100,000-year-old millet starches embedded in stone pounding tools in Africa (Mercader, 2009). Since modern humans didn't leave Africa until after that time, it could be that the entire bread technology began in Africa with millet, and when *Homo sapiens* started living in more northern climates where wheat grew, they adapted their recipe to other grains. Bread is our oldest form of biotechnology (Campbell-Platt, 1994; Figure 9.2).

People started cooking wheat grain paste at least 14,500 years ago in the Middle East (Zeldovich, 2018). The Natufians, the prehistoric people who lived in what is today Israel, Jordan, Lebanon, and Syria, harvested a wild grain called einkorn and ground it with round stones on rock platforms or in hollow rock vessels. They mixed this ground grain with water and baked the dough in clay ovens into a flatbread much like today's pita bread. These clay ovens called "tinru" were really just large pots with a small fire at the bottom, usually burning sheep dung. The baker would take flat pancakes of

Figure 9.2 Wheat, einkorn, oat, sorghum, barley, and rye. Image by author Christine Schnittka.

dough and press them onto the inner wall of the clay pot/oven (Rova, 2014; Figure 9.3).

> The word, tinru, (from the Akkadian word, 𒁷𒀭 pronounced "tinuru") means mud fire. Today we call this oven "tannur" in Israel and Iraq and all over the middle east, "tandir" in Turkey, and "tandoor" in India.

In South America 12,000 years ago, at about the same time that corn was domesticated, people took dried corn and cooked it in a solution of ashes and water to dissolve the outer skin on the kernel. Today this process is called nixtamalization from a Nahuatl word meaning ash water. After nixtamalization, people dry the corn kernels again, grind them up, mix them with water, flattened the dough, and baked the patties on a griddle pan into tortillas.

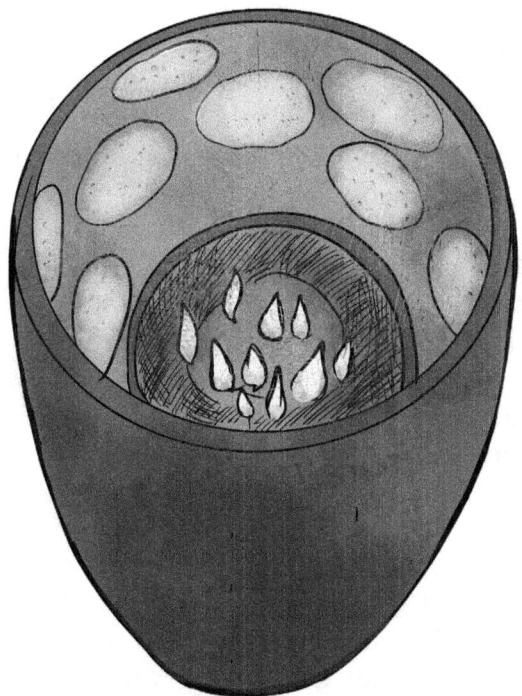

Figure 9.3 Tinru. Image by author Christine Schnittka.

The word "tortilla" is a Spanish name given to this corn bread meaning "little cake." People native to South America called the little flatbreads tlaxcalli, pupusa, or arepa. The ashes made the water alkaline, and in addition to dissolving the inedible seed coat, freed up vital nutrients.

> The word "leaven" comes from the Latin word "levare," which means "to lift." We have many words today derived from this Latin word, such as "lever" (a long rod or stick for lifting), the "Levant" (the region where this yeast bread was first developed, where Israel, Jordan, Syria, and Lebanon are today.
>
> When a grain is ground up and moistened with water, naturally occurring yeast cells are part of the mixture. Given enough time, warmth, and moisture, these yeast organisms will do what all living creatures do—eat and excrete. They eat the natural sugars in the grain and excrete both alcohol and the carbon dioxide gas that makes the dough puff up.

The difference between a flat tortilla and a fluffy loaf of sandwich bread is gas bubbles. One natural way to make gas bubbles is with yeast. Yeast, a fungus that floats in the air and thrives on the natural sugars in fruits and grains, is a wonderful addition to dough. Evidence of the first yeast breads is about 8,000 years old. A dough with yeast will puff up with carbon dioxide gas. After cooking, it is called "leavened bread."

When yeast breads were first invented, one could not purchase yeast from a store. About 5,000 years ago, the Egyptians started isolating and growing yeast so it could be easily added to a bread dough. The Egyptians would brew beer from the same grains they made bread from and would skim the foam off the beer to inoculate the bread dough. They didn't know what was causing grain tea to turn into beer and grain paste to turn into leavened dough, but it worked. From Egypt, the biotechnology of leavened bread spread throughout the world, to Europe and Asia, including Italy, where our next bread story takes place.

In the year 79 CE, a volcano erupted, burying the Italian city of Pompei in ash. Over the past 150 years, modern archaeologists and anthropologists have uncovered the lives of people instantly frozen in time when Mt. Vesuvius asphyxiated them all. One discovery they made was of their bread. Their bread was round in shape, with eight radial indentations, making it appear similar to today's pizza. It had been leavened with a mixture of wild yeast and lactobacillus, the type of bacteria used to make yogurt and cheese. Pliny the Elder (whose real name was Gaius Plinius Secundus) was a Roman writer living at the time when Mt. Vesuvius erupted (Figure 9.4).

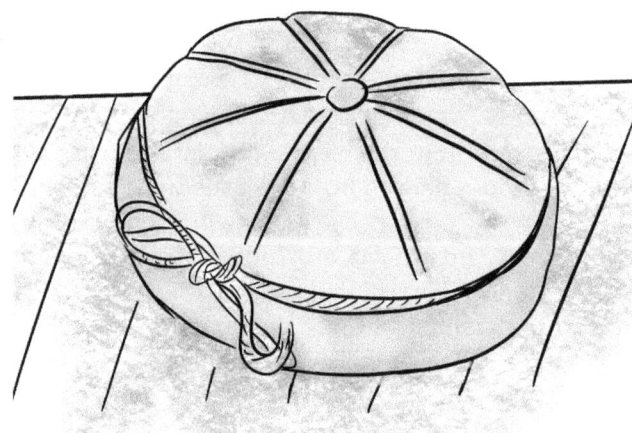

Figure 9.4 Pompei bread. Image by author Christine Schnittka.

He wrote in his book, *Naturalis Historia*, "It is very evident that the principle which causes the dough to rise is of an acid nature, and it is equally evident that those persons who are dieted upon fermented bread are stronger in body."

Pliny the Elder and his nephew, Pliny the Younger, were firsthand witnesses to the destruction wrought by this volcano, and it killed the elder Pliny. Just 17 years old, Pliny the Younger wrote about what he witnessed and about his uncle, who died trying to escape the toxic volcanic fumes (Bostock & Riley, 1855).

Yeast breads were also made in China. In northern China 2,000 years ago, wheat was used to produce the leavened bread, 饅頭, pronounced, "mantou." Baking in ovens was not common, so the dough was steamed in a colander over boiling water. The little steamed mantou looked like eggs or marshmallows. The Uighurs, a group of people living in northern China call them اتنام pronounced "manta," which means "bread prepared in steam." These steamed buns are still popular today!

Today, bread making is industrialized. Wheat is harvested by machine, processed by machine, the nutritious bran is removed by machine, dough is kneaded by machine, bread is sliced by machine, and bagged into plastic by machine. Commercial bread contains additives that make it mold resistant, and vitamins and minerals added to replace the natural nutrients that are removed or degraded during machine processing. So, the time-honored process of making bread by hand is a lost art, craft, and science (Figure 9.5).

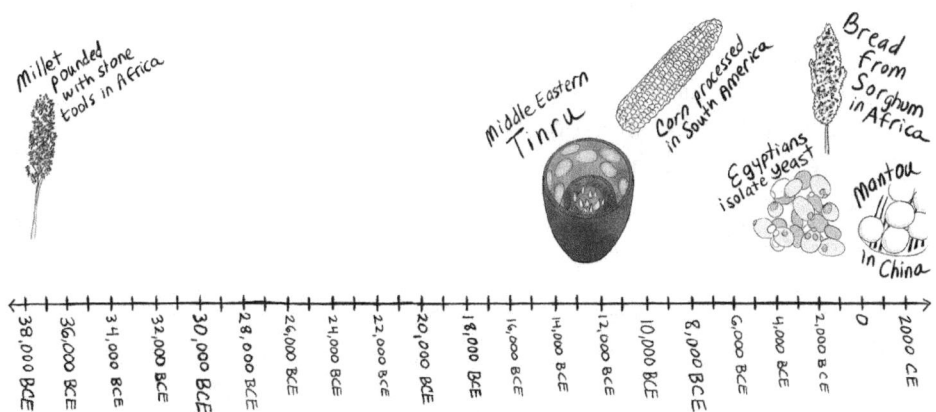

Figure 9.5 Timeline of bread history. Image by author Christine Schnittka.

Meeting the Standards

Teaching this chapter as written focuses on STEAM principles that include: historical elements that influenced technological advancements, engineering principles including iterative design, criteria and constraints, and scientific measurement principles as well as data collection and analysis. For more detailed information regarding which specific standards are covered in this unit, please refer to our website: https://steamcrafts.weebly.com/.

Materials

- All-purpose flour
- Masa harina corn flour
- Water in a pitcher
- Funnels
- Balloons
- Empty plastic water bottles
- A glass beverage bottle
- Bowls for mixing
- Teaspoons
- Salt
- Oat flour
- Yeast
- Sugar
- Vegetable oil
- Baking powder
- Cupcake pans
- Cupcake liners
- Bowls, spoons, and dough scrapers (rulers work)
- Measuring cups and spoons
- Oven mitts and tongs
- Electric skillet
- Toaster oven

Safety

- Determine allergies and intolerances prior to doing this activity.
- Students should not be using an oven without oven mitts and close supervision.
- All students should wear aprons to protect their clothing.

The Lesson

> **The BSCS 5E Instructional Model for Bread Making**
>
> The lessons in this book are designed around the BSCS 5E instructional model designed by the Biological Sciences Curriculum Study (Bybee, 2009). Based on Dewey's model of reflective thinking (Dewey, 1938), Piagetian theory (Piaget, 1955), and other learning cycle models that followed, the five phases of this model are: Engage, Explore, Explain, Elaborate, and Evaluate. The purpose and summary for each phase are explained in the sections that follow.

- To find accompanying presentations, student handouts, and more be sure to visit our website: https://steamcrafts.weebly.com/.

Engage: Eating Bread

Purpose

The purpose of the Engage phase of this lesson is to build excitement about making bread, and to initiate curiosity about it and how it is made. It's also a chance for the teacher to find out what prior knowledge students have about bread.

Figure 9.6 A variety of breads. Image by author Christine Schnittka.

Overview

The teacher brings several types of bread to class: white sliced bread, matzah, tortillas, a baguette, bagels, pumpernickel bread, etc., trying to provide a diverse array of bread types and including some non-traditional breads. Students explore these and begin to determine what makes them similar and different from each other.

Teachers: bring a diverse array of bread to class. Include some non-traditional breads if possible. Avoid sweet breads like cookies, cakes, and croissants if you want to avoid sugar. You can set up a buffet and let students sample what they are interested in, or create family style baskets on group tables. Be aware of any allergies or food intolerances that students may have and plan accordingly (Figure 9.6).

Probing Questions to Ask

As students are trying out different breads, you can ask some questions to find out what they know.

What do all these breads have in common?

- Students may comment on textures or colors or the holes they see in a slice of bread. In reality, what they have in common is that they are cooked, solid food made from a pulverized grain.

How are they different from each other?

- Students may notice different surface effects, different shapes, and different textures. The differences are in how the doughs are shaped and cooked, whether a leavening is added, whether eggs, oils, or milk are included in the recipe, and how the dough is treated prior to cooking.

What is it about this food that makes it bread?

- Students may say that "flour" makes something bread. It is true that a ground grain is a flour, but there are many types of flours: wheat, rice, oat, barley, etc.

What ingredients do you think are in bread?

- Breads usually contain four ingredients: flour, water, salt, and yeast. However, some breads, like matzah, only contain flour, water, and salt. Corn tortillas only contain masa (a flour made from corn treated with lime), salt, and water. Some breads contain eggs, milk, and butter, as well as flour, water, salt, and yeast.

What feelings do you think that bread gives people across the world?

- ◆ Students may know that bread fills the hungry tummy and that bread gives people the feeling of comfort.

Tell students that they are going to make bread from scratch. Ask them if they have ever made bread before. By the end of the Engage phase of this lesson, you will have gotten students interested in bread and determined their prior knowledge about it.

- Student handouts and instructions for this activity can be found on our website https://steamcrafts.weebly.com/.

Explore: Bread Dough

Purpose
The purpose of the Explore phase of this lesson is to allow students to all have experiences with the materials that make bread prior to learning any new content. Some students have different levels of experience with bread dough and yeast. This phase attempts to level that field of knowledge in order to have a more concrete foundation to build further understanding.

Overview
In this phase of the lesson, students will gain common experiences with yeast, flour, kneading, and shaping dough.

Probing Questions to Ask
As students are exploring the components of bread, you can ask some questions to find out what they know.
Where do you think flour comes from? Trees? Grass? Flowers?

- ◆ Students may think that flour comes from flowers. It comes from grass!

What ingredients do you think are in bread?

- ◆ Students may say, "flour" but have no other ideas. Flour is indeed the primary and necessary ingredient.

Is bread alive?

- ◆ While cooked bread is not alive, some of the ingredients of bread were once alive! Flour comes from grass fruit and seeds, and yeast comes from fungi.

Where do the holes in bread come from?

- ◆ Students may have no idea, but the holes come from carbon dioxide, as gas.

Yeast

Have students work in groups. Provide each group with a pitcher of warm water, a funnel, an empty plastic water bottle, a packet of yeast, a balloon, and 30 ml (two tablespoons) of sugar. Have students make a prediction of what will happen when water, yeast, and sugar are mixed.

Instruct them to put the funnel in the empty water bottle, pour in the yeast and sugar, add water until the bottle is half full, and then slip the balloon on top. They could also use the funnel to put the sugar and yeast directly into the balloon, and then after slipping the balloon onto the bottle with warm water, upend the balloon so the contents spill into the water.

Have them swirl the contents until mixed and observe what happens. The yeast needs time to consume enough sugar to produce enough gas to inflate the balloon. From experience, it starts to work right away, but takes 30 minutes to fill the balloon (Figure 9.7).

Yeast Questions to Ask

Why do you think the balloon is inflating? What do you think is inside the balloon? What do you think this has to do with bread?

Baking Powder

While waiting for the yeast to produce gas, the teacher should do a demonstration for the class, repeating the activity with baking powder in a glass bottle and boiling water. Check to make sure the baking powder has not expired, because it will not react vigorously if it is too old. Have the water boiling in an electric kettle since baking powder needs a temperature of over 48°C (120°F) to really work. Hot tap water will still produce a reaction, but it will be about half as productive. Put the funnel into the balloon and add one tablespoon of baking powder so it falls inside the balloon. Use the funnel to pour boiling water into the glass soda bottle until it's half full. Then, carefully slip the balloon onto the opening, lift the balloon to dump the contents, and observe.

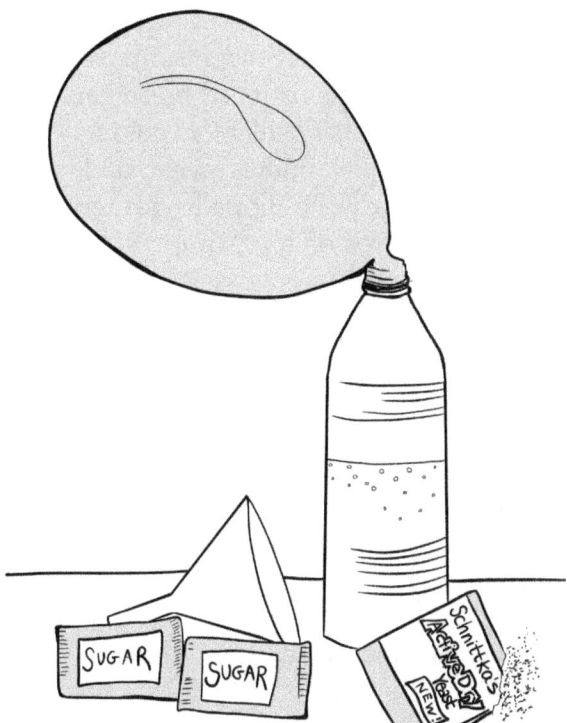

Figure 9.7 Active yeast in a bottle. Image by author Christine Schnittka.

The balloon will inflate immediately to about half the size of what the yeast balloon will inflate to.

Baking Powder Questions to Ask
Why do you think the balloon is inflating? What do you think is inside the balloon now that it has blown up? What do you think this has to do with bread?

Ask students to compare the two activities. Which one took longer to inflate the balloon? Which one made the balloon get bigger? How might this impact bread?

Doughs

Have students work in groups of four. Provide each group with a pitcher of warm water, some flour, some masa corn flour, some oil, some teaspoons, and a small mixing bowl. After placing the desired amount of flour and salt in the bowl, have them add water one teaspoon at a time while stirring, until a ball forms.

About 30 grams (1/4 cup) of flour or masa mixed with a pinch of salt requires about 30 ml (1/8 cup) of water to form a ball. This is the perfect amount to make one tortilla.

Have students knead the ball until it's elastic and smooth, then roll it out with a rolling pin on a floured surface. Students can work in groups and share one rolling pin between them. This flattened bread can easily be placed on a paper plate and carried to an electric skillet for cooking. Just a tiny bit of oil on the skillet is enough, and a couple minutes on each side will make the tortilla perfectly cooked. The tortilla can be flipped with tongs. I love to eat mine warm with a little butter smeared on top. Yum!

The objective is to have students make close observations of what they see and smell after mixing water into the flours and stirring until it forms a ball that can be kneaded, and make close observations as the flatbread cooks.

Dough Questions to Ask
How did the dough feel in your hands?
What do you think holds the flour particles together?

- Students may think that the water holds the particles together.

Why do you think the yeast makes bubbles?

- Yeast makes bubbles because they are living microbes that excrete carbon dioxide.

Why do you think the baking powder makes bubbles?

- Baking powder chemically reacts with hot water and produces carbon dioxide too.

Why do you think the dough with salt was harder to knead?

- Salt helps gluten molecules bond together.

Why do you think the dough with salt and oil was easier to knead?

- Oil interferes with gluten bonds, so the dough is softer.

Clean Up

A dough scraper is a vital tool when cleaning up floury surfaces. If a dough scraper is not available, a ruler edge will work too. Put scraped dough and flour in a trash can, not the sink. After scraping the flour and dried dough, counters should be wiped down.

- Student handouts and instructions for this activity can be found on our website https://steamcrafts.weebly.com/.

Explain: The STEAM Concepts

Purpose
The purpose of the Explain phase of this lesson is to allow students to gain new scientific knowledge and understanding of how bread works, how baking soda and powder work, and how yeast works so that they can make informed design decisions in a later phase.

Overview
In this phase of the lesson, you should first ask your students to explain their new reasonings and understandings. It's very important in this phase of the lesson to find out what students are thinking before teaching them the STEAM concepts of bread. They will learn about how all the ingredients in bread work together, how bread is from the fruit of grasses, and how the fungi, yeast, work to make bread fluffy and delicious.

Bread Science

Most bread contains crushed grain, water, and salt. Some breads contain fat such as butter or olive oil. Some contain yeast as a leavener, while others contain baking powder. In this section, the science of grains, water, yeast, salt, and baking powder will be explained.

Bread Questions to Ask
What do you think bread is made from?

- ◆ Bread is made from ground up grains.

What do you think each ingredient is for?

- ◆ Breads usually contain four ingredients: flour, water, salt, and yeast. The flour is the main ingredient which contains a lot of protein and carbohydrates. Water helps chemical reactions happen and keeps the microbes well hydrated.

What would happen if you left out one or two ingredients?

- If you left out one of two ingredients, the bread might not be fluffy or might fall apart easily.

Can you make bread from just dry ingredients? No water or milk?

- No. Bread needs to be made from a paste containing water and flour.

Can you make bread without flour?

- It depends. There are many substitutes that are used to make gluten-free bread.

Can you make bread without yeast?

- Yes, bread made with baking soda instead of yeast is called quick bread.

Bread Science: The Basics
Grains

Bread is made from ground up grains. Grains are tiny, dry fruits of a flowering grass plant. Inside each tiny fruit is one seed. There are 12,000 different types of grasses in the world, and together they are the most important plant on Earth because over half of the food we eat comes from grasses and 70% of all the plants grown for food are grasses (Constable, 1985). A grass that produces a food that humans either eat or feed to animals is called cereal. When you wake up in the morning and eat your cereal, you are eating grass fruit!

Grasses grow on every continent, including Antarctica. Because we mow our lawns, we are not used to seeing the fruits of grasses, and many people would be surprised to learn that grasses even produce fruits. Of all the grasses in the world, there are less than a dozen varieties that are cereals, producing edible grains. Barley, corn, oats, rice, rye, sorghum, wheat, and millet are the most common ones we eat. These plants, these grasses called cereals, feed the world. The word "cereal" comes from the Roman goddess Ceres, who was responsible for agriculture. Access to cereals for humans is like access to petroleum for cars. It is a concentrated, nutrient, and calorie-rich source of food.

People throughout history have thrived the most in areas where there was an abundance of cereals. When humans started farming cereals, they abandoned their nomadic hunter-gatherer lifestyles, built towns, and were able to grow in population. Science writer Nigel Calder said, "The master of the planet Earth is now identifiable; it is grass" (Calder, 1983).

Grasses have hollow stems, and the leaves grow from the bottom of each blade, so the plant is not hurt when an animal munches on it. When a grass plant goes into bloom, the flowers are on a stalk that sticks up above the leaves. If you forget to mow your lawn, eventually you will see these stalks emerge with small flowers called spikelets. Because grasses are pollinated by the wind, the flowers do not need to be colorful or attractive to pollinators.

Grasses are monocots, which means that a grass seed does not have two separate halves (cotyledons) that can split apart, like a lima bean splits apart into two halves. A grass seedling will only have one leaf, not two, like a lima bean plant has two leaves when it sprouts. Being a monocot also means that the veins on the leaf, a blade of grass, are parallel. The roots of a grass plant are fibrous and lack a main root (Figure 9.8).

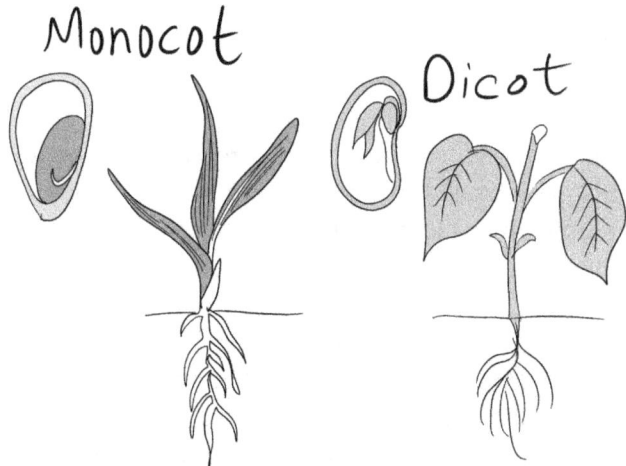

Figure 9.8 Monocot vs dicot seed and seedling. Image by author Christine Schnittka.

Yeast: Saccharomyces Cerevisiae

Yeast is a single-celled fungus which floats in the air and lands on all sorts of things. Your cup of orange juice, if left out on the kitchen counter for two days, may pick up some yeast particles and start getting bubbly and smelly. Grapes growing in a vineyard will pick up yeast particles, and when the grapes are crushed for wine, the yeast is already there to do its science. Barley, rye, wheat, and other grains will pick up yeast particles too. That may be the origin of yeast bread! If you mix a crushed grain (flour) with water and let it sit out in a wet, warm place, the yeast may start its work if other fungi and bacteria don't get to work first. This is how one makes a sourdough starter (Figure 9.9).

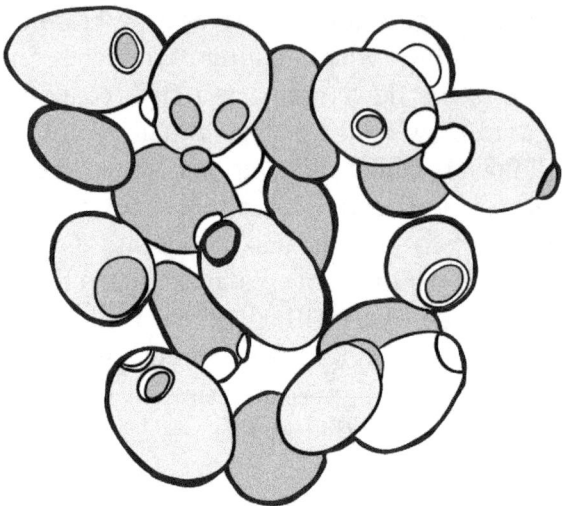

Figure 9.9 Yeast budding. Image by author Christine Schnittka.

Baking Powder

As a child, on days we did not have yeast bread to eat, we had quick bread, a bread made not with yeast but with baking powder. The bread rises in the oven as it is cooking. Since delicious flavors are not developed by yeast, quick breads often have sugar, milk, and butter added. Banana bread and zucchini bread are two popular quick breads. The same gas, carbon dioxide, is produced, but it happens by a chemical reaction between the two ingredients in the baking powder, the alkaline sodium bicarbonate ($NaHCO_3$) and either the acid cream of tartar ($KHC_4H_4O_6$) or the acid, sodium aluminum sulfate ($NaAl(SO_4)_2$). I try to avoid ingesting aluminum, so I purchase baking powder made with cream of tartar. When heated, the chemical reaction takes place and bubbles of carbon dioxide puff up the bread.

$$NaHCO_3 + KHC_4H_4O_6 \rightarrow KNaC_4H_4O_6 + H_2O + CO_2$$

Bread Science: The Details

Grains

Corn

Zea mays evolved in southern Mexico from a wild grass called teosinte that didn't have the large and juicy ears of corn we know and love today. Teosinte ears were only a couple of inches long and contained only about 12 kernels each. The indigenous Americans used selective breeding to create the variety we consume today. The pollen is located on the male flowers at the top of each stalk. The female flowers are located where the ears of corn grow.

Wheat

Wheat, of which there are many species, is classified in the genus, *Triticum*. Today we primarily grow six species of wheat: common wheat, durum, spelt, emmer, khorasan, and einkorn. A grain of wheat is the fruit, and it contains protein, fat, carbohydrates, fiber, and iron. Inside each grain of wheat is the seed portion, which consists of a tiny embryo of a wheat plant. This seed portion is called the "germ" and it's what wheat germ is made from. This little germ contains fat which spoils sooner than the rest of the grain. Spoiled or rancid fat tastes off and while it is not bad for you if eaten occasionally, a regular diet of rancid fat is not a good idea. Once, my mother bought too many packages of wheat germ and gave me one of them. It turned rancid before I could use it because it contained so much fat. (We will tell you more about rancid fat in the soap chapter.) The skin or outer layer of the wheat grain is called bran. Wheat bran is full of B-vitamins and fiber. Most flour mills remove both the germ and the bran, leaving behind only the endosperm. The endosperm is supposed to help the little embryo grow, giving it nutrients and physically protecting it from damage during sprouting. What is fascinating is that the endosperm forms separately from the embryo and is actually a separate organism. Pollen contains sperm to fertilize an egg. Yes, plants make eggs. One sperm cell will fertilize the egg cell to make the embryo, while a second sperm cell will fertilize a separate cell, the "central cell," to form the endosperm (Li & Yang, 2020). Wheat contains gluten, which is a sticky protein, and so when yeast produces carbon dioxide in a dough, the gas bubbles do not readily pop. Gluten can cause digestive, autoimmune, and inflammatory problems in about 1%–2% of people.

Oat

Avena sativa is a grain with the most protein of any cereal. Oats do not contain the same type of gluten proteins that wheat has, so people who have problems with wheat gluten often eat oat breads. We are used to seeing oats that have been crushed or rolled, not whole. An oat grain has a thick outer hull that must be removed before eating, unlike wheat which can be ground up whole. The inside of an oat grain, once the hull is removed, is called a groat. Groats contain a lot of fats, and so they spoil quickly and go rancid. To prevent groats from spoiling, they are heat treated, which kills the germ and prevents the grain from sprouting. You can make oatmeal in your fridge overnight (overnight oats) without having to cook the oats because they are already cooked!

Yeast

The Dutch scientist, Anton van Leeuwenhoek, first spotted yeast under a microscope he built in 1680, but he did not know what these globular, budding cells were for. In 1859, the Dutch scientist J. H. van den Broek discovered that yeast cells produce gas and alcohol and gave yeast its name from the Old English word, "gist," which means "dirt" and "jest," which means "foam." Yeast indeed makes foam!

Yeast is a single celled organism that feeds on glucose. The waste excreted by yeast is carbon dioxide and alcohol. The chemical formula for glucose is $C_6H_{12}O_6$. The chemical formula for ethanol, the alcohol produced by yeast, is C_2H_5OH. One molecule of glucose becomes two molecules of alcohol and two molecules of carbon dioxide.

$$C_6H_{12}O_6 \rightarrow 2C_2H_5OH + 2CO_2$$

When making bread, yeast gets the glucose it needs from the endosperm portion of the grain. This endosperm is made of starch, which is a form of glucose for storage. When a plant stores glucose as starch, the glucose molecules join together. Starch does not taste sweet, but if the bonds between the glucose molecules are broken apart, it does. To break these bonds and turn starch into glucose, an enzyme is needed. That enzyme, amylase, is already present in the skin of seed grains—the bran. When wheat grains are processed to remove the bran, some will remain. When you add water to flour, this enzyme in the bran remnant called amylase will start to break the starch down into sugar. The more finely ground up the wheat is, the easier it is for amylase to break down starches into sugars. Highly processed foods can cause health problems because the flour is more finely ground and the amylase has an easier time doing its enzymatic work, and subsequently more sugar ends up in the bloodstream of the person eating the processed food (Angelidis et al., 2016). So, make bread at home for good health!

The longer yeast is allowed to consume the sugars in the flour, the more carbon dioxide is created, and the fluffier the bread dough becomes. Also, when yeast is given enough time to consume sugars in bread dough, the flavorful alcohol, ethanol, is produced. In 1961, the Chorleywood bread process was invented in Great Britain for high volume bread production. The dough is placed in high-speed mixers and placed in a vacuum chamber. The yeast acts on the dough for about 45 minutes before it is baked (Cauvain & Young, 2006). When you make bread at home, it takes two hours or more for the dough to be ready to bake. This slower process makes a healthier and better tasting bread, which is one more reason to bake bread at home.

Nixtamalization

If you have ever bought ground corn flour, masa harina, you have noticed that the ingredients are corn and lime. I used to think that meant that lime juice was added. Actually, the dried corn is cooked in limewater, which is calcium hydroxide dissolved in water. When dried corn is cooked in this alkaline solution, an important chemical change called nixtamalization ensues. This process was invented by the people who lived in what is today, Mexico and Central America. The word "nixtli" means "ashes," and "tamalli" means "cooked maize masa." Instead of using calcium hydroxide, some people in the region used ashes for their alkaline solution. Nixtamalization frees up the vitamin B3 in the corn, adds calcium from the limewater solution, and deactivates toxins from the molds that are commonly present in dried corn (Palencia et al., 2003). This makes corn breads healthy, full of nutrients, and able to sustain a growing civilization.

Salt

No chapter on bread is complete without discussing salt. Having made yeast bread without salt, I can tell you that its role is not just one of flavor. When yeast bread is made, it needs to be kneaded by hand or in a mixer. This makes the gluten protein strands stretch and stick together forming a web that makes the dough feel stiffer and stiffer the more you knead it. The more this gluten matrix develops, the better the bread will hold the carbon dioxide bubbles and hold its shape. When making long baguette loaves, they will flatten like oval pancakes if the dough is not kneaded enough to "develop the gluten." The gluten does not need to be created—it is already there—but as the dough is kneaded, the gluten matrix becomes more complex and tangled. However, without salt, there is only so much webbing that can take place between strands of gluten.

The gluten strands are positively charged and naturally repel each other and refuse to stick together. When salt (NaCl) is dissolved in a liquid, the sodium and chlorine separate into ions. Negatively charged chlorine ions bond with positive areas on the gluten molecule. This neutralizes the charge on the gluten, so the strands stop repelling each other. If you knead your dough until you can stretch it thin and see light through it, the gluten is well webbed and connected. Bread bakers call this the windowpane test. If oil is added to a dough, like in some recipes for focaccia or pizza dough, the oil coats the gluten molecules and prevents them from sticking together and the dough can more easily be rolled out flat.

Probing Questions to Ask

What are the ingredients in bread?

- ◆ Bread, by definition, needs to contain ground up grain and water. The grain can be wheat, rye, oat, rice, corn, einkorn, or any other grain. Flour is the name for ground up grains.

What is the role of yeast in bread?

- Yeast is a fungus that digests the sugars in the dough and produces carbon dioxide gas and the alcohol, ethanol. It adds flavor to the bread and gives it a light, fluffy texture. The alcohol evaporates when the bread is cooked.

What is the role of baking powder in bread?

- Baking powder contains two ingredients which react with each other when wet and warm and produces carbon dioxide gas. This fluffs up the bread dough. Without yeast or baking powder, the bread is flat.

Explain what gluten is, and how it works in bread.

- Gluten is a protein found in wheat flour which is sticky like glue. It forms long strands. When dough is kneaded, the gluten strands stick to each other and give the dough shape. The gluten helps trap the carbon dioxide bubbles so they stay in the dough.

Elaborate: Bread Art, Craft, Technology, and Engineering

Purpose
The purpose of the Elaborate phase of this lesson is to apply the science of bread to craft, art, technology, and engineering. Now that your students have experimented with bread dough and learned about the science of bread and history of bread making, it's time to engineer some bread!

Overview
After making a bread by following some specific instructions, students can engineer their own bread (Figure 9.10).

The Challenge
The challenge for this phase of the lesson is to have students invent a new type of bread and make it. Perhaps you want your students to invent a bread that is gluten free and flat like a cracker. Perhaps you want them to invent a bread that is light and fluffy but can be prepared and cooked in under an hour. Or, perhaps their challenge will be to invent a sandwich bread sized for miniature cucumber sandwiches. Younger students can be challenged to take a dough made by the teacher and form a particular shape.

Figure 9.10 Bread supplies. Image by author Christine Schnittka.

Instead of having this activity be trial-and-error free-for-all, make sure students are making purposeful decisions based on the science they learned and experiences they had in the Explore phase of this lesson. Have them work in groups of 3–4.

Probing Questions to Ask
- What are the properties of the bread you need to make?
- What are the limitations you must work around?
- Which ingredients will you require to produce the bread you need?
- How can you vary these ingredients?
- What equipment will you need?
- What safety considerations will you have to think about?
- How will you keep track of your ingredients, process, and results?

Have students work on a small scale—making muffin-sized bread loaves or pancake-sized flatbreads. Provide a toaster oven or two and an electric skillet as well as muffin tins and muffin tin liners.

Some general rules of thumb:

- Typical yeast breads include 2.5 ml (1/2 teaspoon) of salt for every cup of flour.

- Typical yeast breads include 2.5 ml (1/2 teaspoon) of yeast for every cup of flour.
- You will typically need 79 ml (1/3 cup) of water for a cup of flour.
- Yeast bread typically cooks at 176°C (350°F).
- Corn tortillas usually have 177 ml (3/4 cup) of water for every cup of masa harina corn flour.
- Corn tortillas can be pressed or rolled between two Ziploc bags, peeled away from the bags, and then cooked in an electric skillet.
- Bread without yeast will often include 5 ml (one teaspoon) of baking powder for 120 grams (one cup) of flour.
- Bread without yeast will often also include 118 ml (1/2 cup) of milk for every 120 grams (one cup) of flour, 10 ml (a couple teaspoons) of oil, a pinch of salt, and a bit of sugar.

Have each group plan out their design, write out their recipe, and get it approved by the teacher. Have the group justify their decisions based on what they learned. For example, why are they using salt? Why are they using milk instead of water? Why are they using masa instead of flour?

- What happens if less water is used?
- What happens if more or less salt is used?
- What happens if milk replaces water?
- What happens if oil is added to bread dough?
- What happens if yeast and sugar are added to a corn tortilla dough?

The "breads" can be cooked in muffin liners that have the group name and recipe name written on the bottom.

The "breads" should be evaluated after cooking. The teacher could cook the breads one day, and the students could sample them the next day, taking notes on the texture, flavor, and success of the design.

Engineers always redesign their products and try again when the product does not live up to expectations. The teacher can plan on a couple days of baking and evaluating!

Evaluate: What Did They Learn?

After making bread, ask your students to write the answers to the following questions to see what they learned. A form to collect the answers to these questions from your students is provided on our website https://steamcrafts.weebly.com./

1. What is bread?

    ◆ Bread is any food that is a solid, cooked, cereal paste.

2. What is biotechnology? Is bread a biotechnology?

    ◆ Technologies are inventions. Bread was invented. A biotechnology is an invention that uses the living world. Since bread is made from the fruit and seeds of grasses, it's a biotechnology.

3. Where in the world was bread first invented?

    ◆ There is evidence that it was invented separately in Africa, in South America, and in the Middle East, using different grains, however the oldest evidence is in Africa.

4. What are the grains used to make flour for bread?

    ◆ Barley, corn, oats, rice, rye, sorghum, wheat, and millet are the most common ones we eat. These plants are grasses. The fruit of the grass is the grain we grind to make flour.

5. How can you cook bread? What technologies allow for bread cooking?

    ◆ Bread can be cooked inside a clay pot (a technology), cooked in an oven (a technology), and steamed in a bamboo basket (a technology) over boiling water in a pot (a technology).

6. What are the ingredients in bread and what do they do?

    ◆ The flour is the food. Water allows the gluten strands to bond to each other, and water helps the yeast find the sugars from the flour. Salt helps the gluten strands bond. Oil prevents the gluten strands from bonding. Yeast makes flavor and holes in the bread. Baking powder makes holes in the bread. Sugar gives the yeast something to eat.

7. What does kneading do?

    ◆ Kneading helps gluten strands bond because it forces them into contact with each other.

8. What breads did you make? What ingredients did you use, and why were they chosen?

Summary

Making bread is an ancient craft that people all over the world have been practicing for over 10,000 years. From corn in South America to rice in Asia, figuring out how to turn the same grass that flocks of sheep and goats and cows ate into food for people sparked agriculture and settled villages. Our civilization as we know it today would be quite different without the grasses, grains, and breads that feed and nourish us. Learning the science, history, engineering, math, and craft of bread helps us see how proximal we are to the natural world, and how we can use our minds and hands to create technologies that connect us to the grasses of the fields. After making a tortilla, a pita pocket, or a loaf of sandwich bread, one never looks at bread the same way, nor takes it for granted. If stranded on a deserted island, we should hope that it was full of grasses, because with the knowledge our ancestors passed down to us, we would have food to eat for the rest of our lives.

Contemporary Bread Artisans

Making bread is still a relevant art and craft today. Artists and craftspeople around the world are still creating and using grains, and doing fascinating things with them. For links to examine modern bread artisans, please see our website https://steamcrafts.weebly.com/.

References

Angelidis, G., Protonotariou, S., Mandala, I., & Rosell, C. M. (2016). Jet milling effect on wheat flour characteristics and starch hydrolysis. *Journal of Food Science and Technology, 53*, 784–791.

Bostock, J., & Riley, H. T. (1855). Pliny the elder. *The Natural History.* https://www.perseus.tufts.edu/hopper/text?doc=Perseus%3atext%3a1999.02.0137

Bybee, R. W. (2009). *The BSCS 5E instructional model and 21st century skills*. National Academies Board on Science Education.

Calder, N. (1983). *Timescale: An atlas of the fourth dimension*. Viking Press.

Cauvain, S. P., & Young, L. S. (2006). *The Chorleywood bread process*. Woodhead Publishing.

Campbell-Platt, G. (1994). Fermented foods—A world perspective. *Food Research International, 27*(3), 253–257.

Constable, G. (1985). *Grasslands and Tundra: Planet Earth*. Time Life Books.

Dewey, J. (1938). *Experience and education*. Macmillan.

Li, H. J., & Yang, W. C. (2020). Central cell in flowering plants: Specification, signaling, and evolution. *Frontiers in Plant Science, 11*, 590307.

Mercader, J. (2009). Mozambican grass seed consumption during the Middle Stone Age. *Science, 326*(5960), 1680–1683.

Palencia, E., Torres, O., Hagler, W., Meredith, F.I., Williams, L., & Riley, R.T. (2003). Total fumonisins are reduced in tortillas using the traditional nixtamalization method of Mayan communities. *The Journal of Nutrition, 133*(10), 3200–3203.

Piaget, J. (1955). The construction of reality in the child. *Journal of Consulting Psychology, 19*(1), 77.

Rova, E. (2014). Tannurs, tannur concentrations and centralised bread production at Tell Beydar and elsewhere: An overview. *Paleonutrition and Food Practices in the Ancient Near East: Towards a Multidisciplinary Approach, 14*, 121–170.

Zeldovich, L. (2018). 14,000-year-old piece of bread rewrites the history of baking and farming. https://www.npr.org/sections/thesalt/2018/07/24/631583427/14-000-year-old-piece-of-bread-rewrites-the-history-of-baking-and-farming

10

Clay Creations

Introduction

As a 12-year-old, I learned to play a yellow plastic recorder, and annoyed my parents, sisters, and friends with my squeaky attempt at tune playing. It fascinated me to take the recorder apart into pieces, dissect the mouthpiece to clean it, and experiment with different ways of playing it. Each of my children has a recorder of his own, and now we have enough recorders in the house for a quintet. As an adult, I picked up pottery as a hobby, and one of the first things I made was a clay flute. As a child, I never knew about the ancient origins of flutes, whistles, and other wind instruments, nor did I consider the science, math, or engineering that went into designing an instrument. In this chapter, you will learn how to use clay and the craft of pottery to teach an interdisciplinary STEAM unit on musical instruments to your students. You will learn the science and history of using clay to make music and learn how to engage your students in this fascinating, ancient activity. Your students will learn about properties of earth materials, how sound is created inside hollow vessels, and learn about contemporary artists who work with clay to make music (Figure 10.1).

 ## Wind Instrument History

For thousands of years across the world, people made musical instruments out of natural materials like gourds, hollow bones, animal horns, and clay. In South and

DOI: 10.4324/9781003428312-10

Clay Creations ◆ 217

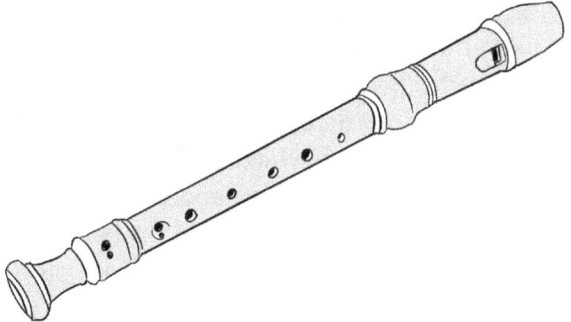

Figure 10.1 Plastic recorder. Image by author Christine Schnittka.

Central America 2,500 years ago, the Peruvians, Hopi, Mayans, Incas, Aztecs, and others made wind instruments from clay and decorated them with the images of animals or people. These wind instruments had four or five holes, sometimes had two chambers, and sometimes contained hidden chambers which allowed for a wide variety of musical notes (Broad, 1988). Clay gave the instrument makers the ability to form these flutes into a myriad of shapes, and by firing the clay to make it as hard as rock, many of them have survived to this day. In addition to wind instruments, ancient people also made rattles and drums from clay. In the city of Kish, which is today's Iraq, 5,000-year-old rattles were found which contain little pellets and still make sounds when shaken. In China, 2,000 years ago, people made the 埙 pronounced, "xun," which was a small clay egg-shaped whistle with several holes to make different notes. The Chinese also made semi-enclosed bells from clay 4,000 years ago, which could be hung from a cord and resemble little metal bells still manufactured today (Figure 10.2).

Figure 10.2 Xun and other wind instruments. Images drawn by author Christine Schnittka from images found at the Metropolitan Museum in the public domain.

Why did people make and play these musical instruments? The Aztecs used their wind instruments called tlapitzalli, to imitate birds and communicate with the spirit world (Both, 2007). The story of an individual chosen to play the instrument while climbing up to the top of a temple is a macabre one, and not appropriate for youth, but which can be read (Sahagún, 1950–1982, Book 2: 65). The Chinese played the egg-shaped xun to communicate sorrow through music. Many people around the world probably played clay musical instruments for the same reasons we play them today- to express and communicate emotions.

More recently, in 1853, an Italian baker named Giuseppe Donati created a little whistle in the style of the ancient South and Central American instruments, and he called it an "ocarina." Ocarina is the Italian word for "little goose." Donati made ocarinas of all shapes and sizes so that people could make music together. While the clay whistle was popularized by Donati 150 years ago, it was actually created by people all over the world thousands of years ago. Today, people all over the world still make and play clay whistles for fun, for a hobby, to make art, and to make music (Figure 10.3).

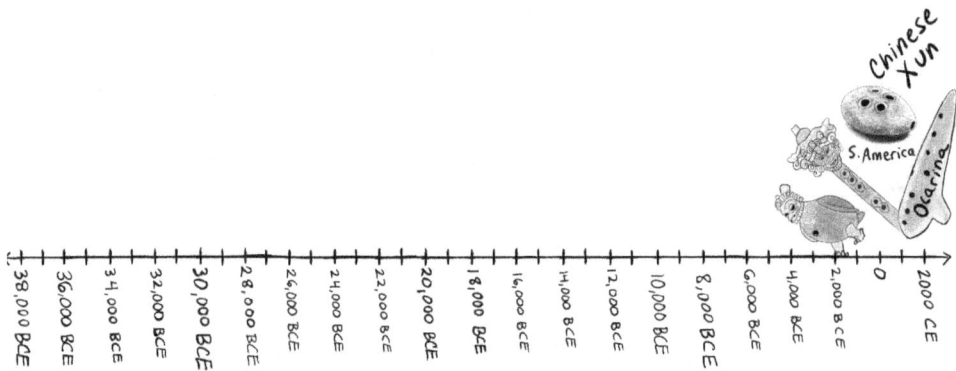

Figure 10.3 Wind instrument timeline. Image by author Christine Schnittka.

Meeting the Standards

Teaching this chapter as written focuses on STEAM principles that include: historical elements that influenced technological advancements, engineering principles including iterative design, criteria and constraints, and scientific measurement principles as well as data collection and analysis. For more detailed information regarding which specific standards are covered in this unit, please refer to our website: https://steamcrafts.weebly.com/.

Materials

- Collection of instruments such as tambourines, maracas, xylophones, harmonicas, kazoos, recorders, a ukulele, etc.
- Deck of playing cards
- Tuning forks
- ¼ kg (½ pound) of clay per student
- Bucket of water for washing hands after clay play
- Towels for drying hands
- Towels for washing tables after clay play
- Narrow-opening bottles (glass soda bottles)
- Water in small pitchers
- Paper towels for clean-up
- Craft sticks
- Toothpicks
- Clay
- A big bucket, bowl, or dish pan for washing up
- Lots of kitchen towels

Safety

- The only danger in working with clay involves breathing clay dust. To avoid this, be sure to clean up all clay residue with a wet cloth before it dries and gets dusty. Do not let youth sand or otherwise abrade dry clay objects, and thus create dust. The Amaco brand of air-dry clay contains a plasticizer which prevents dry clay items from breaking down into dust easily.

The Lesson

> **The BSCS 5E Instructional Model for Clay Instrument Making**
>
> The lessons in this book are designed around the BSCS 5E instructional model designed by the Biological Sciences Curriculum Study (Bybee, 2009). Based on Dewey's model of reflective thinking (Dewey, 1938), Piagetian theory (Piaget, 1955), and other learning cycle models that followed, the five phases of this model are: Engage, Explore, Explain, Elaborate, and Evaluate. The purpose and summary for each phase are explained in the sections that follow.

- To find accompanying presentations, student handouts, and more be sure to visit our website: https://steamcrafts.weebly.com/.

Engage: Making Music

Purpose
The purpose of the Engage phase of this lesson is to build excitement about making musical instruments, and to initiate curiosity about them and how they work.

Overview
The teacher brings several types of simple musical instruments to class for students to try out: tambourines, maracas, xylophones, harmonicas, kazoos, recorders, a ukulele, etc. Students discuss how they might make a musical instrument out of clay.

Note to the Teacher: There are collections that can be purchased online that are very reasonably priced and contain most of these. In order to prevent the spread of germs, the teacher should demonstrate how to make the wind instruments work but allow students to try out all the others. They can be passed around or set up at stations around the room.

Probing Questions to Ask
As students are trying out different contemporary musical instruments, you can ask some questions to find out what they know.

What do all these instruments have in common?

- The instruments will vary in the method of making music, but they all can produce a sound.

How are they different from each other?

- The instruments will differ in terms of the materials they are made of, the method of producing the sound, and the type of sound. Some will make a sound that is musical, and others will produce a sound that more rhythmic, like a drum or rattle.

What is it about the instrument that allows it to make sound?

- Vibrations! Students may not be able to come to this conclusion, but regardless of the type of instrument, it makes a vibration in the air which reaches the human ear.

How do you think these musical instruments work to make sound?

- ◆ Depending on the age and background knowledge of the students, they may not be able to conclude that vibrations make these sounds. Students may think that the air splits or goes fast for wind instruments to work.

What emotions do you think each instrument communicates?

- ◆ Happiness, sadness, fear, anger … the same emotions we communicate through music today were used by our ancestors.

Tell students that they are going to make musical instruments out of clay. Ask them if they have ever worked with clay before. Have them discuss which instruments could be made from clay, which sounds could be produced by a clay instrument. Can a ukulele be made from clay? Can a xylophone be made from clay? How about a rattle? A flute?

- Student handouts and instructions for this activity can be found on our website https://steamcrafts.weebly.com/.

Explore: Clay Play!

Purpose
The purpose of the Explore phase of this lesson is to allow students to all have experiences with clay before using it to design and construct a musical instrument.

Some students have different levels of experience with clay and music. This phase attempts to level that field of knowledge so that students have a more concrete foundation on which to build further understanding.

Overview
Students can use the handouts found on our website https://steamcrafts.weebly.com/ to try the challenges in this lesson. Students conduct an experiment with soil to see where clay is present. Next, they play with clay to experience its properties and abilities. Finally, they make pinch pots, an essential skill needed to make most musical instruments from clay.

Clay

Students may have had experiences with Play-Doh or other types of synthetic clays, but aside from making mud pies in the dirt (do kids still make mud pies?) playing with actual clay may be a new experience. To provide your students with some clay for this phase of the lesson, it can be purchased or harvested! It is much easier to purchase clay, but clay can be harvested by digging up soil, drying it, crushing it, mixing it with water, and straining it.

Digging Clay

Depending on where you live, you can probably find clay in your backyard, schoolyard, or down by a creek in your neighborhood. Because clay particles stay suspended in water for a long time and are carried long distances by running water, clay is often found deposited in the banks of creeks and streams. If you have ever seen dry, cracked mud on the ground from a dried-up stream, you can try to pick up some flat sections of the cracked, dry mud. These top sections are full of clay and can be harvested and reconstituted into workable clay.

Clay will look different from normal soil. When wet, it will stick together into a mud pie. When dry, it will be dusty and cracked. It might be reddish, or it might even be yellow. It will be made from very small, smooth particles that feel like dust on your fingers when dry.

Clay is a natural earth material made from very small particles of the same minerals that rocks are made from. Clay usually forms where rocks break down into small mineral particles, which is why clays are often found near creeks where these minerals are deposited. Clay is just very very eroded rock. Silt is still eroded rock, but the particles are larger. If you dig up a clump of dirt from your front yard, most likely, 20% of it will be clay and the remainder will be silt, sand, pebbles, and partially decomposed organic matter. When looking for clay, collect some soil and let it dry out. Then, mix the dried soil that you suspect has a high concentration of clay with water, shake it until everything is mixed, and then let it settle. Clay and silt particles will initially stay suspended while sand will sink to the bottom. A day later, you will see layers of sand, silt, and clay. You can measure the clay content this way as a percentage of the soil (Figure 10.4).

If you succeed in finding some pure clay, dig it up and let it dry out completely. Then, break it up into small parts, removing any pebbles, sticks, or other non-clay parts. You can use your hands or a hammer to break it up. Be sure to put on a face mask to keep clay dust out of your nose and lungs! Once it's dry and broken into small pieces, add water and make a mud slip or

Figure 10.4 Jars of soil after settling into differentiated bands. Image by author Christine Schnittka.

slurry. To get more lumps out, you can put your mud slip through a kitchen spaghetti strainer. Now, just let your mud slip dry enough that it can be formed into a ball. I like to pour my mud slip into a pillowcase, tie it up with a rope, and hang it to drain. After a week or so, the pillowcase will only contain workable clay. Then, I put the clay into a sealed plastic bag for using later.

If you wish to remove clay from soil which contains a lot of silt and sand, pour off the suspended clay slurry into the pillowcase, and return the silt and sand to the Earth.

Digging and processing clay is very rewarding work. However, if you want to provide your students with some clay the easy way, you can buy it.

Buying Clay

If you can't or don't want to dig clay, you can buy some online. You can get potter's clay that requires a kiln to harden, or you can purchase clay that contains a plasticizer that hardens when dry. Here are some sources with good prices:

- Rocky Mountain Clay–Terra Cotta Low Fire Cone 06–Red Rock Red Clay (2.2 kg or 5 pounds)
- Aurora Pottery–Whiteware Clay (Lo-Fire)–EM-342 (2.2 kg or 5 pounds)
- Amaco–Air Dry Clay (No kiln required). Gray, terracotta, or white

Once you have some clay, have students investigate its properties. Students can work alone or in small groups to explore this material. You can have them do the activities below with their clay and draw or write about what happens.

You want students to discover that clay behaves in a particular way. It can be squashed, rolled, and flattened. It cannot be stretched like a rubber band. When moist, it bends easily.

Clay Play

Use the student handout on our website https://steamcrafts.weebly.com/to guide students in their clay play.

Pinch Pots

Pinch pots, or thumb pots, are the oldest and simplest forms to make with clay.

After playing with the clay, instruct students to take a ball of clay in their non-dominant hand (their left hand if they are right-handed) and stick their dominant hand thumb into the center of the clay a bit more than halfway down. Then, rotate the clay while pinching the sides. As they do this, they are making a small pot (Figure 10.5).

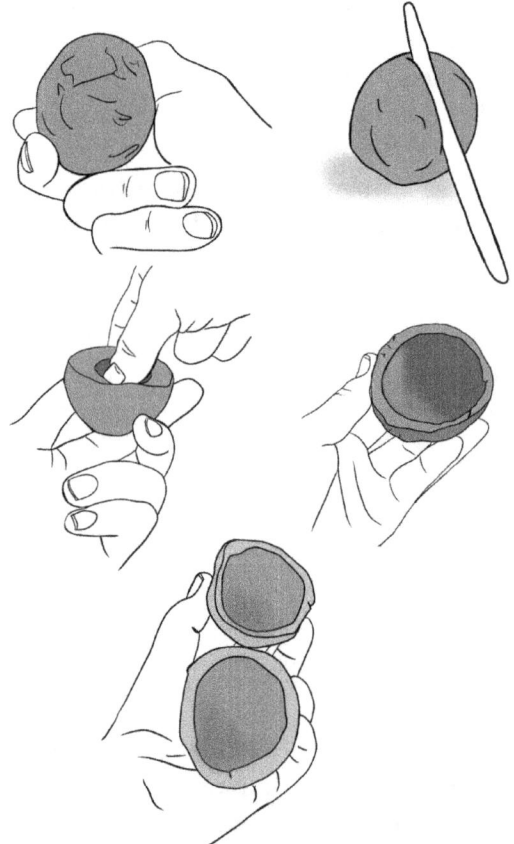

Figure 10.5 Process of creating a pinch pot. Image by author Christine Schnittka.

Students may become frustrated making these pinch pots. They may pinch too much and end up with a large, floppy bowl. Their pot might crack at the sides. The top might be uneven. Remind them that it's only clay, that they can squish up their wonky pot and start over. If their pinch pot gets too dried out during formation and starts to crack, allow them to put the clay into a reclaim bucket and start over with a fresh lump. You can always mist these slightly dried-out lumps with water, seal up the container they are in, and reclaim the clay in the future. Never throw clay away.

Working with clay this way teaches children to be patient with themselves, try again, and develop resiliency (Berberian, 2019; Jang & Choi, 2012).

Be sure to have a discussion with students about how clay behaves. It can be pressed, but not stretched too easily. Ask students these questions and have them construct a model (mental or on paper with a pencil) for clay's behavior.

Probing Questions to Ask

Why do you think clay behaves differently than Silly Putty does?

- ◆ Silly Putty is made from silicone, and silicone molecules are long, sticky, and wavy. As you pull on the putty, the molecules slide next to each other and straighten out. Clay is not made of long molecules at all.

Why do you think clay breaks when you stretch it?

- ◆ Clay particles do not stick to each other in the way that silicone molecules will stick to each other. The attraction between the clay particles is easily broken with a little tug.

Why do you think clay flops over if you try to make a tall tower?

- ◆ When clay has moisture, there are water molecules in between the clay particles. The water molecules are attracted to the clay particles and allow them to move a bit in all directions. Imagine, instead of sticking Lego bricks together, you put chewing gum between each one. The stack of Lego bricks could bend and sway as the chewing gum moves. The water molecules in the clay act like that chewing gum. Once a clay tower dries, there are no more water molecules giving it flexibility. If you try to bend the dry clay tower, it will break when the clay particles separate from each other.

Pinch pots can be used to make whistles, bells, and rattles. Have students become proficient at this task so that they can complete the challenge later in the lesson. Have students try to make four identical pinch pots. The way to do this is to take two balls of clay, each about the size of a golf ball, and carefully divide them in half with a craft stick. Then, when a pinch pot is made with each half, each is about the same size. Later, students will take these four pinch pots and put them together to make two hollow spheres.

Before making musical instruments from the pinch pots, it's wise to let them harden a bit, but not too much. To accomplish this, let them sit out for a few hours, then put them in a sealed container. You can use plastic bags or plastic boxes to keep them from drying out more. The perfect amount of dryness results in clay that feels like a chocolate bar. You can carve into it and even cut it with a plastic knife or a toothpick, and it holds its shape. If the clay is not dry enough, it will deflect too much when pressed.

Drying stages: When clay is soft, it feels like Play-Doh. As it dries, it changes into something more like soft milk chocolate, and then hardened dark chocolate, and finally a brick. It's best to make a whistle when it's in one of the chocolate stages.

Clean up: Do not pour clay water down the drain, as the clay particles will settle in pipes and cause clogs. I usually provide a bucket for rinsing off hands and pour the bucket outside afterward. Alternatively, you can let the clay settle in the bucket, and then pour the water down a drain and wipe out the clay residue with a paper towel and throw it in the trash.

- Student handouts and instructions for this activity can be found on our website https://steamcrafts.weebly.com/.

Explain: The STEAM Concepts

Purpose
The purpose of the Explain phase of this lesson is to allow students to gain new scientific knowledge and understanding of how clay works, how sound works, and how musical instruments work so that they can make informed design decisions in a later phase.

Overview
A presentation found on our website https://steamcrafts.weebly.com/ discusses different examples of clay and music science that can be used. In this phase of the lesson, you should first ask your students to explain their new reasonings and understandings. It's very important in this phase of the lesson to find out

what students are thinking before teaching them the STEAM concepts of clay, sound, and musical instruments. What follows is a discussion of the basics and the details of clay and sound science.

Clay Science: The Basics

Ask students to imagine that they have a very powerful microscope, and that they are looking at clay with it. Ask them to draw or articulate what they think they would see through this microscope. They will probably imagine that clay is made from small balls, like very small pieces of sand. Next, show students an actual microscopic image of clay. Notice that clay is made of flat particles which resemble a deck of cards (Figure 10.6).

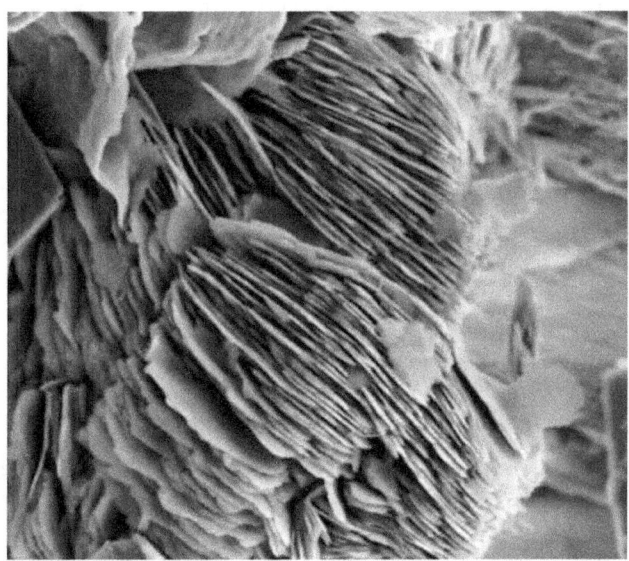

Figure 10.6 Microscopic view of kaolinite particles. "Kaolinit yüzeyleri kitap gibi sayfa aralıklarına su germez hydrogen bağlantı O H yeşil" by Ayratayrat is licensed under CC BY-SA 4.0.

Clay Questions to Ask

Ask students, "How do you think these flat particles make clay behave?"

◆ Students may be able to articulate that the flat particles can slide over each other.

Show students a stack of playing cards or a stack of index cards. Ask them how this stack behaves when squished or pushed on.

- ♦ When squished, the cards in the deck just get closer to each other. Nothing breaks.

If we dipped all the playing cards in water and then made a stack, how would the stack behave when we pushed on it?

- ♦ When we push on a wet deck of cards, the water gets squeezed out from between each card.

Ask students how the deck of cards behaves when stretched.

- ♦ You can't stretch a deck of cards. The cards just separate from each other.

Now, ask what happens if you try to stretch a deck of wet cards.

- ♦ A wet deck of cards will hold up for a little when stretched but will still break. The water acts as a sort of glue to keep the cards together with some pulling force applied, but not much.

These flat mineral particles also slide over each other when wet, making clay slippery. Look at how the particles of clay (the mineral kaolinite) resemble cards in a card deck.

Clay Science: The Details

The most common mineral in clay is kaolinite which has the chemical formula, $Al_2Si_2O_5(OH)_4$. Kaolinite molecules form crystals shaped like flat hexagons. Kaolinite comes from eroded granite, the rock from which many statues and kitchen countertops are made. Imagine a granite statue eroding over many years into clay that can be gathered and formed into a new statue, one made of clay (Figure 10.7).

> One summer, I was visiting Israel where most buildings are made from a limestone called Jerusalem Stone. After it rains, a white mud can collect in low places. When it dries, you can pick up pieces of this cracked dry mud. I showed a piece of this mud to someone who lives in Israel, and he said that some people collect it and make pottery from it. This makes sense! Rain is slightly acidic, and it dissolves the limestone structures into different types of clay minerals.

Clay particles stick to each other very well when they are wet. The hydrogen atoms in a water molecules will stick to the oxygen atoms on the clay

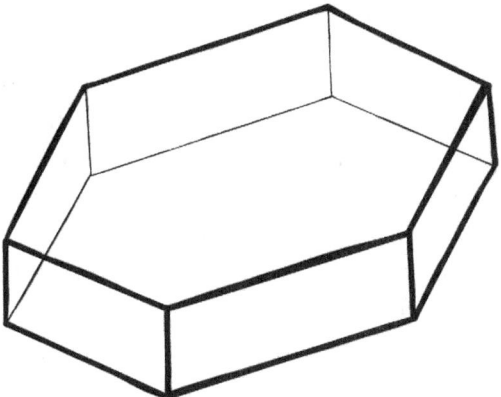

Figure 10.7 Hexagonal prism. Image by author Christine Schnittka.

particles, and oxygen atoms on the water molecules will stick to hydrogen atoms on the clay particles. This is due to hydrogen bonds. The hydrogen atom is positively charged, and the oxygen atom is negatively charged. Since opposite charges attract each other, this creates weak bonds. When the water in between two clay particles evaporates, the particles get closer together and the clay shrinks. This shrinkage allows the oxygen and hydrogen atoms to get close enough to bond to each other without the water in between. However, the bond is a weak one, and can easily be broken when pulled apart. With water in between the particles, the clay particles stick to each other better. But, when dry, there are fewer bonding sites, and the dry clay item is easily broken (Figure 10.8).

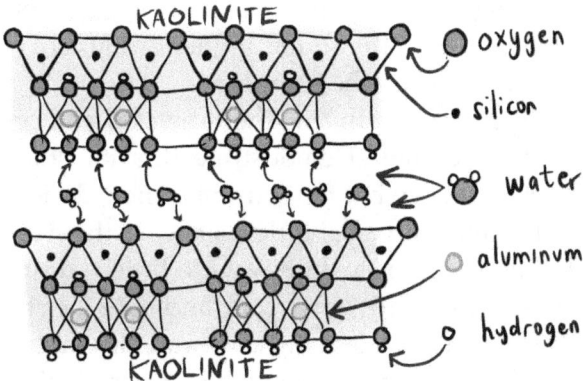

Figure 10.8 Cross-section view between two layers of kaolinite. Image adapted by author Christine Schnittka from "Structure & Reactivity in Organic, Biological and Inorganic Chemistry" by Chris Schaller.

When you want to attach two pieces of clay together, you score (roughen up) the two surfaces with a sharp point and wet them. The roughness creates bonding sites at many angles, and the water helps with the temporary bonding. When dry, the connection is less likely to fail with all those attachments in different directions. I did an experiment where I stuck two pieces of clay together three ways: (a) no scoring/no water, (b) scoring/no water, and (c) scoring and water. When I tried to pull each joint apart after drying, the two with scoring stayed stuck together well, but the connection with no scoring broke apart right away. See Figure 10.9 to visualize how a rough surface locks into another rough surface with bonding sites in all orientations.

Figure 10.9 Improving bonding sites between surfaces by scoring clay. Image created by author Christine Schnittka.

Sound Science: The Basics

When you blow across the opening of a bottle, like a glass soda bottle or a large ceramic jug, it makes a sound. A large ceramic jug makes a different sound than a glass soda bottle. Blowing across a large jug with a narrow opening makes a low, deep musical sound. Blowing across a smaller bottle with a narrow opening makes a higher pitched musical sound. The amount of air inside the bottle makes the sound higher or lower. The more space for air to vibrate, the lower pitched the sound.

Students can experiment with this themselves if you provide them with bottles with narrow openings. Demonstrate this for students by blowing across a bottle to show them what the sound is. Then, divide students up into groups and provide them with one bottle each. Give them access to water and task them with filling their bottle with water a little at a time so there is less air inside. Have them blow across the bottle and note the change in the pitch. The sound will be higher with less air to vibrate. If you have time, you can fill each bottle with different amounts of water and have the class play a song using each bottle as a note (Figure 10.10).

Figure 10.10 Narrow mouthed glass bottle. Image created by author Christine Schnittka.

When you blow into an ocarina or a whistle, you are primarily blowing ACROSS an opening. The mouthpiece just directs air across the opening, not into the opening (but some of it does indeed go into the chamber).

When you blow across a bottle, the air inside the bottle vibrates like a wiggling, jiggling bowl of Jello! Sound is caused by vibrations. The vibrating air makes a sound that travels to your ear and vibrates your eardrum, which vibrates your little, tiny ear bones, which vibrates the fluid in your cochlea (the snail-looking thing in the picture), which sends a message to your brain (Figure 10.11).

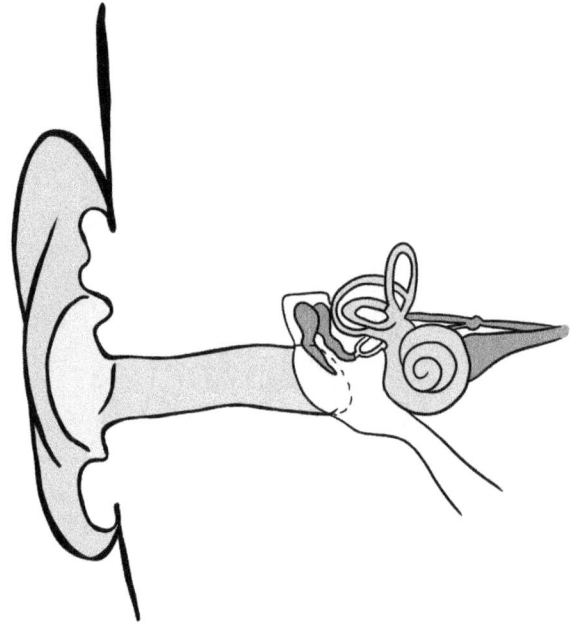

Figure 10.11 Inner ear anatomy. Image created by author Christine Schnittka.

Sound Questions to Ask

Ask students: Why do you think the bottle makes a sound when you blow across it?

- When you blow across the bottle opening, the fast-moving air creates a lower pressure zone. Air in the bottle rises up to fill this low-pressure zone but is pushed back down because of the air stream. This repeats itself over and over hundreds of times each second, causing a vibration of the air in the bottle.

What happens to the sound when you add water to the bottle?

- Adding water displaces air, and so less air vibrates when you blow. Less air means less mass, which means that the air has less inertia and can vibrate faster.

Why do you think the water changes the sound that the bottle makes?

♦ The water reduces the amount of air that can vibrate.

What if we added sand or cornflakes or something else to the bottle? How do you think the sound would change?

♦ If the amount of air changes, the sound will change.

Do the following demonstration for the class. Hang something very light from a string and tie the string up to the ceiling or other object so it can hang freely. Next, hang something much heavier the same way. You could choose a piece of popcorn and a book.
Ask students to predict what will happen when you blow on each of them.

♦ The popcorn will sway but the book will not.

Why do you think that will happen?

♦ The popcorn is light and the book is heavy.

Yes, it takes more energy and force to get a heavy object moving. A heavy object has more inertia than a light object. The same thing happens when you have more air in your bottle. The more air in the bottle, the more force is needed to get it moving, and when it does move, it moves slowly.
A vibration is a movement that goes back and forth over and over again. When objects vibrate slowly, they produce a low sound. When objects vibrate quickly, they make a high-pitched sound. You can demonstrate this with tuning forks. Larger tuning forks produce a lower pitched sound. Hang a light object, like a piece of popcorn, from a string and touch the popcorn to a vibrating tuning fork to prove that the fork is indeed vibrating.
Do you know why a fast vibration makes a high-pitched sound?

♦ Students in grades 3-8 are not likely to know why fast vibrations make high-pitched sounds. It all has to do with your brain! Your brain interprets fast vibrations as high pitches.

Sound Science: The Details

The faster that air vibrates, the higher pitched the sound. The slower the vibration, the lower pitched the sound. This is because of how your ears and brain work. A bigger ocarina has more air inside, and this air needs more energy to vibrate, so it doesn't vibrate as fast, and the sound is a lower pitch. A tiny ocarina does not have much air inside, so it is easier to get going. It vibrates faster, and you hear a higher pitch. Some whistles are SO high pitched, people can't hear them, only certain animals can. Dog whistles are tiny whistles with a small amount of air inside. The air vibrations push on a dog's eardrum and the dog hears the sound, but your brain does not interpret these vibrations as sound because they are too fast.

Ask students if they have ever had a cold or flu or Covid. Ask them if it ever changed their voice. Some will say yes that it made their voice lower. Why? Your voice comes from vibrations of your vocal cords in your throat. When you are sick, these flaps of tissue can get inflamed and swollen. Swollen tissue has more mass and cannot vibrate as fast as normal tissue. Slower vibrating vocal cords lead to a lower pitched voice.

Inside your ear, as shown in Figure 10.11, little bones connect your eardrum to the fluid in the cochlea. These are the smallest bones in the human body. When your eardrum vibrates, it makes the first little bone, the malleus, often called the hammer, vibrate. When the malleus vibrates, it makes the incus, often called the anvil, vibrate. A vibrating incus makes the stapes, often called the stirrup, vibrate. Why three bones and not just have the eardrum push on the cochlea directly? The bones are situated so that they act like levers, and they amplify the force.

The vibrating bones touch the fluid-filled cochlea. The cochlea is filled with fluid and tiny hairs which sway in the fluid. These tiny hairs send signals to the brain and sounds are being detected. The tiny hairs at the opening to the cochlea register high notes while the tiny hairs deep within the cochlea register low notes.

Mathematics

The frequency of the note that your whistle makes depends on the amount of air inside the whistle, the area of the opening (the square window you cut), and the thickness of the clay at the window. Advanced students may enjoy seeing and analyzing this formula. The frequency is the number of vibrations per second. The frequency can be predicted based on the following formula and measurements:

$$f = \frac{c}{2\pi}\sqrt{\frac{A}{VL}}$$

c = the speed of sound in air
V = the volume of the interior space.
A = the area of the openings
L = the thickness of the clay material
The bigger the frequency, f, the higher the pitch.

Mathematical Questions to Ask

Ask students, what happens if V gets bigger?

- If the volume inside the ocarina increases, the number under the square root symbol will get smaller, and the frequency will get smaller resulting in a lower pitch.

What happens if A gets bigger?

- If the area of the opening gets bigger, the number under the square root symbol will get larger, and the frequency will get larger, resulting in a higher pitched note. We usually make A bigger by adding holes in the instrument, which can be covered or uncovered by the fingers.

What happens if L gets bigger?

- If the thickness of the clay, L, gets bigger, the number under the square root symbol will get smaller, and the frequency will decrease, resulting in a lower pitch.

Elaborate: Clay Art, Craft, Technology, and Engineering

Purpose
The purpose of the Elaborate phase of this lesson is to apply the science of clay to craft, art, technology, and engineering. Now that your students have experimented with clay and learned about the science of clay and history of clay instruments, it's time to engineer some clay instruments!

Overview
After making a clay instrument by following some specific instructions, students can engineer their own instrument. They will make pinch pots, attach them to each other, and either make a wind instrument, a rattle, or a bell.

The instruments in this chapter involve hollow spheres. Whether a flute, a rattle, or a bell, students will need to first make a hollow sphere out of clay. Have them take the two identical pinch pots they made and stick them together. This works best if the pots have had time to dry out a bit. Resting overnight under loosely placed plastic should do the trick.

Once each student has made one or two hollow spheres about the size of their fist, have students wrap them in a paper towel with their name written on it. Collect them and set them aside, covered loosely with plastic wrap or a plastic grocery bag. Letting these harden a bit before the next step will make engineering an instrument much easier.

To Make a Rattle

Rattles need to have pellets inside! These pellets can be added before the two pinch pots are sealed up, or they can be added to the sphere. To add them to the sphere, simply cut a small hole in the sphere or a little doorway flap, insert the pellets (balls of clay, little metal jingle bells, marbles), then seal up the hole with more clay or the plug that was cut out. Students can vary the size, shape, and pellet materials. They can add small holes to change the sounds. I find that small holes really help. Having a handle will also change the sound that the rattle makes. Unless they are fired in a kiln, a rattle with a long handle will not stand up to the force of being shaken, but a short handle will be fine. Also, egg-shaped rattles can be made from Amaco air-dry clay and withstand the forces of being shaken (Figure 10.12).

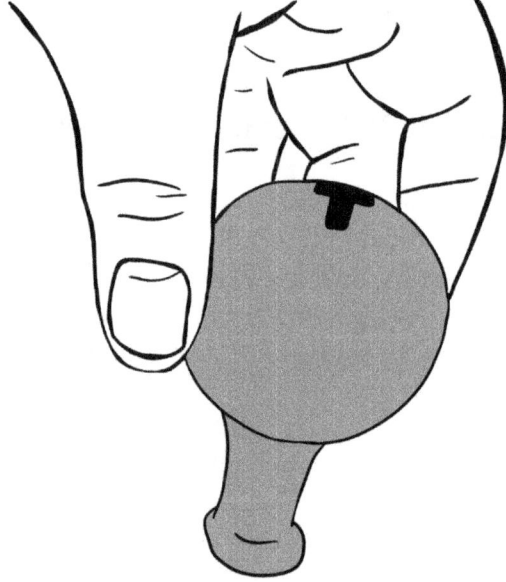

Figure 10.12 Handmade rattle. Image created by author Christine Schnittka.

To Make a Bell

How is a bell different from a rattle? A bell has more open areas whereas a rattle is more closed. A bell made from clay can be held in the hand and shaken or hung from a string and hit with a stick. How does a bell sound differently than a rattle? A semi-enclosed bell can be made by sealing two pinch pots to make a sphere. Once the sphere has hardened somewhat, cut slits into the sphere and add a little bit of clay to allow a string to go through (Figure 10.13).

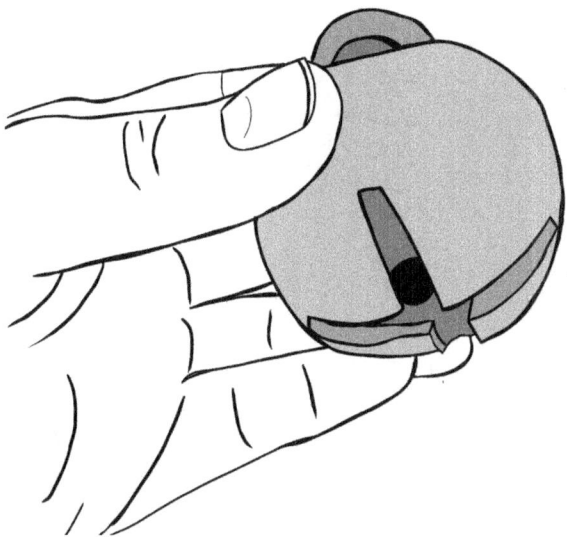

Figure 10.13 Handmade bell. Image created by author Christine Schnittka.

To Make a Wind Instrument

Many musical instruments have mouthpieces. While the xun does not have a mouthpiece, it will be easier for students to play their clay whistle if it has one (Figure 10.14).

Figure 10.14 Brass whistle. Image created by author Christine Schnittka.

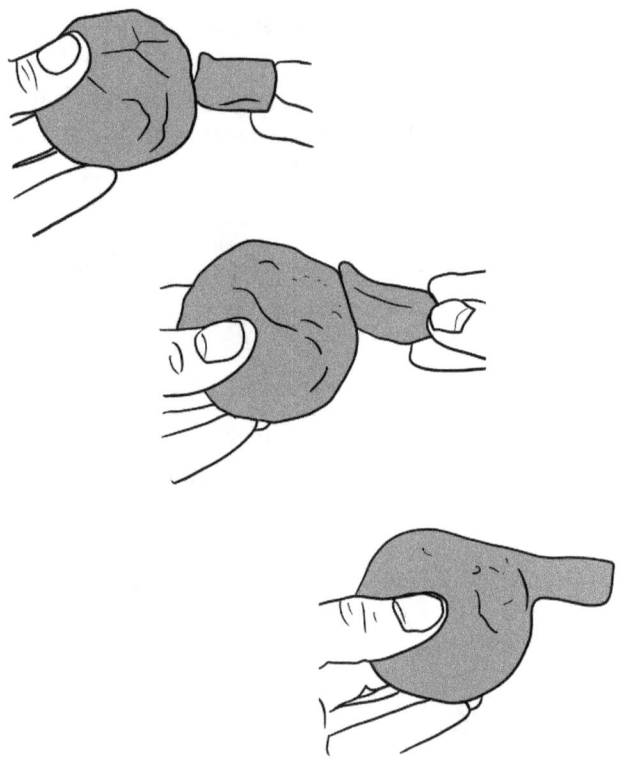

Figure 10.15 Clay whistle mouthpiece formation. Image created by author Christine Schnittka.

Take a piece of clay about the size of your thumb and shape it into a mouthpiece. Instead of putting the mouthpiece in the middle of your hollow sphere, try putting it toward the top so it looks like a whistle, the kind of whistle a sports coach might blow to get the players' attention. To do this, shape the mouthpiece a bit (Figure 10.15).

The next two steps are very important in making the whistle. Take a craft stick and stick it into the mouthpiece so that it punctures the hollow ball created with the two pinch pots (Figure 10.16).

Leave the popsicle stick in the whistle while the square window (the voicing) is cut. Use a toothpick to draw a square window above the craft stick, just as wide as the craft stick, just after the mouthpiece meets the hollow sphere (Figure 10.17).

Next, use a toothpick to first make a nice, neat, 45-degree ramp at the far end of the square window so the air makes a nice exit. Make sure to shape the ramp on the FAR side of the window. A cross section of the ramp looks like this (Figure 10.18).

After cutting the ramp, cut the rest of the square and remove the plug of clay. The air you blow will go through the mouthpiece, and some air will go down into your whistle, while some air will escape through the window.

Clay Creations ◆ 239

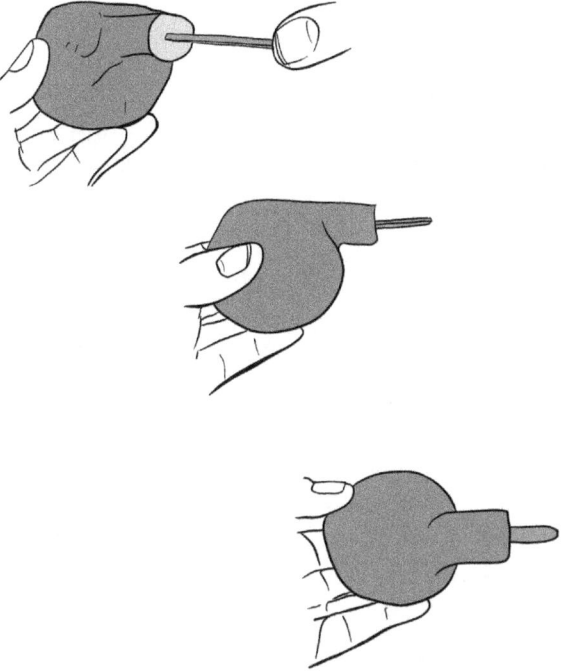

Figure 10.16 Whistle mouthpiece hole. Image created by author Christine Schnittka.

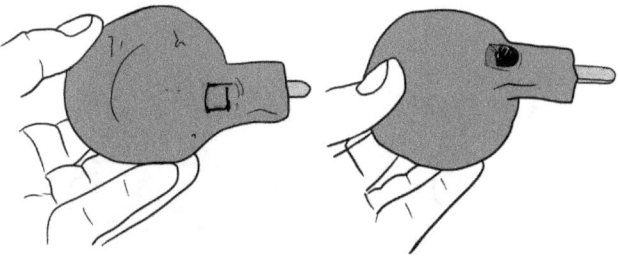

Figure 10.17 Creating the voicing for the whistle. Image created by author Christine Schnittka.

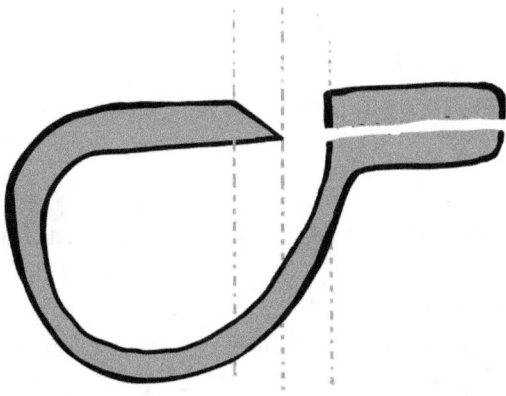

Figure 10.18 Cross section of the inside of a whistle. Image created by author Christine Schnittka.

Since these two steps are very tricky, you may want to watch the instructional videos linked on our website.

Finally, remove the popsicle stick and look into the hollow cavity. Can you see into the cavity? Can your craft stick descend into the cavity? Now blow! Does your whistle work? No? It usually does not work the first time. You may need to clean up the ramp and the window and get rid of clay lumps that don't belong in the airway.

Can students make two whistles—one big and one small? Listen to the difference in the pitch.

Can students make one whistle with thick walls and one with thin walls?

Can students make one whistle with a large opening and one with a small opening?

Students can decorate their whistles with clay. Just be sure they scratch and wet the clay where they are attaching pieces, or the pieces will fall off when dry. I have loaded my kiln many times with students' adorable whistles, only to have ears, tails, or feet drop off (Figure 10.19).

Figure 10.19 Whistle art. Image created by author Christine Schnittka.

The Challenge

The challenge for this phase of the lesson is to have students create a unique musical instrument that makes a sound that they like (high pitched/low pitched). They can even add additional holes to make different musical notes. See https://steamcrafts.weebly.com/ for student handouts that provide students with images and instructions for how to make the whistle.

The site also has links to many tutorial videos that are helpful with this challenge.

Perhaps students could design an instrument that makes a specific sound. For instance, have them try to imitate a particular modern instrument, or you can challenge students to make an instrument which imitates a particular animal. Have students choose a bird to imitate!

Evaluate: What Did They Learn?

After making clay instruments, ask your students to write the answers to the following questions to see what they learned. A form to collect the answers to these questions from your students is provided on our website https://steamcrafts.weebly.com/.

1. Thousands of years ago, people made musical instruments out of clay. What kinds of instruments did they make?

    ◆ Percussion instruments (rattles and bells) and wind instruments (flutes, whistles, and ocarinas) are two types in this lesson.

2. Why did people make musical instruments?

    ◆ Sometimes they just wanted to make nice music. Other times, they wanted to express emotions. They imitated animal sounds with these instruments and tried to use them to communicate with the supernatural realm.

3. Why do you think clay was chosen as a material to make musical instruments?

    ◆ Clay is easy to form into any shape. Clay is easy to dig up and is found all over the world. After being baked in an oven or in a fire, a clay instrument will last a very long time.

4. What makes clay so easy to form into shapes, and what causes it to harden when dry?

    ◆ When clay is wet, water gets between the flat particles, allowing them to slide next to each other. Once the water evaporates, the particles cannot slide anymore but they are attracted to each other because of hydrogen bonds.

5. Why do hollow musical instruments make notes when they are blown into?

   ♦ The stream of breath across the opening of the instrument creates lower pressure, which causes air in the hollow cavity to vibrate. Vibrations cause sounds and notes.

6. Why does a big ocarina make a lower note than a small one?

   ♦ A large mass of air will vibrate slower than a small mass of air just like a large mountain of Jello will vibrate slower than a small hill of Jello.

7. How does the ear hear musical notes?

   ♦ Vibrations in the air move the eardrum, which moves the little bones behind the ear drum, which presses on the fluid in the cochlea, and sends a nerve impulse to the brain.

8. How can you change your ocarina to produce different notes?

   ♦ If the thickness of the walls changes, if the space inside the ocarina changes, and if the size of the opening or number of openings changes, the note will change.

Summary

Making music is an ancient craft, and people have been making music from natural materials for thousands of years. Wood, bone, leather, metals, and clay have all been used for this purpose. Clay is easy to manipulate and doesn't require any special tools. Clay can be formed into percussion instruments as well as wind instruments. Working with clay is emotionally soothing, and it helps students learn patience, resilience, and the benefits of failure in a design process. When making an instrument from clay, students can learn about the history of the culture that made that particular instrument, they can learn about the scientific properties of the earth material, and they can learn about how vibrations cause sounds in the ear and brain. Students can engineer a wide variety of musical instruments depending on the nature of the problem or challenge provided to them. If the teacher doesn't have access to a kiln, air dry clay can be used. All clay that is not formed into instruments can be reconstituted with a bit of water. Clay is free to dig up, and inexpensive to purchase ready-made. Clay is a wonderful material!

Contemporary Clay Instrument Artisans

Making musical instruments from clay is still a relevant art and craft today. Artists and craftspeople around the world work with clay to make beautiful music.

For links to examine modern clay instrument artisans, please see our website https://steamcrafts.weebly.com/.

References

Berberian, M. (2019). Creative problem solving in art therapy: An overview of benefits to promote resilience. In: Bergerian, M. & Davis, B. (Eds) *Art Therapy Practices for Resilient Youth* (pp.13–32).

Both, A. A. (2007). Aztec music culture. *The World of Music, 49*(2), 91–104.

Broad, W. J. (1988, March 29). Complex whistles found to play key roles in Inca and Maya life. *New York Times*. Section C, p. 1.

Bybee, R. W. (2009). *The BSCS 5E instructional model and 21st century skills*. National Academies Board on Science Education.

Dewey, J. (1938). *Experience and education*. Macmillan.

Jang, H., & Choi, S. (2012). Increasing ego-resilience using clay with low SES (Social Economic Status) adolescents in group art therapy. *The Arts in Psychotherapy, 39*(4), 245–250.

Piaget, J. (1955). The construction of reality in the child. *Journal of Consulting Psychology, 19*(1), 77.

Sahagún, B. (1950–1982). *The Florentine Codex* (translated from the Aztec into English by Anderson, A. J. O., & Dibble, C. E.). The School of American Research and the University of Utah.

11
Conclusion

In today's plugged-in, screens-on, digital world, it's easy to forget the importance of our primitive skills, the ones our ancestors developed and needed to survive (Figure 11.1). Our brains and hands evolved to work together to do intricate tasks that required precise motor control (Napier, 1956; Young, 2003). As our human ancestors' brains evolved, and they rose up on two legs freeing the hands, there was so much they could do to enhance their survival and enrich their lives (Tuttle, 1967). They could throw rocks at predators, or take sticks in their hands to defend themselves, and by living longer, increase their reproductive success (Young, 2003). Perhaps tool making, in turn, expanded their brains, as tool-use is correlated with bigger brains (Lundborg, 2014). Primates living today have hands too, and they can use their hands in all the mechanical ways that we use them, but the purposive action is missing because their brains lack the capacity (Napier, 1956). However, when a small number of primates figures out how to use a particular tool, like a hammer to crack nuts, other primates emulate this behavior, and then practice it and learn how to use tools more efficiently (Fuhrmann et al., 2014). It's the brain-hand connection that is so intrinsically human.

The idea of a "homunculus" (Latin for "little man") was invented during the Middle Ages in Europe, as philosophers tried to determine how a human developed in utero before birth. Some postulated that the tiniest human baby was simply a miniature version of an adult. The idea of a "cortical homunculus" was invented by American neurosurgeon Wilder Penfield in the 1950s. By stimulating the human brain in different regions while the patient was under local anesthesia, he and his colleagues Edwin Boldrey and Theodore

DOI: 10.4324/9781003428312-11

Figure 11.1 Playtime. Image created by author Christine Schnittka.

Rasmussen mapped the 3mm thick outer layer of the brain, the neocortex, the most recently evolved portion of the cerebral cortex, and deduced which sections were associated with different parts of the body (Penfield & Rasmussen, 1950). They discovered that a very large portion of the neocortex is devoted to the hand. Later on, the British artist, Sharon Price-James, created sculptures of the human body where the percentage of the neocortex devoted to different parts was represented to scale. The most obvious part of this homunculus is its exceedingly large hands (Figure 11.2).

Other species, including those without hands, also manipulate their environments to solve problems. From termites and ants who build mounds and tunnels, to wasps and bees who make complex hives, and spiders who spin and construct intricate webs, the living world is replete with makers of all kinds. Birds such as African Weavers use many different types of knots to construct their nests. They use blades of grass to create temperature-controlled nests to raise their young safely under the scorching sun of the African savannah. Similarly, great apes such as orangutans and gorillas tie together leaves and vines to make nests that they use to rest in during the day and to sleep in during the night. But unlike Weaver birds, which have a genetic basis for their knot-making abilities, great apes must learn how to tie knots by watching their mothers and other members of the group, much like ourselves. This apprenticeship model is an ancient one, as our deep ancestors learned the skills they needed to survive this way too. Imagine if each one of us had to invent soap, cheese, bread, fabric, paper, dyes, candles, musical instruments, and string by ourselves. We could not do it in one lifetime. Humans needed to have passed these skills and this knowledge down from one generation to the next generation.

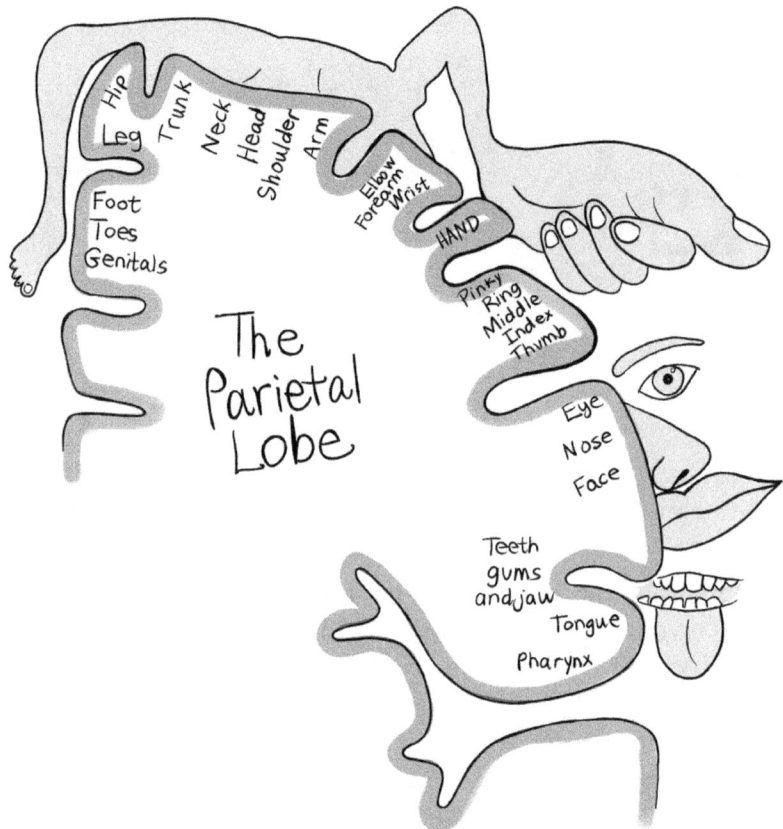

Figure 11.2 The mapped neocortex. Image created by author Christine Schnittka from an image by OpenStax College. CC BY 3.0

It's the next generation now. How are children using their hands to learn in schools? Sheri Leafgren said it best:

> Keeping children apart—apart from nature, apart from the material world—and especially apart from one another—is an overt mechanism of school. Spend time in an elementary classroom, and you will hear, "Keep your hands to yourself," "Mind your own business," "Keep your eyes on your work," "Don't touch," and "Put that down!" Children are placed behind desks, on chairs, in lines, and under one's thumb.
>
> (Leafgren, 2011, p. 36)

Children naturally seek experiences with their bodies and especially their hands. They learn about the world through their senses, and Leafgren (2009) compares the restrictions placed on schoolchildren to infant swaddling, a practice which keeps children safe, but limits their learning, as it is with their sense of touch that they learn (Tuan, 2005).

When I (Schnittka) was a middle school science teacher back in the '90s and early 2000s, my classroom was a place for physical interactions. We made. We crafted. We dissected everything. Our hands were busy, and our minds followed along. Visiting my co-author Amanda Haynes's classroom leaves me with the same impression. It's a place for doing. Haynes has collected every type of material you can think of, and sorted and organized them all into bins and drawers, and engages her STEAM students in get-your-hands-dirty activities all day long.

My dear friend, Cheikhouna Ka, who assisted with this chapter, is a PhD student in biological sciences at Auburn University. When he was a child in Senegal, a small country on the western coast of Africa, he lived with his grandmother in a town without formal education, and so he complimented the religious tutoring he received from his great uncle with physical experiences in the natural world. He became an autodidact by using his hands to explore, making things from natural materials, dissecting old discarded junk that he found, and thus exercising his hand-brain connection. After arriving in the United States at age 14 with no formal math, history, English, or science education, he was able to quickly make up for eight years of lost schooling and flourish in ways few American youth ever do. I can't help but think that the early experiences he had with his hands fostered his remarkable intellectual development.

We have lost our connection to ourselves.

A study that just came out in JAMA Pediatrics describes a possibly causal relationship between screen time in early childhood and atypical sensory processing (Heffler et al., 2024). Children who have atypical sensory processing can have difficulties with all of their senses, including touch. While the study poses no theory to explain this relationship, could it be that children who see the world on a screen, but do not FEEL or experience or touch or manipulate this world, do not exercise their cerebral cortexes as they should be exercised? Are specific areas of the neocortex pruned away with lack of use? Future studies will certainly help us understand the mechanism behind this finding, but now **you** know that it might be possible to damage the brains of children if they experience this plugged-in, screens-on, digital world too much, and use their hands too little.

This book is a small primer on how to engage youth in hand-making while they learn requisite knowledge about science, history, engineering, and math, in the hopes that it inspires teachers to let kids be human. It can be used in part or in whole. Chapters can be divided up into individual lessons, which have coordinating handouts, presentations, design challenges, rubrics, and even summative assessments on our website https://steamcrafts.weebly.com/.

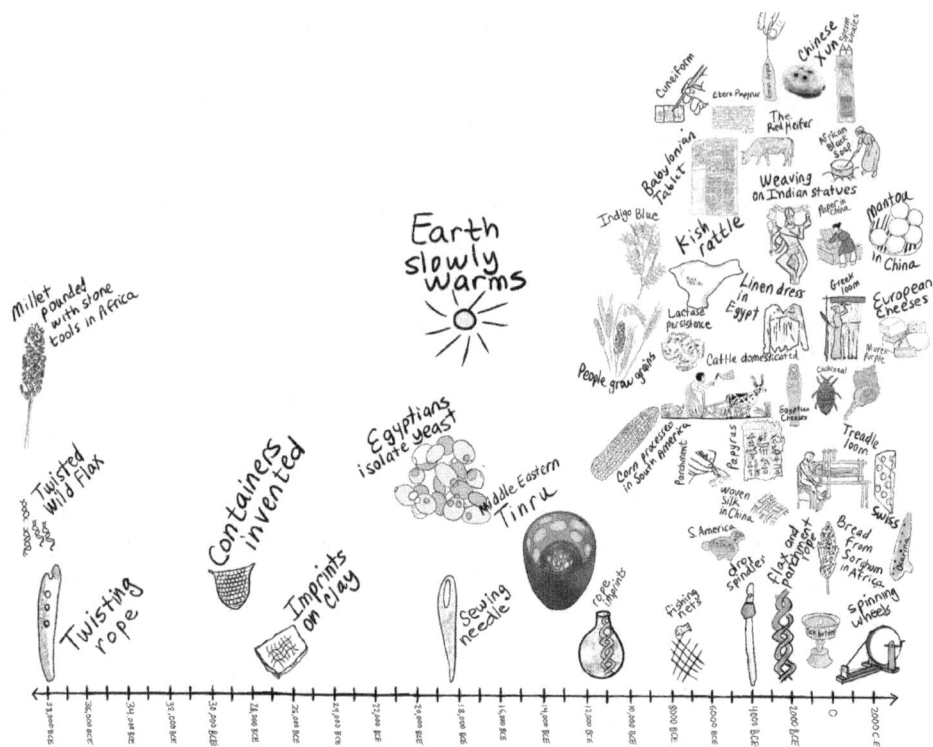

Figure 11.3 Timeline of crafts. Image created by author Christine Schnittka.

Since many similar materials are used throughout the book, it is wise to seek out activities that complement each other financially. Combining the cheese and bread chapters can lead to a classroom feast! Combining the fibers, natural dyeing, and weaving chapters makes sense as well. Candles and soap both use oils. The chapter on paper builds on the concepts learned in the fibers chapter. The chapter on clay stands alone, or does it? In most of these chapters, the fact that the material world is built up from small particles bonded to each other only through the electrostatic hydrogen bonds, is a common thread. The chemistry informs the physics, which informs the biology, which informs the engineering, and shapes the history of the craft (Figure 11.3).

Please let us know if this book has had an impact on your teaching!
~ Amanda and Chris

References

Fuhrmann, D., Ravignani, A., Marshall-Pescini, S., & Whiten, A. (2014). Synchrony and motor mimicking in chimpanzee observational learning. *Scientific Reports*, 4(1), 5283.

Heffler, K. F., Acharya, B., Subedi, K., & Bennett, D. S. (2024). Early-Life digital media experiences and development of atypical sensory processing. *JAMA Pediatrics, 178*(3), 266–273.

Leafgren, S. L. (2009). The subversive nature of touch in the kindergarten schoolroom. In: De Souza, M. (Ed), *International handbook of education for spirituality, care and wellbeing*, pp. 836–852. Springer Science and Business Media.

Leafgren, S. L. (2011). "Hands at your sides!" The severing of body and mind in the elementary school. *Journal of Curriculum Theorizing, 27*(2), 35–50.

Lundborg, G. (2014). The hand, the brain and tools. In: Lundborg, G. (Ed), *The hand and the brain: From Lucy's thumb to the thought-controlled robotic hand*, pp. 31–36. Springer.

Napier, J. R. (1956). The prehensile movements of the human hand. *The Journal of Bone and Joint Surgery, 38*(4), 902–913.

Penfield, W., & Rasmussen, T. (1950). *The cerebral cortex of man: Clinical study of localization of function*. Macmillan.

Tuan, Y. (2005). The pleasures of touch. In: Classen, C. (Ed.), *The book of touch*, pp. 74–79. Routledge.

Tuttle, R. H. (1967). Knuckle-walking and the evolution of hominoid hands. *American Journal of Physical Anthropology, 26*(2), 171–206.

Young, R. W. (2003). Evolution of the human hand: The role of throwing and clubbing. *Journal of Anatomy, 202*(1), 165–174.

For Product Safety Concerns and Information please contact our EU representative GPSR@taylorandfrancis.com
Taylor & Francis Verlag GmbH, Kaufingerstraße 24, 80331 München, Germany

www.ingramcontent.com/pod-product-compliance
Lightning Source LLC
Chambersburg PA
CBHW060510300426
44112CB00017B/2607